AFFECT

Psychoanalytic Theory and Practice

AFFECT

Psychoanalytic Theory
and Practice

Edited by

MORTON B. CANTOR, M.D.

and

MYRON L. GLUCKSMAN, M.D.

A Wiley-Interscience Publication

JOHN WILEY & SONS

New York · Chichester · Brisbane · Toronto · Singapore

Library of Congress Cataloging in Publication Data:

Main entry under title:

Affect: psychoanalytic theory and practice.

  "Selected papers from the Journal of the American
Academy of Psychoanalysis."

  "A Wiley-Interscience publication."
  Includes index.
  1. Affective disorders—Addresses, essays, lectures.
2. Affect (Psychology)—Addresses, essays, lectures.
3. Depression, Mental—Addresses, essays, lectures.
4. Psychoanalysis—Addresses, essays, lectures.
I. Cantor, Morton B. II. Glucksman, Myron L.
III. Journal of the American Academy of Psychoanalysis.

[DNLM: 1. Affect—Collected works. 2. Psychoanalytic
theory—Collected works. 3. Psychoanalytic therapy—
Collected works. BF 511 A256]
RC537.A28   1984   616.89   83-14574
ISBN 0-471-88071-X

Printed in the United States of America

10 9 8 7 6 5 4 3 2 1

Preface

The presentation of this collection of papers follows the twenty-fifth anniversary of the American Academy of Psychoanalysis. It was in 1956 that outstanding psychoanalysts from all over the country came together with the strong feeling that psychoanalysis needed protection "from the dangers of premature standardization and a rigidly enforced conformism," as noted in an *Archives of General Psychiatry* editorial. An Academy of Psychoanalysis was founded with the primary purpose "to serve as a forum of exchanging ideas of common interest for psychoanalysts and representatives of related disciplines" in this country and abroad.

The Academy has grown by welcoming diversity, questioning the status quo, and responding to changing sociocultural approaches and new biochemicophysical data. This has led to investigating fresh and broadening innovations in viewing psychoanalytic theory and practice.

From 1958 through 1971 the contributions of the Academy, as reviewed in its semiannual meetings, were published in annual volumes, *Science and Psychoanalysis*, edited by Jules Masserman. In 1972, *The Journal of the American Academy of Psychoanalysis* was founded under the editorship of Silvano Arieti. The contents of the journal went beyond the proceedings of the Academy meetings and welcomed papers independent of our meetings from contributors of various disciplines from all over the world.

The nucleus of this book arose from an Academy meeting, "Affect: Psychoanalytic Theory and Practice," held in New York City from November 29 to December 2, 1979. The meeting was organized by Myron L. Glucksman, Chairman of that Program Committee. Papers from that meeting were reviewed, selected and edited for publication in the journal. The response to that meeting and issue of the journal excited a great deal of interest and the idea for this book was born. Many of those selected papers as well as a group of related articles from previous issues of the journal are included in this book.

We would like to specifically acknowledge the help of the Editorial Board of the journal; Ian Alger, Chairman of the Committee on Programs of the Academy, who first suggested the topic; and Vivian Mendelsohn, the Academy Administrative Director, and her staff.

MORTON B. CANTOR, M.D.

Scarsdale, New York
July 1983

Contents

PART 3. **Continued**

Introduction

MYRON L. GLUCKSMAN

Affect is perhaps the most central and challenging subject in psychoanalysis. The selected papers in this volume examine some of the theoretical, developmental, clinical, and treatment aspects of this topic. In a broad sense, affects are an indispensable part of human experience and form the very foundation of human relationships. Emotions are essential to the concept of self, providing us with the uniqueness and vitality that contribute to our individual identities. They are the necessary signals which give meaning to our verbal and nonverbal communications. As therapists, we constantly attend to the ebb and flow of our patients' feelings and moods. Indeed, when we examine patients, we invariably evaluate the quality, intensity, and appropriateness of their affects. Many patients seek help because they suffer from serious affective disturbances. Some enter treatment in order to alleviate intolerable feelings — anxiety, sadness, anger, guilt, shame, despair, boredom. Certain individuals find it difficult if not impossible to express their feelings, while others remain virtually unaware of their inner emotional experience. No doubt, the most commonly asked question during therapy is some variation of "How do you feel about that?" Changes in mood, unexplained feelings, involuntary sounds, gestures, and facial expressions often are the initial clues that help therapists identify important memories, irrational beliefs, and basic conflicts in their patients. Our own feelings during sessions aid us in empathizing with and understanding our patients' internal affective states. Without question, affects provide us with an enormous amount of information about ourselves and those with whom we communicate, whether it be in therapy or in our social and work relationships.

The terms "affect," "mood," "feeling," and "emotion" are used interchangeably in the literature, although some authors distinguish among them. For example, Greenson defines moods as "chronic complex affective states." In his paper "Theoretical and Clinical Considerations of Affects in Psychoanalysis," Drellich

1

reviews the various definitions of affect and concludes that the majority of psychoanalytic authors view affect as a "subjective feeling tone or feeling quality which is often, but not invariably, accompanied by discernible physiological or motoric reactions." There seems to be general agreement that affects are behavioral events which are subjectively experienced, often observed by others, and usually accompanied by physiological changes. Drellich details the evolution of Freud's concept of affect, noting that he first equated it with libido and psychic energy. Freud subsequently viewed affects as "representations" of unconscious drives consisting of two components, including motor or secretory discharges and subjective feelings. Other investigators, including Fenichel, Lewin, Jacobson, and Rappaport, further refined the "drive-discharge" theory of affect. Drellich points out that Brierly and Novey were among the first psychoanalysts to emphasize the role affects play in interpersonal communication. Although affects continued to be considered discharge phenomena linked to instinctual drives, the emergence of the interpersonal and adaptive theories of behavior influenced clinicians to focus more on their communicative aspects.

Stone informs us that Descartes described 49 emotions in his treatise "Passiones Animae," written in 1650. He considered six of them — admiration, love, hate, desire, joy, and sorrow — primary emotions. The remainder either were modified versions of the six or were composed of two or more of them. Like Descartes, contemporary investigators such as Dahl, Stengel, and DeRivera define eight basic emotions: love, surprise, anger, fear, contentment, joy, depression, and anxiety. They describe a spectrum of affects composed of emotional pairs (e.g., love–hate) based on the primary affects and classified according to three dimensions. The first dimension relates to whether an emotion is concerned with another person or with the self; the second refers to whether the predominant attitude is one of attraction or repulsion; the third indicates whether the emotion is directed to something or someone, or whether it is experienced as derived from something or someone.

Knapp, in his paper "Core Processes in the Organization of Emotions," presents a model of emotion that includes affects as derivatives of instinctual drives and as signals which aid us in reacting to others. He cites three important elements that constitute the core of emotional organization: (1) hedonic evaluation (appraisal of incoming stimuli), (2) activation–deactivation (regulation of affects), and (3) expressive mobilization (flight–fight responses and their variations). Knapp emphasizes the role of memory, symbolization, and cognition in the development of the affective system. He reminds us that "idiosymbolic processes" such as personal memories and nondiscursive imagery are connected to feelings.

There is little doubt that infants experience and "learn" affects prior to the development of language and cognition. In "The Origins of Affect — Normal and Pathological," Kestenbaum points out that pleasurable and unpleasurable feelings occur in the context of mother–infant attachment behavior. She emphasizes that the potential for pleasurable affects is innate and depends on the availability of a "good-enough mother." It is the mother who transmits and reinforces pleasurable feelings in the infant by means of touching, caressing, fondling, smiling, and other vocal, or tactile behaviors. The infant's innate drive for mastery, achievement, and activity is another potential source of pleasurable affects if it receives positive reinforcement. Bennett, in his paper "Early Emotion," stresses the infant's repertoire of facial expressions, including the smile, which evoke emotional responses in the mother. He states that it is the visual, vocal, motor interplay between mother and infant which determines the infant's affectively charged internal representations of its relationship with the mother. Both Kestenbaum and Bennett point to disturbances in the attachment process which result in pathological affects. Kestenbaum describes "joyless" children who are humorless and unable to form human bonds. They have been subject to frequent separations or losses and are the victims of child abuse, abandonment, and mothers who are too psychotic or depressed to respond to them in an affectively appropriate way. Bennett notes that disturbance of the attachment process may also be the result of congenital abnormalities including blindness, deafness, Down's Syndrome and esophageal atresia.

The evolution of two specific pathological affects, anxiety and depression, is discussed in the papers by Schecter and by Bemporad and Wilson. Schecter outlines the development of stranger anxiety, separation anxiety, anxiety by contagion, and anxiety through loss of love or security. He observes that "most types of early anxiety derive from some form of disruption of a good 'external' interpersonal relationship as well as of a good internal object relationship." Bemporad and Wilson point out that clinical depression truly comparable to that which is seen in adults does not occur in infancy and childhood. Children may experience feelings of sadness or dysphoria, but they are incapable of becoming depressed because they do not possess a full cognitive self-representation. Moreover, they have an undeveloped time sense so that they are unable to experience hopelessness and despair. It is not until adolescence that they achieve a fully developed concept of time and can relate the present to the future. The severe depressions sometimes seen in adolescents are in part due to their exaggerated cognitive distortions untempered by adult experience. Therefore, seemingly trivial events assume monumental importance and lead to feelings of insurmountable finality and desperation.

Numerous psychoanalysts, including Schur, Brenner, and Arieti, have commented on the central role of cognition in the affective process. Brenner notes that affects originate in childhood when ideas first become associated with sensations of pleasure and unpleasure. According to him, gradations of pleasure and unpleasure together with their associated ideation constitute affects. Arieti divides emotion into three orders, depending on the level of cognitive work involved: (1) "protoemotions," such as fear and rage, require a minimum of cognitive work; (2) "second-order" emotions, such as anxiety and anger, are evoked by inner objects or images, necessitating symbolic cognition; and (3) "third-order" emotions, including depression, love, and joy, require more complex cognitive processes relating to the past, present, and future. In her paper "Cognitive Aspects of Affects and Other Feeling States with Clinical Applications," Spiegel stresses the informational and evaluative functions of affect. This entails "cognitive monitoring" at different levels of awareness. Emotions, then, are intimately connected with cognition both developmentally and through a continual feedback mechanism which helps determine their quality, intensity, expression, or nonexpression. Emotions and cognition appear to have a complementary relationship, although, as Modell states, "Ideas are only meaningful when they are 'invested' with affect."

In their respective papers on depression, Arieti and Bemporad emphasize how important it is for the therapist to utilize transference reactions in confronting the patient with his or her depressive modes of interaction. Arieti and Bemporad focus on enabling the patient to relate to the therapist not as a dominant but as a significant third person who wants to help the patient in a mutually cooperative way.

The role of affect in interpersonal transactions is most elo-
quently described by Bonime in his paper "Anger as a Basis for a
Sense of Self." Bonime describes the various manifestations of
pathological anger (violence, rebellion, stubbornness, sophisticated
self-control) used to protect the individual and to maintain his or
her sense of identity. Bonime has elsewhere demonstrated how the
depressed person engages in depressive "practices" including
manipulation, competitiveness, intolerance to influence from
others, avoidance of responsibility, and unwillingness to give gratification to others. A subliminal sense of entrapment in these
practices and their inevitable painful consequences result in
inescapable despair.

In "Interpretation of Affect and Affective Interpretation,"
Mohacsy and Silver advocate the active use of the analyst's affect
in identifying and interpreting the patient's feelings. They agree
with Arlow in regard to the two stages of empathy in the psychoanalytic process. First, the analyst identifies with the patient and
the former's unconscious "reverberates in response to the patient's
unconscious." In effect, the analyst develops an empathic, internalized working model of the patient. This process evolves into a
second stage in which this temporary identification changes from
the analyst thinking and feeling *with* the patient to feeling and
thinking *about* the patient. Therefore, interpretation occurs as a
result of transient affective identification, cognitive appraisal, and,
finally, the use of affective coloring in giving the interpretation.
All of these papers emphasize the communicative importance of
affect in the therapeutic relationship. That is, the analyst helps the
patient recognize and express feelings through active monitoring
and selective use of his own affects. To a large extent, therapy
focuses more on the adaptive, defensive, and transactional roles
of affects and less on their function as mediators of instinctual
discharge.

The psychoanalytic literature contains a number of papers concerned with specific emotions in addition to anxiety and depression; these include boredom, smugness, arrogance, enthusiasm,
sarcasm, vengeance, gloating, jealousy, and shame. In this book,
Green examines anticipation, hope, and despair; Satran explores
the phenomenon of loneliness, and Tauber describes disordered
affect in the obsessional character.

Since the turn of the century, psychoanalysis has been concerned not only with the relationship between affect and psychopathology but also with the relationship between affect and phys-

ical illness. Freud, whose first patients displayed functional somatic symptoms, explained their pathogenesis through the mechanism of "conversion." He postulated that affects connected with unacceptable ideas were denied, displaced, symbolized and "converted" into somatic channels. Conversion symptoms continue to be seen in clinical practice, yet the psychophysiological mechanisms leading to their occurrence are no better understood than they were by Freud. Since the 1930s a great deal of research has been devoted to understanding the role played by affects in the etiology of both functional and organic disorders. Alexander proposed that the emotions accompanying specific intrapsychic conflicts promoted physiological changes which, if sustained, resulted in organic pathology (e.g., duodenal ulcer, bronchial asthma). Subsequent investigators demonstrated that the pathogenesis of these illnesses is far more complex than Alexander's "core conflict" theory suggests. Engel and Schmale observed that the onset of many organic illnesses is preceded by actual, threatened, or symbolic object loss. According to Engel, when object loss is accompanied by feelings of helplessness and hopelessness a "conservation–withdrawal" state may result, rendering the individual less resistant to a variety of pathogenic factors. Current thinking about the etiology of both functional and organic illness emphasizes the interplay of genetic, biological, social, and intrapsychic factors in which affect plays an important but not exclusive role.

Knapp discusses patients with "alexithymia," a term introduced by Nemiah and Sifneos to describe patients with somatic symptoms who have great difficulty in recognizing and expressing their feelings. These patients are unable to distinguish one emotion from another, tend to be concrete in their thinking, and have impaired self and object representation. Hoppe, who studied patients with interhemispheric commissurotomies, suggested that alexithymic individuals have functional commissurotomies. Nondominant (right) hemisphere phenomena, including idiosymbolic imagery and somatic sensations, cannot be elaborated and verbalized through the dominant (left) hemisphere so that somatic symptoms develop. Krystal explains alexithymic patients in terms of a developmental disturbance. According to him, the mother–child interaction promotes differentiation, verbalization, and desomatization of emotions so that they become useful as signals to the self and others. During this period the child develops affectively toned object and self representations, as well as the capacity for affect tolerance. If the mother–child relationship is affectively disturbed, emotions are neither differentiated nor verbalized, and the ability to become acquainted with one's feelings as well as the capacity to translate them into language is impaired. Krystal contends that these individuals focus on external reality, are unimaginative, and are prone to experience feelings as vague somatic sensations or frank physical symptoms. Every analyst has faced the challenge of treating patients who "somatize"; many of these individuals simply cannot identify, experience, and express their feelings. By the same token, there are many patients who have a similar impairment of their affective life yet do not manifest somatic symptoms. Some of these individuals construct an array of defenses against feelings they perceive as intolerable and overwhelming. The analyst's task remains the same in treating these patients (alexithymic or not); that is, the aberrations in their affective development must be identified and their affective inhibitions "worked-through" to the point where they can experience and verbalize their feelings.

The papers in this book do not directly address the neurochemical substrate of affect, nor do they examine the disturbances in brain amine metabolism connected with the major affective illnesses. This is not to say that practicing psychoanalysts are not aware of the profound impact the antidepressant drugs and lithium have had on the treatment of unipolar and bipolar affective disorders. The discovery of the naturally occurring opioid peptides in the central nervous system may also have relevance for the future treatment of these disorders. Although there is a close relationship among affective intensity, certain hormonal levels, and autonomic nervous system activity, there is little evidence to date for an association between specific neurochemical changes and discrete affects such as guilt, shame, and joy. Nevertheless, as our knowledge of the physiology of affects expands, it will become the psychoanalyst's task to correlate the biology of normal and pathological affects with psychodynamic information pertaining to each patient.

The papers selected for this book do not pretend to include the vast amount of knowledge available in the psychoanalytic literature regarding affect. They were chosen in order to present some of the current thinking and work in the field. If they stimulate the reader's curiosity and perhaps provide further possibilities in the treatment of certain patients, then their inclusion in this volume will have been well justified.

PART ONE

Theoretical Aspects Of Affect

ONE

Psychoanalytic Theories Of Affect

MARVIN G. DRELLICH

It is my intention herein to present an overview of the classical theory of affects with special attention to the historical development of these theories. This review must include the changes
in classical theory, the controversies which have existed in the
past and some of the controversies which persist at the present
time.

It is easiest, to begin with, to note the two large areas of agreement among analysts of all persuasions. First, everyone seems to
agree that affects are phenomena of the utmost importance in the
human experience. Affects are vital events of everyday life and are
of vital importance for understanding normal human behavior as
well as understanding all aspects of psychopathology. Affects are a
central consideration in the psychoanalytic process. Distressful
affects, especially anxiety and depression, are the reasons that
patients seek psychotherapeutic or psychoanalytic help. The
patient's affects are among the most important data which the
psychoanalyst monitors in the psychoanalytic process and they are
most profoundly affected by successful psychoanalytic treatment.

The second area of agreement is that we do not possess a satisfactory or a unitary theory of affects. Many attempts have been
made to construct a consistent and inclusive metapsychology of
affects. Some of these theories have been brilliant, creative and
often very useful, especially when they have been primarily
clinical in emphasis. Nevertheless, a majority of writers invariably
begin their publications on affect theory by asserting that this area
remains extremely obscure. The essence of affects is nonverbal and

nonconceptual while affect theory is inevitably an attempt to conceptualize the nonconceptual and to verbalize the nonverbal. Still, we must try to understand these ubiquitous, elusive phenomena.

CONCEPTS OF AFFECT IN THE DEVELOPMENT OF PSYCHOANALYSIS

Freud's earliest preanalytic psychotherapy in the 1880's was essentially a cathartic or tension-releasing procedure. Neurosis was regarded as due to an excess accumulation of strangulated affect or emotions which were directly tied to forgotten but disturbing memories. Treatment consisted of bringing unconscious memories into consciousness, using hypnosis. Remembering traumatic events with a full abreaction (release) of associated emotions was essential for a cure. This oversimplified view of therapy was, of course, abandoned by Freud as his theories of psychopathology became more sophisticated. Yet even today his first concepts are not altogether meaningless. We are still aware of the importance of the patient's emotional responses in the analytic process, although we are more concerned with consistent and appropriate emotional participation and less with massive abreactions of affect.

Freud's first theoretical formulation dates from 1894 when he wrote, "In mental functions something is to be distinguished − a quota of affect or sum of excitation − which possesses all the characteristics of a quantity." At that time Freud equated "quota or affect" with "sum of excitation," and seems to have used the terms synonymously. This corresponds to the time when he was concerned with the "actual neuroses," where the affect (anxiety) was thought to be dammed-up libido, and therapy was largely a cathartic process aimed at discharging or draining the dammed-up affect, thereby relieving anxiety and reducing the pathological impact of repressed ideas.

In equating affects with the quantity of psychic energy, Freud was operating within the neuronal or neurophysiological model of the psychic apparatus as outlined in the *Project,* which he had prepared in 1895, but which was not published in his lifetime.

With the publication of the *Interpretation of Dreams* in 1900 (1953), Freud's model of the psychic apparatus became at last a largely psychological rather than neurophysiological construct, but the influence of the earlier model is clearly seen in his economic hypothesis, the theory of cathexis, and the primary and secondary processes. He defined affects as "motor and secretary discharge processes" which are controlled by the unconscious. They were no longer regarded as exactly the same as drive, energy, or libido, but were instead "representations" serving as safety valves and indicators of the unconscious drive. The idea of a "safety valve" implies a massive expression or display of emotional behavior and not a subtle, subjective feeling state.

Freud's differentiation of affect and drive in 1915 was further clarified in the two metapsychological papers (1957a,b). The unknown energy of "cathexis" (the instinctual energy or drive energy) was described as having two phenomena associated with it: (1) an affect or affect charge and (2) ideas or memory traces. Both affects and ideas are "representations" of the drive, but are not synonymous with drive. "Affects and emotions," he said, "correspond to processes of discharge, the final manifestations of which are perceived as feelings" (1957a). By this statement he implied that the affect itself consists of two components: (1) motor or secretary discharge processes and (2) the purely subjective phenomena which we call "feelings" or "emotions." In his *Introductory Lectures,* delivered in 1915 (1963), he made this explicit. He defined an affect as "something highly composite." It "includes in the first place particular motor innervations or discharges and secondarily certain feelings . . . of pleasure and unpleasure which, as we say, give the affect its keynote."

Freud's concept of affects as representations of, but not identical with, drives, and his description of the discharge component and purely subjective component are the starting points for all subsequent classical analytic formulations involving affect. There is one detail which Freud clarified which I feel needs to be underlined. He said in 1915 (1957a), "Strictly speaking . . . there are no unconscious affects as there are unconscious ideas." When an idea and its associated affect are repressed, the idea is unchanged except for its being unconscious, but the affect becomes only "*a potential disposition* which is prevented from developing further." Freud asserted that, by definition, affects are conscious phenomena and hence we cannot properly speak of unconscious anxiety, unconscious guilt or unconscious grief — but only of the potential to develop such affects. Pulver (1971) devoted an entire paper to the question of unconscious affects. He concluded that it *is* possible to speak of unconscious affects and was quite persuasive but by no means conclusive on this question. For the time being I believe the matter remains unsettled.

When Freud proposed his structural hypothesis in 1923 (1961) he called attention to the affects as ego functions. While focusing mainly on anxiety, he retained the view of affects as discharge processes but added that affects "can be experienced only by the Ego." Initially the infant's ego *endures* an affect (affect discharge plus feelings) passively, but gradually the ego "tames" the affects, reduces their intensity, and indeed learns to produce affect actively to serve as a signal. This theory implicitly indicated that affects are communications, not only intrapsychically, but also in an extended sense, at the interpersonal level as well. This concept of the signal and communication function of affects in the service of the ego obviously has the most profound dynamic and clinical implications for psychoanalytic science.

I will make no attempt to summarize the psychoanalytic literature [this has been reviewed by Rapaport (1953), Jacobson (1953), Kaywin (1960), Arnold (1960) and Valenstein (1962) among others], but will mention some significant details which have been added to Freud's basic concept of affects.

In 1929, Jones showed that affects which originally serve as signals to the ego in the service of defense may themselves become intolerable and an individual may have to develop new affect signals to warn against the earlier painful affects. These "secondary affects" are thus seen to serve as defense against other affects, and not merely defense against instinctual impulses.

In 1937, Brierley tried to stir interest in affects when she wrote, "In spite of this temporary eclipse in theory, in practice affect has never lost its importance . . . no analyst fails to pay attention to his patient's feelings . . . all [patients] complain of some disorder of feeling and tend to estimate their own progress by changes in their feelings." She made the additional point that affects ought not be regarded as discharge phenomena but rather as purely subjective experiences or tension phenomena impelling toward discharge or action. This distinction permitted her to focus on affect as a signal to the individual himself about himself and about the outside world. She even recognized the importance of communication of affect between individuals as an essential element in "rapport" and "empathy."

Unfortunately, Brierley was 25 years ahead of her times. Little heed was paid to her insights and suggestions. Subsequent papers continued to focus on the tension discharge function of affects in the framework of the theory of libidinal cathexes. The signal function and communication function of affects received precious little attention.

In 1941, Fenichel devoted a paper to affects in the framework of the expanding interest in ego-psychology. He emphasized that children and "neurotic personalities" have acute emotional spells, outbursts or discharges. The ego's increasing strength that comes with maturity "gets the upper hand" over the affects. The ego may be said to develop some mastery over affects, to bind the affects, and use them for its purpose. Further, he went into great detail to describe defenses against intense and overwhelming affects. Every known defense is employed against intense affects: blocking or inhibition of affects, delayed outbursts of affect, displacement, "affects equivalents" (as when excess eating and obesity are an equivalent of depression), reaction formations or "counter affects" (as when impotence is a defense against guilt), and finally, isolation and projection of affects.

He declared that the "normal person" is master of his affects, whereas the weak ego is mastered by its affects. In 1945 he went further and stated that "instinctual drives are warded off . . . because of anxiety or guilt feelings . . . *thus in the last analysis any defense is a defense against affects."*

In 1950 Lewin devoted a small volume to the *Psychoanalysis of Elation,* in which he anticipated the increased attention to certain specific affects which was to follow in subsequent years. He introduced the term "screen affect" to designate an affect which screens, denies or wards off a significantly more painful affective state.

Jacobson's papers (1953, 1954, 1957) represent a serious, painstaking attempt to understand affects in terms of the structural theory and the psychic discharge processes. She stated that affects of pleasure and unpleasure control the psychic life and serve as "indicators" or signals serving the regulation of the entire psychic economy. She modified Freud's view that pleasure is relief of tension and unpleasure is accumulation of tension. Instead, she suggested that the pleasure–unpleasure affects are expressions of both rising and falling of tension. "The psychic organization may show a striving for *cycles of pleasure* alternating between excitement (tension) and relief (discharge)." She asserted that "What turns us into human beings is not only the organization of our thought processes but also the organization of a wide range of feelings, emotional attitudes and affective states." She suggested that maturation of the ego involves greater capacity to endure affective tensions without discharge and the opening-up of innumerable new channels or pathways for affective discharge.

Rapaport's paper, "On the Psychoanalytic Theory of Affects"

(1953), seems to have been a turning point. He presented an exhaustive and critical review of psychoanalytic theories of affect and offered an outline of a theory of affects. His attention to the role of affects in the therapeutic process is summed up in his statement, "The liberation and proper handling of affects is a crucial element in therapy. Clarification of the theory of affects should be a step toward a metapsychological theory of technique and therapy."

Rapaport's work seems to have stimulated a substantial number of theoretical and clinical papers on affects in the past three decades. The emphasis in these publications has been on the clinical and therapeutic importance of affects, including the liberating and handling of the patient's affects, the role of the analyst's affects, the dynamics of empathy and intuition and the inevitable and perpetual problems of "What is therapeutic in psychoanalysis?"

Greenson (1954) wrote one of his many valuable papers putting stress on the defenses which the ego develops against painful affects. He drew attention to the psychopathology of "moods," which he defined as chronic complex affective states, which function as continuous defensive processes serving to deny an intolerable affective condition.

Szasz's book on *Pain and Pleasure* (1957) classified pain as an affect, and in his typically provocative way suggested that the distinction between physical pain and psychic pain is not valid. Both are affects, both function as signals about the integrity of the organism, and both have a capacity to communicate and inform others about the individual's physical or mental state of being. Szasz pointed out that most psychoanalytic concern with affect has dealt with powerful or negative affect, and consequently a psychoanalytic theory of pleasure and positive affect was lacking. His own formulations stressed the importance of affects as signals to label or define the quality of relationship between the ego and the object. His concepts focus on the role of affects in object relationships and minimal attention is paid to the purely intrapsychic vicissitudes of energy and affect.

Novey's (1959, 1961, 1962) interest in affect was primarily clinical. In addition to its signal function he listed four other functions of affect: (1) discharge processes with or without an object relationship; (2) motivators or inhibitors of behavior; (3) devices for communication; and (4) means of eliciting or inhibiting behavioral responses in others. He said that affects are not passive discharge channels for drives but rather they are dynamic forces with direction which impel toward action. His views seem to have finally brought back Brierley's neglected concepts of the dynamic function of affects. Novey concluded that, "The tension and/or discharge theories of affect are primarily concerned with crisis phenomena (massive affect attacks) and fail to center attention on the continuing mood states of man."

TOWARD A DEFINITION OF AFFECT

When we seek a consistent definition of affect we find no agreement as to what affects actually are. Some authors use the terms affect, feeling, and emotion synonymously and interchangeably. Others make a sharp distinction between the inner subjective experience and the expressive phenomena, that is the motor, secretory or physiological discharge processes. Here too we find no agreement about terminology. Fenichel (1941) suggested that the word "emotion" should designate the "feeling sensations themselves" and "affect" should refer to the "outcome of those sensations, the discharge phenomena." Rapaport (1950) supported the use of the term "affect" for the conscious, subjective feeling experience and the word "emotion" for the "objective," physiological and motor discharge manifestations — the exact reverse of the definitions suggested by Fenichel. For Jacobson (1953), "The term *affect* refers to the whole set of psychophysiological discharge phenomena which are physiological insofar as they express themselves in bodily changes and psychological insofar as they are perceived as feelings." Novey (1959) speaks of emotions and affects as complex psychological, physiological and motor phenomena and prefers the word "feeling" to delimit the subjectively experienced aspects of affects. Kaywin (1960) described affects as the subjective "tonal perceptions" ordinarily called feelings and distinguished these from the "reaction patterns" of expression or discharge in response to the affects.

Blau (1955) was adamant in insisting that affect is purely subjective. "It exists only when the individual feels or perceives it," and "should not be confused with its expressive counterparts."

Authors who include the physiological and motor reactions within their definition of affect are, for the most part, those who are concerned with the relationship between instincts and affects. Their theoretical formulations are primarily involved with the vicissitudes of psychic energy, the apportionment of psychic energy between the three psychic "structures," the cathexis of internal objects with drive energy and similar intrapsychic phenomena. They give far less attention to the subjective phenomena, the feelings or moods, and to the role which external objects play in evoking feelings.

Those who define affect as the subjective feeling, or feeling tone, generally regard the physiological and motor discharge processes as *responses to* or results of the "emotions felt." These authors are far more concerned with the importance of affects in human interaction than they are with intrapsychic energy transfer. Valenstein (1962) exemplifies the group who "take up the question of affects in association with considerations of the theory of therapy, concern over what is curative in psychoanalytic therapy, problems of working through . . . the analyst–patient relationship, communication in analysis and in human relations in general."

I see more and more writers identified with the second group, placing major emphasis on the subjective feeling tone or feeling quality which is often, but not invariably, accompanied by discernible physiological or motoric reactions. Affect is experienced as pure sensation; hence it is essentially nonverbal and nonconceptual. Affects are never experienced as localized phenomena, hence they are states of the organism as a whole. Arnold (1960) has pointed out that there is no intransitive verb in the English language to denote the experiencing of any emotion, except the verb "to feel." Indeed, if one says "I feel angry, I feel sad, I feel confident," or "I feel enthusiastic," it is exactly the same as saying, "I *am* angry, I *am* sad, I *am* confident," or "I *am* enthusiastic." This indicates the extent to which a person's affective or *feeling* state is experienced as virtually identical with the quality of his *being* at a given moment in time.

Affects are independent of specific sense organs, although the stimuli perceived by the sense organs have a great deal to do with determining one's affective state.

The *function* of affect as viewed by most psychoanalysts is primarily to signal, label, or define the qualitative state of one's being in relation to the perceived environment and to the needs, values and defenses within oneself.

As we *perceive* the situation outside ourselves, especially the behavior and attitudes of the significant persons in our life, as we perceive the state of our own body, the substance of our thoughts, ideas, fantasies and dreams, some kind of inner evaluation or appraisal is made. This nonverbal, nonconceptual appraisal or evaluation is one essential part of the affect. In addition, I believe that the affect includes an impulse or inclination to act. The impulse may not be conceptualized or verbally labeled as such, but analytic exploration reveals that it is an integral part of the affect. It may be an impulse to act so as to continue, sustain, or encourage a situation which evokes positive or pleasurable affects or it may be an impulse to act so as to avoid or change the stimuli which evoke negative or unpleasurable affects. It is probable that the physiological changes associated with strong affects are preparations for carrying out the behavioral responses which are being impelled by the affect. This view of affect as including the tendency to act coincides with Brierley's (1937) formulation, which designated affects as being "tensions impelling toward discharge," but not the discharge or behavioral phenomena themselves.

In response to what one becomes aware of in his environment or in himself, one may experience feelings which might be translated into phrases such as "I fear him, I hate her, I want that, I am frustrated by them" or "I'm ashamed of myself, I am disgusted with my appearance, I'm proud of myself, I feel guilty for what I've done" "I like the way he smiled at me," etc. These are all statements which rather crudely indicate how an individual is *affected* by the perception of outer or inner phenomena, and there is in each instance a greater or lesser impulse, urge or inclination to act. Without the subject being aware of these words, the total affect is translated, "I fear him and want to run away" or "I hate her and would like to hurt her" or "I'm ashamed of myself and want to hide from others and from myself," or "It feels good to have him smile at me that way and I'd like to do something to have it continue or repeated."

Affects label the present but also label the past and future as well. Remembering a past blunder of gaucherie evokes shame or embarrassment, perhaps severe enough to make one wince or blush. Anticipating a remote or imminent danger evokes fear which, it is superfluous to mention, almost invariably labels the dangerous impact of what may or what will happen.

It is almost certain that affects are present in pre-verbal children, in fact, some affect must be present at that point in development when a sense of the distinction between the "self" and the "non-self" begins to emerge. Affect, even at this early age, is knowable only through some kind of self-awareness or subjectivity. Much later in life we call this introspection, but it remains true throughout life that we can only know our own affects through introspection or self-scrutiny. Knowing the affects of others is, in the last analysis, also knowable only by introspection. For example, as we see the subtle movements of posture and gesture, as we hear the intonation and expression of another person's voice, as we study the mimetic muscles, as we notice the involuntary vasomotor phenomena accompanying the affects of another person, as we hear the verbal expletives, the sighs, the groans — as we perceive all this evidence of what another person is feeling, we actually understand his feelings because we recognize something which we have ourselves once felt. There is aroused in us a corresponding affect which we once felt and now feel again. In this way we really "know" what the other person is feeling. The words anxiety, guilt, joy, and enthusiasm are truly meaningful only insofar as they evoke very small but identifiable feelings which the listener perceives introspectively and subjectively.

CLASSIFICATION OF AFFECTS

There are, of course, many, many different emotions and no list could be complete. Some affects may be qualitatively alike, but are subjectively distinguishable from each other by their intensity or duration. Apprehensiveness, anxiety, panic, and dread may serve as examples of affects which are probably subjectively different intensities of the same quality of feeling. Sadness, grief, and depression are probably also similar in quality but subjectively different in terms of their intensity and duration. I am well aware that there are very significant genetic and dynamic differences between these qualitatively similar affects. I am, for the moment, merely indicating that there is resemblance between the subjectively experienced feeling tone of the affects within each group.

Other affects seem to have unique qualities which we readily distinguish by introspectively sampling such feelings from our own affect reservoir. This group includes guilt, shame, envy, awe, jealousy, disgust, rage, bitterness, and boredom as some of the so-called negative or unpleasure affects, and joy, pride, enthusiasm, confidence, gratitude, and whimsicality as a few of the so-called positive or pleasure affects. Each one *feels* distinctly different from the others, although we are often hard pressed to define verbally the differences between them.

Several attempts to classify affects have been made by psycho-analytic authors. Negative affects serve to label or evaluate a situation, activity, or inner condition as dangerous, unfavorable, undesirable, unsatisfying or not likely to be satisfying — hence, impelling the individual to discontinue or avoid the provoking stimulus if at all possible. Positive affects indicate to the discriminatory process within oneself that the inner or outer situation or activity is in some way favorable, desirable, satisfying, or potentially satisfying, and hence it ought to be sustained or repeated. Positive and negative affects loosely correspond to Freud's concept of pleasure and pain feelings without the original emphasis on tension accumulation and discharge. We must recognize that all affect cannot easily be classified as positive or negative. Feelings of elation or nostalgia, for example, are often felt to have both positive and negative qualities.

Glover (1939) divided affects into two groups, tension affects and discharge affects, consistent with his predominant cathectic orientation. Jacobson's (1953) classification described simple and compound affects arising either from *intra*-systemic tension, that is tension within the id, or within the ego, or arising from *inter*-systemic tensions, for example, tensions between the ego and the id or tensions between the ego and superego.

Ostow (1955, 1961), drawing heavily from studies in ethology, suggested that there are two distinct kinds of pleasurable affects: (1) Pleasure affects associated with anticipatory actions — sitting down in preparation for a meal and looking at the food, for example, and (2) pleasure affects associated with performance or consummation, for example, actually eating the meal.

Engel (1962) proposed that affects can be classified as either *signal-scanning affects* which "have a warning or signal function . . . yielding judgments of good or bad, success or failure, pleasure or unpleasure," or *drive-discharge affects* which "show more discharge quality. The feeling state [being] more directly the expression of drive seeking discharge." Green (1977) classified appetitive affects and inhibitory affects.

It seems to me that no satisfactory classification has yet evolved. The existing schemes tend to blunt or obscure the subtle characteristics which distinguish the individual affects in a given category.

It is understandable that among the specific emotional states, anxiety and depression have received the most attention and intensive study, an emphasis which is consistent with their central importance in clinical psychopathology. Other individual affects have begun to receive more detailed study, mostly since 1950, when Lewin published his imaginative and challenging volume on *The Psychoanalysis of Elation.*

We have had the separate studies by Greenson (1949, 1953) and Bieber (1951) on apathy, boredom and inertia. Greeacre (1956) wrote about the experience of awe in childhood, Greenson (1962) has a paper on enthusiasm, Klein (1957) on envy and gratitude, James Alexander (1960) on the psychology of bitterness and Rangell (1963) on friendliness, to mention just a few. Some of these studies may be definitive statements about the particular affect, but in most instances these emotions still have secrets which are waiting to be unlocked by focused psychoanalytic exploration. There are, of course, still other affects about which little or nothing has yet been said.

In the past two decades new questions have been posed and preliminary answers have been offered regarding affect theory. Attention has been directed to the developmental aspects of affect. In 1967 a panel of the American Psychoanalytic Association addressed the issue of affect development. Moore (1967) asserted that emotional expression can only develop in the context of object relations. Schur (1967) emphasized the role of affect in the cognitive function of the ego, where the minute-to-minute data, the internal and external perceptions, are evaluated by means of affects and ideas. In practical terms, affects are evaluators in development and continue to so function throughout life. Modell (1971) offered the provocative view that affects are primarily signals which serve the needs of the group.

Brenner (1974) fashioned a detailed theory of affect development. "One may safely assume that early in life, before any substantial degree of ego development has taken place, all affects can be divided into pleasurable and unpleasurable. [All] subjective emotional experiences of later life derive from [these two feeling states]."

Other psychoanalysts have studied the relationship between affects and neurophysiology. Krystal (1974, 1978) made some useful correlations between clinical observations of pleasure, pain and brain physiology. He pointed out that separate pleasure centers and distress centers have been found in the brain and he used data to explain such thorny problems as the masochist deriving pleasure from pain, the pleasure associated with thrills and danger and the libidinization of many distressful affects. Basch (1974) separated affects and' emotions. He suggested that affects are purely subjective phenomena; they are nonconceptual and are generated by the old brain. Emotions he believed to be affect plus idea or content. Emotions, therefore, are conceptual and are generated by neocortical areas of the brain.

References

Alexander, J. (1960), The psychology of bitterness, *Int. J. Psychoanal.*, **41**, 514-520.

Arnold, B. (1960), *Emotions and Personality*, Columbia University Press, New York.

Basch, M. F. (1976), The concept of affect: A re-examination, *J. Am. Psychoanal. Assoc.*, **24**, 759-778.

Bieber, I. (1951), Boredom and inertia, *Am. J. Psychotherapy*, **5**, 215-225.

Blau, A. (1955), A unitary hypothesis of emotion. 1. Anxiety, emotions of displeasure and affective disorders, *Psychoanal. Q.*, **24**, 75-103.

Brenner, C. (1974), On the nature and development of affects: A unified theory, *Psychoanal. Q.*, **43**, 532-556.

Brierley, M. (1937), Affects in theory and practice, *Int. J. Psychoanal.*, **18**, 256-269.

Engel, G. (1962), Anxiety and depression-withdrawal; the primary affects of unpleasure, *Int. J. Psychoanal.*, **43**, 89-97.

Fenichel, O. (1941), The ego and the affects, *Psychoanal. Rev.*, **28**, 47-60.

Fenichel, O. (1945), *The Psychoanalytic Theory of the Neuroses*, W. W. Norton, New York.

Frank, L. K. (1954), *Feelings and Emotions*, Random House, New York.

Freud, S. (1962), *The Neuro-Psychoses of Defense*, in *Standard Edition*, Vol. 3, Hogarth, London.

Freud, S. (1895), *Project for a Scientific Psychology*, in M. Bonaparte, A. Freud, and E. Kris (Eds.) (1954), *The Origins of Psychoanalysis*, Basic Books, New York.

Freud, S. (1953), *The Interpretation of Dreams*, in *Standard Edition*, Vols. 4 and 5, Hogarth, London.

Freud, S. (1957a), *The Unconscious*, in *Standard Edition*, Vol. 14, Hogarth, London.

Freud, S. (1957b), *Repression*, in *Standard Edition*, Vol. 14, Hogarth, London.

Freud, S. (1963), *Introductory Lectures on Psychoanalysis*, in *Standard Edition*, Vols. 15 and 16, Hogarth, London.

Freud, S. (1961), *The Ego and the Id*, in *Standard Edition*, Vol. 19, Hogarth, London.

Glover, E. (1939), The psychoanalysis of affects, *Int. J. Psychoanal.*, **20**, 299-307.

Green, A. (1977), Conceptions of affect, *Int. J. Psychoanal.*, **58**, 129-156.

Greenacre, P. (1956), Experiences of awe in childhood, *Psychoanal. Study Child*, **11**, 9-30.

Greenson, R. R. (1949), The psychology of apathy, *Psychoanal. Q.*, **18**, 290-302.

Greenson, R. R. (1953), On boredom, *J. Am. Psychoanal. Assoc.*, **1**, 7-21.

Greenson, R. R. (1954), On moods and introjects, *Bull. Menninger Clin.*, **18**, 1-11.

Greenson, R. R. (1962), On enthusiasm, *J. Am. Psychoanal. Assoc.*, **10**, 3-21.

Jacobson, E. (1953), The affects and their pleasure-unpleasure qualities in relation to the psychic discharge processes, in *Drives, Affects, Behavior*, edited by R. Loewenstein, International Universities Press, New York.

Jacobson, E. (1954), The self and the object world: Vicissitudes of their infantile cathexes and their influence on ideational and affective development, *Psychoanal. Study Child*, **9**, 75-127.

Jacobson, E. (1957), Normal and pathological moods: Their nature and function, *Psychoanal. Study Child*, **12**, 73-113.

Joffe, W. G. and J. Sandler (1968), Comments on the psychoanalytic psychology of adaptation, with special reference to the role of affects and the representational world, *Int. J. Psychoanal.*, **49**, 445-454.

Jones, E. (1929), Fear, guilt and hate, in (1961) *Papers on Psychoanalysis*, The Beacon Press, Boston.

Kaywin, L. (1960), An epigenetic approach to the psychoanalytic theory of instincts and affects, *J. Am. Psychoanal. Assoc.*, **8**, 613-658.

Klein, M. (1957), *Envy and Gratitude: A Study of Unconscious Forces*, Basic Books, New York.

Krystal, H. (1974), The genetic development of affects and affect regression, *Ann. Psychoanal.*, **2**, 98-126.

Krystal, H. (1978), Aspects of affect theory, *Bull. Menninger Clin.*, **41**, 1-26.

Lewin, B. D. (1950), *The Psychoanalysis of Elation*, W. W. Norton, New York.

Löfgren, L. B. (1967), Report of panel: Psychoanalytic theory of affects, *J. Am. Psychoanal. Assoc.*, **16**, 638-650.

Modell, A. H. (1971), The origin of certain forms of pre-oedipal guilt and the implications for a psychoanalytic theory of affects, *Int. J. Psychoanal.*, 52, 337-346.

Modell, A. H. (1979), Affects and complementarity of biological and historical meaning, *Ann. Psychoanal.*, 6, 167-180.

Moore, B. E. (1967), Some genetic and developmental considerations in regard to affect, in Löfgren (Ed.), Report of panel: Psychoanalytic theory of affects, *J. Am. Psychoanal. Assoc.*, 16, 638-650.

Novey, S. (1959), A clinical view of affect theory in psychoanalysis, *Int. J. Psychoanal.*, 40, 94-104.

Novey, S. (1961), Further considerations on affect theory in psychoanalysis, *Int. J. Psychoanal.*, 42, 21-31.

Novey, S. (1962), The principle of "working through" in psychoanalysis, *J. Am. Psychoanal. Assoc.*, 10, 658-676.

Ostow, M. (1955), A psychoanalytic contribution to the study of brain function, *Psychoanal. Q.*, 24, 383-423.

Ostow, M. (1961), Affect in psychoanalytic theory, *Psychoanal. Psychoanal. Rev.*, 48, 83-93.

Pulver, S. E. (1971), Can affects be unconscious?, *Int. J. Psychoanal.*, 52, 347-354.

Rangel, L. (1963), On friendship, *J. Am. Psychoanal. Assoc.*, 11, 3-54.

Rapaport, D. (1950), *Emotions and Memory*, International Universities Press, New York.

Rapaport, D. (1953), On the psychoanalytic theory of affects, *Int. J. Psychoanal.*, 34, 177-198.

Szasz, T. S. (1957), *Pain and Pleasure*, Basic Books, New York.

Schur, M. (1967), Comments on unconscious affects and the 'signal' concept, in Löfgren (Ed.), Report of panel: Psychoanalytic theory of affects, *J. Am. Psychoanal. Assoc.*, 16, 638-650.

Valenstein, A. F. (1962), Affects, emotional reliving and insight in the psychoanalytic process, *Int. J. Psychoanal.*, 43, 315-324.

TWO

Modern Concepts Of Emotion As Prefigured In Descartes' "Passions Of The Soul"

M. H. STONE

Although emotions — or, as they tend to be called in the psychoanalytic community, affects — play a central role in all psychological systems dealing with human interactions, few theoreticians, whether modern or ancient, have busied themselves with the construction of models for categorizing all the various nuances of emotion and their interrelationships.

Juan Luis Vives (1492–1540) wrote extensively on the "passions," the medieval term for the emotions, describing a number of the most important: love, hate, resentment, envy, jealousy, and hope. Further passages on self-love and anger are to be found in his *Introductio ad Sapientiam* (1524). Elsewhere Vives spoke of how the passions of the soul, ". . . in opposition to reason, are always girded and prepared for battle, and that if they conquer, the result is the bitterest perdition to man." He advocated rigid control over the passions, ". . . lest they beat down our strength" (1531).

Harvey, the great cardiac physiologist, noted the influence of emotion upon the body: ". . . in almost every affection, appetite, hope or fear, our body suffers, the countenance changes, and the blood appears to course hither and thither." He drew attention to

Presented at The Payne Whitney Clinic, Seminar on History of Psychiatry, March 14, 1979. The author wishes to express his gratitude to Drs. Hartvig Dahl, Otto Kernberg, and Arnold Cooper for their careful reading of this article in manuscript form, and for their valuable comments and suggestions.

the blushing that tends to accompany modesty, to the fiery appearance of the eyes during anger, to the distension of the genitals with blood during lust, etc. (Alexander and Selesnick, p. 96).

In the modern period one of the early psychologists to advance a systematic theory of the emotions was William James (1890). Although he emphasized the dynamic nature of psychological processes, his theory of emotions was mechanistic. He maintained, for example, that emotions constitute a kind of subjective awareness of physiological responses, as though *anger* were the awareness of increased heartbeat and muscle tension (the James–Lange theory of emotion).*

Despite innumerable references in Freud's works to affects of one kind or another, Freud tended not to focus on individual emotions, either to catalog or describe them, but instead dwelt with affective phenomena on a higher level of abstraction. Thus, in the *Introductory Lectures* he writes, "An affect includes . . . particular motor innovations or discharges and secondly, certain feelings; the latter are of two kinds — perceptions of the motor actions that have occurred and the direct feelings of pleasure or unpleasure which . . . give the affect its keynote" (p. 395).

Psychoanalytic pioneers who developed comprehensive theories about emotions include Rado and Franz Alexander.

Rado (1956) divided affects into the "welfare" emotions (love, joy, pride, pleasurable desire) and the "emergency" emotions (fear, rage, guilty fear, guilty rage). This division already implies a teleological notion of ultimate purpose, in the sense that the emergency emotions have survival value for the individual, since they are called into play in critical situations requiring immediate all-or-none reactions. Reactions to which we apply the label "emotional" tend to be massive, all-encompassing; they dominate and indeed characterize the state of the individual during the time they hold sway. Rado of course recognized not only the genuine utility of the emergency emotions during true emergencies but also their dis-utility during situations incorrectly perceived as threatening by a neurotic or psychotic individual. Emotions, in general, Rado regarded as ". . . central mechanisms both for the

---

*James also held that the cerebral cortex was little more than a surface for the ". . . projection of every sensitive spot and every muscle in the body." He saw no reason to posit any special brain centers that subserve emotion (1890, p. 473).

arousal of the peripheral organism and for the peripheral disposal of superabundant central excitation" (p. 339).

Franz Alexander evolved an approach to the understanding of the emotions where *continuous interaction of bodily and psychic influences* was stressed. This approach was accordingly known as *psychosomatic* and represented an effort to integrate and circumvent what was for so long regarded as an essential dualism between body and soul. Processes such as facial flush in anger, explosive laughter upon hearing a joke, sobbing upon the receipt of devastating news, are first ". . . perceived subjectively as emotions" and then ". . . *objectively* observed as changes in body functions" (Alexander, p. 389). It is this chain of events that Alexander subsumed under the heading of "psychosomatic phenomena." Because we are indivisible organisms with respect to mental and somatic processes, he advocated simultaneous study of psychological and physiological events in those undertaking the investigation of emotions.

More recently, Kernberg (1976) has reexamined affects from the vantage point of object-relations theory. He regards affect dispositions as "primary motivational systems which integrate the perception of central (pleasurable or unpleasurable) states. . ." (p. 87). In addition, he sees physiological discharge phenomena, inborn perceptive and behavior patterns and stimuli that impinge on our special sense organs as fundamental ingredients of affective life. Elsewhere, Kernberg expresses the view that affects have a particular *raison d'être* for the individual, insofar as they serve to ". . . increase the perception of external and internal stimuli. . ." (p. 104), which, in turn, promotes the fixation of memory traces, for just those events that are critical to the welfare of the individual. Interestingly, Descartes had an inchoate notion of a very similar nature, regarding the survival value of the *passiones.* Kernberg also underlines the importance of affects in the pleasure/pain dimension of human behavior. In this connection he draws attention to the model proposed by Mac Lean (1967), in which the central nervous system is seen as consisting of (1) a primitive ("reptilian") brain with (mainly hypothalamic) pleasure and pain centers, (2) a limbic brain, housing "affective memory," and finally (3) a neocortical brain, which ". . . relates to the higher level cognitive functions that, by implication, are less involved in early, affect-laden learning" (Kernberg, 1976, p. 87).

We may wish to think of the pleasure/pain dimension as a

manifestation of a feedback system operating in an "advisory" capacity vis-à-vis the rest of the organism: the self is warned against what is bad for its welfare or survival and is advised about what is beneficial. Since affects figure both in this feedback system and also in the memory-enhancing mechanism that strengthens this system, both functions are quite interrelated. Descartes' awareness of this interrelationship is apparent throughout the *Passiones,* as we shall see below.

DAHL'S PSYCHOANALYTIC MODEL OF MOTIVATION

Recently, Dahl (1978) has made an important contribution to psychoanalytic metapsychology regarding the emotions. Building on de Rivera's decisional theory of emotions (1962; cited in Dahl, 1978), Dahl postulates that the emotions can best be understood as appetites and as messages. Characteristic of emotions is a chain of structural components beginning with (a) a perceptual experience, followed by (b) an implicit wish (customarily for "perceptual identity" with some former and remembered state of satisfaction), and completed by (c) a consummatory act, such as, in the case of love, physical approach or mating with the loved one. The buildup toward a consummatory act relates specifically to wishes involving external objects.

The model advocated by Dahl and Stengel (1978) represents a simplification of a six-dimensional schema proposed by de Rivera (1977). Dahl and Stengel's model emphasizes three dimensions. The first, or *"it-me"* dimension, relates to whether any given emotion concerns another person or object *(it)* or the self *(me).* The second relates to whether the predominant attitude is one of *attraction* or of *repulsion.* The last identifies whether the emotion is directed to something or someone, or whether it is experienced as derived *from* something or someone. When the *me* emotions are involved, the terms *positive* versus *negative* are used to denote the *"attraction/repulsion"* dimension of the *it* emotions. Similarly, in the *me* emotions, *passive* and *active* replace *from* and *to.* This model, built upon three dimensions, each of which can vary in two ways, generates an eight-category universe of fundamental emotions, as outlined in the logic tree of Figure 1.

According to this system, the four basic emotional appetites are *love, surprise, anger,* and *fear.* We are not trained to think

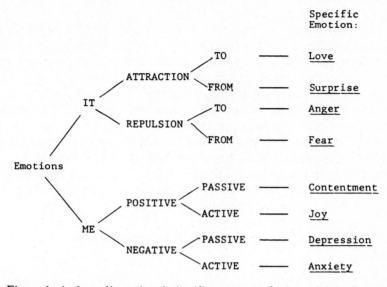

Figure 1. A three-dimensional classificatory tree. [Adapted from Dahl and Stengel (1979), p. 273.]

of anger or fear as appetitive, but it is part of the conceptual elegance of Dahl's model that it can make a convincing case for such an argument. Fear, for example, generates the desire to *escape* from the threatening object; *escape* is fear's natural consummatory act. By the same token, to *anger* may be said to correspond to the natural inclination to *get rid of* the offending object. Even *surprise* inspires the consummatory act of *beholding* whatever is the source of our fascination.

The *me* emotions are similarly divided into four basic categories: *contentment, joy, depression,* and *anxiety,* the two former deriving from the experience of *pleasure;* the latter, from *displeasure.* These emotions are also said to relate to whether the individual's mission is perceived by him as already accomplished (in which case, *contentment*), going well (elation, or *joy*), has already failed (leading to *depression*), or is not going well (bringing about distress or *anxiety*).

As with Rado, Dahl presents a convincing teleological hypothesis that "Powerful survival advantages would accrue to those specimens that best 'knew' (perceived) when to be attracted and when to be repulsed, when to approach and when to withdraw, when to relate to an object and when to attend it's own internal evaluative messages" (1978, p. 404).

The profundity, as well as the utility, of Dahl's model lies in its reduction of an often bewildering and forbidding collection of physio-psycho-logical phenomena to a simple vocabulary containing only a few pairs of opposites: *attraction/repulsion; me/it; to/from; negative/positive; passive/active.* The clarity of thought regarding the whole subject of emotions, to which this model conduces, finds expression in Dahl's nontrivial observation (1978, p. 399) that certain *"positive-me"* emotions are (a) essential to life, yet (b) incapable of being satisfied by a consummatory act that the individual could initiate. The infant, for example, will not survive unless it becomes the object of *someone else's* appetite of love (here in the nonsexual sense of needing to *care for another person*). As Dahl points out, ". . . there is no consummatory act that the child can perform to satisfy his wish to be loved."

DESCARTES AND THE *PASSIONES ANIMAE*

The preceding brief review of some of the contemporary systems for classifying and analyzing the emotions will serve to highlight Descartes' achievement in this area; the modernity of his treatise on the emotions stands out the more boldly for its having been written over 300 years ago.

Descartes (1596–1650) was a contemporary of William Harvey, whose work on the circulation of the blood deeply influenced his thinking about the emotions. Descartes was also a contemporary of Francis Bacon and of Galileo, both of whom stressed meticulous observation too much, in the opinion of Descartes; at the same time his *own* penchant for deductive, analytical reasoning — uncontaminated by the crass facts of everyday life — was chided by Galileo and Bacon. Descartes was preoccupied with the essence of things, with first causes and with the purity of his own mental resources; he was not a man for details. The principal theoretician behind analytical geometry, Descartes felt that every property of space, including motion, could be translated into numerical form. If the world could be comprehended in terms of extension and motion, then surely geometry was the key to understanding the universe.

It should not be surprising, then, to see the same deductive, geometrical approach at work in Descartes' treatise on the emotions, the *Passiones Animae* (1650), written during the last year of his life. The treatise is comprised of 212 paragraphs or "articles," divided into three main sections.

The first section of the *Passiones* is devoted to the rigorous definition of the passions (i.e., the emotions), coupled with a careful examination of how they may be said to differ from "actions." Though conceptually separable to Descartes, the "soul" (read: the mind) and the body were, at the same time, seen as joined in such a way that various *actions* in the body and various *perceptions* by the sense organs immediately provoke certain *passions* in the soul, here pictured as the momentarily passive (hence the term *passiones*) recipient of these impressions. The soul is thereupon capable of initiating a special breed of *actions* all its own, namely, all our *desires*, which, according to Descartes, proceed directly from the soul and depend only upon the soul (Art. 17). Collectively, our desires can be subsumed under the notion of our Will (*voluntas*). As we shall see further on, *desire* is understood by Descartes as being one of the fundamental passions, but different from the others in being directed toward the *future:* we *want* what we do not yet have. This simple but often overlooked truth happens to be embedded in the basic grammar of many languages, including English, German, and Modern Greek. We express the future tense with the auxiliary "will," a derivative of the primitive notion of Will, as in the expression, "I will eat." The latter implies, "I will desire to eat," with such urgency that "I am actually going to eat in the very near future." The "will" of our contemporary future tense, however, no longer carries this sense of urgency and *voluntas* to quite the same degree, the auxiliary "will" now being something of a dead metaphor. The same may be said for the equivalent expressions in German (Ich *will* essen) or Modern Greek (*thelo na trōgō*: I will that I eat).

We think of the emotions in action terms, because action of some sort (fight, flight, pairing, etc.) so often follows, once an e-motion (accent on the "motion") has made itself felt. But Descartes, like all his philosophical predecessors, chose to emphasize the moment of (passive) impingement on the soul (of various perceptions, etc.) as the "first cause" of the experience we now call emotion. The *subsequent* actions, set in motion by the *passio*, constitute precisely the phenomena, of course, that have led to the shift in connotation of "passion" from a passive experience of the mind to the more action-oriented, if not violent, character of our modern word, *passionate.*

Descartes was nevertheless aware of the paradoxical aspect of his own assertion, for a little further on (Art. 19) he states that ". . . we cannot desire anything without *perceiving* that we desire it" (i.e., without laying down in some fashion a mental representation of our own wish), for which reason, ". . . with respect to the Soul, it is an action to desire something," whilst it is also a ". . . passion to perceive *that* we desire it." Here Descartes seems to be aware of some kind of neurophysiological feedback mechanism (where action invokes perception and memory of the action), at whose nature he could only make the crudest guess. Those familiar with Freud's 1895 *Project for a Scientific Psychology* will recognize the lofty task that Descartes also embarked upon some 250 years before Freud: to explain mental phenomena in terms of some subtle bodily counterparts. It would take us too far afield to examine Descartes' mind–body solution in detail; suffice it to say that Descartes felt that the organ which played a key role in mediating perceptions, and the changes in blood circulation that accompanied the "passions," was the pineal gland. This gland was posited as the seat of the Soul by virtue of its central (as opposed to bilateral) location. As such, it was in a position to integrate messages from the two sides of the brain, was, to that extent, more basic, more fundamental an organ than any which existed in a right and a left form. Besides this, it was unitary and therefore more appealing to Descartes as a likely candidate to be the Soul's bodily house and central station.*

A little further on (Art. 24), Descartes draws a distinction between perceptions related to our body and those related to the Soul. The former comprise what we more often subsume under the rubric of "the Drives," and include hunger, thirst, and other natural appetites; also pain, warmth, and other "affections" one senses as stemming from the body. Those related to the Soul include joy, anger, and other "sentiments": these the soul experiences *passively* (and are thus called "passions"). Insofar as the passions are commonly felt to "shake" the soul, they also may be properly called the e-*motions.* Descartes' position here appears to

---

*As it turns out, the pineal, functioning prominently in the maintenance of circadian biological rhythms, may now be seen, if not as the spiritual inner sanctum Descartes envisioned, at least as the Soul's timekeeper!

embody a theory of the emotions in which they are seen as a class of (or derived from) *intensified* perceptions, whose effects on the individual are much more widespread than are mere perceptions of neutral objects or of people who neither menace nor interest us.

Reminiscent of the James–Lange theory of emotions is a subsequent passage (Art. 38) in which Descartes describes certain movements of the body that accompany the passions, without depending on (prior messages from) the Soul. If certain perceptions stimulate fear, they may at the same time cause a "movement of the spirits" toward nerves serving to move the feet − in order to flee. But the soul also senses this *flight,* which Descartes saw as being initiated at times ". . . just by the disposition of the organs, and without any special contribution from the soul." Descartes does not go so far, however, as to claim that the emotion of fear is just an epiphenomenon accompanying the act of − and the mind's enregistration of − a flight response. One may even see an inchoate vector-analytic approach to the emotions in Descartes' writing, to the extent that he takes into account both the prior state of the individual and the variable intensities of competing emotions:

> The same impressions which a frightening object makes upon the (pineal) gland and which causes fear in some men, can incite others to courage. . .because not all brains are built in the same way. (Art. 39)

Descartes elaborates on this point, invoking the concept of *representations.* He seems here to be speaking of memory-traces; the thought he expresses presages the psychostructural approach to object-relations, and does so within the context of a *pleasure-pain* hypothesis regarding adaptation:

> Our passions can't be directly excited. . . by the action of our Will, but they can be, indirectly, by the representations of the things which are customarily connected with the passions we *want* to have − and contrary to those we would *reject.* (Art. 45)

The remainder of Article 45 includes remarks on the manner in which competing emotions of different intensities are resolved into some *outcome* that expresses the net yield of all the negative and positive influences felt within and impinging upon the individual:

> ... to excite courage in our soul, and to avoid fear, it is not sufficient
> to have the will, but one must also consider the reasons, the objects,
> and the examples [i.e., from our memory − *N.B.*] which persuade us
> that the peril isn't too great, or that there is more security in pursuit
> than in flight.

The second section of the *Passiones* is devoted to the enumera-
tion of the emotions, with special attention being paid to the six
emotions Descartes considered "primary." There is also another
adumbration of a Pleasure–Pain principle in Descartes' comment
that ". . . objects which affect the senses do not cause different
passions in us because of the diversities in the objects, but rather
on account of the different ways they may *harm or help* us"
(italics added; Art. 52).

THE SIX PRIMARY PASSIONS

Although Descartes was to catalog and describe some 49 *passions* in this section (see Table I), there were six that seemed
primary and indivisible. The large remainder were either special
cases or slightly modified versions of these six, or were else "compound" passions composed of two or more of the primary emotional colors he recognized. The "primary" emotions were *admiration, love, hate, desire, joy,* and *sorrow* (the latter used interchangeably with *sadness*).

Concerning *admiration* Descartes expressed himself as follows
(Art. 53):

> When the first encounter with an object surprises us, and we judge it to
> be very different from what we are already familiar with. . .this causes
> us to *admire* it or to be surprised. Because this can happen *before* we
> come to know enough about the object to tell if it would be useful to
> us or not, it seems . . . that admiration is the *first* of the passions.

The desire to learn, and to retain in memory, something about
an unusual event or thing ". . . is in itself a passion" according
to Descartes; namely, that of *curiosity* (Art. 75). It has no opposite: because the object represents nothing new to surprise us,
we regard it without passion [i.e., "dispassionately" − *N.B.*].
Descartes sensed how we *compare* external objects with those
already represented in our memory stores; only what we consider
to be relatively *rare* is deemed worthy of special attention.

TABLE I. The emotions ("passions") described by Descartes.

*Admiration	Envy	*Joy
Affection	Esteem	*Love
Agreeableness	Favor	Mockery
Anger	Fear	Pity
Aversion	Friendship	Pride
Boldness	Generosity	Regret
Cheerfulness	Glory	Remorse
Courage	Gratitude	Repentance
Cowardice	*Hate	*Sadness (Sorrow)
Curiosity	Hope	Scorn
*Desire	Horror	Security
Despair	Humility	Self-satisfaction
Devotion	Indignation	Shame
Disdain	Ingratitude	Titillation
Disgust	Irresolution	Veneration
Dread	Jealousy	Virtuous humility
Emulation		

*Denotes a *primary* emotion.

Elaborating on admiration, Descartes defined (Art. 54) two sets of subspecies, depending on (a) whether the emotion was directed at the self or at others (i.e., at *me* or *it,* in Dahl's language) and (b) whether the emotion was positively or negatively tinged. This could be portrayed as a 2 x 2 table in the manner of Table II:

TABLE II. Subspecies of *admiration.*

Toward other	Toward self	
Esteem	Pride	POSITIVE
Scorn	Humility	NEGATIVE

Derivatives of esteem and scorn also existed, for if those emotions were directed at objects we considered as "free causes capable of doing *good* or *evil*" (Art. 55), they would be experienced as *veneration* or *disdain*, respectively.

Descartes understood *love*, in the most abstract sense, as the emotion that grew out of our conscious awareness that something (or some person) was presented to us as a *good*, as *useful* to us. The opposite of this situation stimulated *hate*.

Descartes felt that one could make useful distinctions with respect to *love* by paying attention to the degree of esteem accompanying our love. A love that is, for example, *less* than that which we feel toward ourselves is experienced as *affection* (much as one might feel toward a pet or a flower). A love equal to what we feel toward ourselves is encountered in *friendship*. A love *greater* that what we feel toward ourselves leads to *devotion*, such as Descartes felt was relevant in particularizing our love toward God (Art. 83).

Reasoning that one doesn't distinguish as many differences among the bad things from which one would separate himself, as among good things, Descartes contended (Art. 84) that there were fewer varieties of *hate* than of love. Whether experience supports this viewpoint is not clear. He did, in any case, distinguish between our response to external (especially visual) perceptions that were in agreement with our nature, as "beautiful" (stimulating the "passion" of *agreeableness*) from those contrary to our nature. The latter were experienced as *ugly* and stimulated *aversion* or *horror*.

With *desire* Descartes introduced the element of time, as mentioned earlier: one desired what one did not already have (or else one desired to avoid an evil that had not yet befallen one); hence this emotion pointed always toward the future. A probabilistic element was added as a refinement to the discussion: if one's estimate of the chances of obtaining a desire was favorable, *hope* was excited. If the chances seemed poor, one felt *fear. Jealousy* was regarded as a species of fear. At further extremes of probability, one began to speak of assurance or *security*, or, if the hope seemed extremely low, *despair*.

Further distinctions (Art. 59) were engendered by considering our capacity to accomplish whatever task or mission was necessitated by our desire. If the task seemed inordinately difficult, we would experience *irresolution, cowardice,* or *dread;* if not too difficult, *courage* or *boldness*. The latter was felt in relation to tasks that, while within our grasp, represented a measure of *danger. Emulation* Descartes also saw as a species of *courage. Remorse* may arise in relation to the past or the present (Art. 60), though elsewhere Descartes speaks of it as primarily a type of *sadness* (Art. 177), stemming from *doubt* whether something one did was good.

The notion of *direction* was important to Descartes in his concept of *desire.* He was aware that his predecessors regarded only the wish *for* something as desire, while the flight from an evil was considered *aversion,* as though that were the opposite of desire (Art. 87). But Descartes pointed out that in seeking riches we flee poverty; in seeking health, we wish to escape illness; and so forth. *Desire* had no opposite for Descartes, who emphasized instead the quality of *movement* in some direction. Movement *toward* a good or *away* from an evil were for him aspects of the same passion. In focusing on movement toward or away, Descartes will be seen to have foreshadowed the theoretical positions of de Rivera and Dahl, for whom the *to/from* axis was one of the essential dimensions of emotion.

Consideration of a *good* which is present in the here-and-now leads to *joy;* of an *evil, sadness.* Descartes clearly perceived these as emotions related to the self (*"me"* emotions) and as *passive* experiences.

With this in mind we can appreciate how Descartes came to regard *mockery* as a special variety of joy: this emotion is elicited by the contemplation of something bad that befalls someone whom we regard as *deserving* the bad outcome. Whether the fate of another is merited or not and whether that fate involves a good or an evil generates, in fact, another 2 × 2 table, which we might characterize as shown in Table III.

TABLE III. Emotional reactions to the fates of other persons.

Other person deserved a good	Other person deserved an evil	
Joy	Envy	Other Person Received a Good
Pity	Mockery	Other Person Received an Evil

Descartes included *pity* and *envy* as species of *sorrow* (Art. 62); namely, as species that were related to our impressions about another person or group of persons. The *joy* he alluded to in this section is also a special case of the more abstract emotion of *joy*: one in which we feel happy for someone who gets something good that he deserved.

In a similar vein, a good that we have done in the past may stimulate, upon our contemplation of it, a type of *joy* known as *self-satisfaction*. Descartes considered this the "sweetest of the passions" (Art. 63), one to be contrasted with its opposite, *remorse* (or "contrition").

Another 2 × 2 table emerges from Descartes' descriptions (Arts. 64–65) of our reactions to good and bad things done either to us or to others (Table IV):

TABLE IV. Variants of *joy* or *sorrow* related to *good* or *evil* done to us or to others.

	Done to self by other(s)	Done to other(s)	
Good	Gratitude	Favor	Variants of joy
Evil	Anger	Indignation	Variants of sorrow

It would appear that Descartes regarded these states as complex emotions, inasmuch as anger and indignation are accompanied by *hate;* gratitude and favor, by *love* (Arts. 192–200).

Other aspects of *joy* and *sorrow* include our reactions to public opinion: a good in us that is made known to others excites the feeling of *glory;* something bad about us made public leads to *shame* (Art. 66).

Time and change in attitudes may lead to still further nuances of *joy* and *sadness*, as when a good that has lasted too long provokes boredom or *disgust,* or when a bad thing, having ended, leads to cheerfulness (a species of joy). A good thing, having ended, induces *regret* (Art. 67).

Descartes also described a number of paradoxical situations

concerning joy and sadness. For example, tickling (titillation), starting out as a joyful emotion, can easily be transformed, were it to become excessive and painful, into a species of sadness. In the theater, the spectacle of someone else's sadness may, if artistically portrayed, stimulate a kind of muted joy — one that is related both to the appreciation of an excellent performance and to the obvious fact that we ourselves are in no physical danger from whatever "harm" befalls the actors (Art. 94). Similarly, the contemplation of an ill once suffered, from which one is now free, is a *pleasure*, and therefore belongs to the family of joyful rather than of sorrowful passions.

The end of the middle section of the treatise is devoted to the bodily accompaniments of different emotions. Descartes, in attempting to explain such phenomena as languor, trembling, fainting, facial redness or pallor, tearfulness and sighing, had little to draw upon except Galenic notions of the four temperaments and some recent discoveries about blood circulation from his contemporary, Harvey. Apart from historians of science, modern readers will find little here either of interest or relevance. One example may suffice: Descartes believed that *anger* was the outcome of certain noxious stimuli, one manifestation of which was the delivery by the bloodstream of unusual amounts of bile (cf. choler = bile; "choleric" = angry) to the higher centers, causing the soul (through the mediation of the pineal) to experience this emotion.

Further remarks on the importance of memory and on his inchoate Pleasure/Pain principle then follow, as Descartes deals with the paradoxical aversion of some people toward experiences others find pleasurable. Inability to enjoy the "smell of roses or the presence of a cat" can come, in Descartes' words, ". . . only from events at the beginning of one's life, from having been seriously hurt in some fashion by these objects . . . or through having been affected by a similar aversion in the mother — *even during pregnancy* [italics mine]. The idea of such an aversion remains imprinted in the brain for the rest of life" (Art. 136).

Love, hate, desire, joy, and *sadness* all pertain to the body, according to Descartes, and are ". . . not given to the soul except insofar as the body is joined to it." The natural usage of the passions is to ". . . incite the soul to contribute to those actions which could serve to preserve the body and render it more perfect" (Art. 137). In this life-enhancing, or if you will, adaptational, task, *joy* and *sadness* are the most important ". . . because the soul is not made at once aware of things which hurt the body except by the feeling of *Pain*, which produces *Sadness*, and then *Hate* (toward the offending agent), and finally *Desire* (to be rid of the noxious influence)." Similarly *Joy* and *Love* promote the retention of pleasurable experiences and objects. Descartes regarded *hate* and *sadness* as ". . . more necessary than *Love* and *Joy*, since the former relate to things which could destroy the body" (Art. 137).

Here Descartes is commenting on the importance of the passions to the survival of the individual, a different concern from the estimation of their relative strengths, about which he had less to say. A generation later, Senault (1671) was to write that the four strongest passions were, in order of their vehemence and intensity, *lust* (or concupiscence), *anger, desire for honor*, and the *fear of death* (pp. 30–31).

Since the passions tend to make us exaggerate our responses, Descartes advocated, as a means of tempering them, the use of *experience* (read: the set of collected and integrated memories) and *reason* (in order to better distinguish the useful from the harmful). As a cautionary note, Descartes mentioned that *joy*, through exciting a *desire* whose cause may be unjustified in the light of subsequent events, can be harmful through rendering us rash. Sadness, in contrast, conduces to restraint and prudence (Art. 143).

Throughout the treatise, including the third section, where many individual emotions are analyzed, Descartes concentrates upon basic emotions, simple emotions (related to one or almost exclusively to one of the basic set), and complex emotions that partake of two or more of the fundamental six. The simple emotions are outlined in Table V.

In Table VI I have summarized the relationships of the four dozen passions described by Descartes to the primary six. From this table it will be clear how even some of the "simple" emotions were regarded as having at least one other subsidiary component.

It should be noted that even the complex emotions, such as *jealousy* and *veneration*, do not contain simultaneous *love* and *hate* toward an object nor simultaneous *joy* and *sadness* in relation to an object. *Humility* is the only "passion" where *love* (toward the self) and *hate* (of one's faults) occur together, but here they are directed at the self. The catalog of Descartes is composed, in other words, of feeling-states that seem distinctive to ordinary people, and thus worthy of a one-word label (irrespective of

TABLE V. Simple emotions or "passions" (related to one or predominantly to one of Descartes' six fundamental passions).

Admiration	Love	Hate	Desire	Joy	Sadness
Esteem	Affection	Aversion	Hope	Mockery	Pity
Scorn	Friendship	Horror	Courage	Glory	Envy
Pride	Devotion		Boldness	Self-satisfaction	Shame
Humility	Agreeableness		Emulation	Cheerfulness	Regret
Curiosity			Security		Disgust
			Fear		
			Despair		
			Irresolution		
			Cowardice		
			Dread		
			Remorse		
			Jealousy		

TABLE VI. Relationships among Descartes' "passions" to the fundamental six.

	Admiration	Love	Hate	Desire	Joy	Sadness
Admiration	(+)					
Affection	+	+				
Agreeableness		+				
Anger			+			+
Aversion			+			
Boldness				+		
Cheerfulness					+	
Courage				+		
Cowardice				+		
Curiosity	+			+		
Desire				(+)		
Despair				+		
Devotion	+	+				
Disdain	+		+			
Disgust						+
Dread				+		
Emulation				+		
Envy			+			+
Esteem	+	+		+		
Favor		+			+	
Fear				+		
Friendship	+	+				
Generosity	+	+				
Glory					+	
Gratitude		+		+	+	

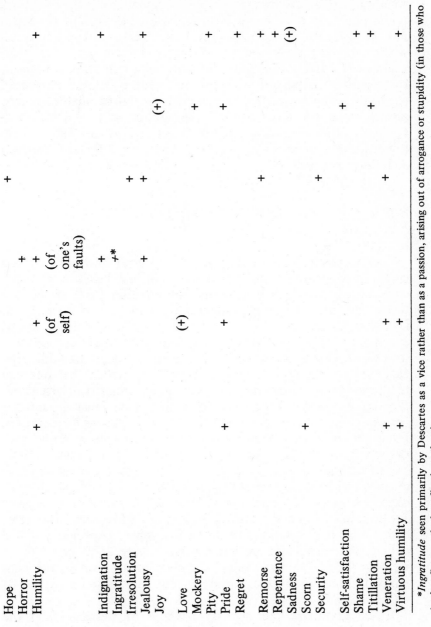

Ingratitude seen primarily by Descartes as a vice rather than as a passion, arising out of arrogance or stupidity (in those who don't reflect on the benefits done them).

whether certain feeling-states appear, upon closer examination, to be made up of several, still more basic, elements). Descartes did not venture far into the psychopathology of the emotions, where one begins to encounter highly ambivalent states characterized by the commingling of "opposite" emotions. *Anguish,* for example, does not come under scrutiny in the *Passiones,* although, using Descartes' own model, we might analyze it into several components. Betrayal in the context of a romantic relationship causes a kind of anguish in which *love* toward and continued *desire* for someone is mixed with *hatred* for the rejection and *sadness* at the loss.

CORRESPONDENCES BETWEEN DESCARTES AND DAHL

Central to the theoretical positions of both Descartes and the contemporary writers, de Rivera and Dahl, is a belief in the existence of certain "primary colors" of emotion from which the whole spectrum of emotional nuances could be reconstructed. Dahl's schema goes a step further in postulating a finite set of emotional pairs (viz., *love–hate*) related to abstract concepts (*to–from; me–it*). These, in turn, arrange themselves like the elements of the periodic table in chemistry, such that one can then predict the existence of "elements" hitherto unsuspected. If a *positive active me* exists (*joy*) then there must be another corresponding to the "position" for a *positive passive me* emotion. For Dahl, the emotion of *contentment* most closely answers to that erstwhile missing element. Descartes also felt *joy* was a basic emotion, but because he did not emphasize the passive/active dimension in relation to JOY, he did not see fit to pair it with *contentment* in the same way as Dahl did. *Contentment* occupies a place in Descartes' catalog, but as we have seen, Descartes understood this "passion" to be, in one sense, a species of *desire* (where the fulfillment of hope was so likely as to bring about *security*) or, in another sense, a species of *joy* (where the contemplation of good things done in the past led to a feeling of *self-satisfaction*).

If we juxtapose the primary passions of Descartes and the eight basic emotions of Dahl, we will note a surprisingly close agreement. A point-by-point comparison of their elements is provided in Table VII.

TABLE VII. Comparison of Descartes primary passions with Dahl's basic emotions.

Descartes' name for the corresponding emotion	Dahl's eight abstract emotional situations	Dahl's name for the corresponding emotion
Admiration	Attraction from it	Surprise
Love	Attraction to it	Love
(Special case of desire)[a]	Repulsion from it	Fear
Hate	Repulsion to it	Anger
Joy	Positive active me	Joy
(Special case of desire or of joy)[b]	Positive passive me	Contentment
(Special case of desire)[c]	Negative active me	Anxiety
Sorrow	Negative passive me	Depression

[a]What is desired won't become available; mission will fail.

[b]Hope of fulfillment (of one's desire) seems certain or contemplation of good things done in the past leads to self-satisfaction.

[c]What is desired requires our effort, but is deemed too difficult to accomplish.

In five instances the emotional labels are identical or virtually so (admiration/surprise; love/love; hate/anger; joy/joy and sorrow/ depression). The latter four are themselves interconnected. On the positive side, for example, joy is the personal *(me)* experience of loving and being loved by another. On the negative side, again, one term relates to the self, another to the interpersonal (or at least, extrapersonal) realm: *sorrow* (or *depression*) is the personal experience arising out of our negative feelings (*hate, anger*) in relation to others. *Anger* is, in fact, a narrower term than *hate,* since we tend to reserve *anger* for situations involving other creatures (most often, other people). One could, for example, speak of "hating" turnips but not of being angry at them.

The close correspondence in these matters between authors separated by 300 years would suggest that they have hit upon something so fundamental about human responsiveness as to be axiomatic — beyond argument, as it were. To a certain extent this may be true. One can make a compelling case that we "hate" what hurts us and "love" what makes us feel especially good, such that our basic emotional vocabulary is wedded inescapably to a pleasure/pain principle itself embedded in our neurophysiological makeup. But it should be equally clear that, beyond these "core" emotions lies a more shadowy realm where the feeling-states one encounters are either mixed or more subtle. Here, especially, our taxonomy will depend increasingly upon matters of utility (in relation to the discussion at hand) rather than on the absolutes of (intense) pleasure or pain. Because Dahl saw great utility in a three-dimensional schema, the eight emotions generated by it appeared "fundamental." *Contentment* occupies as important a place in this model as does *joy*. Descartes, in contrast, was interested primarily in finding an irreducible minimum number of emotional elements, from which all the others could be viewed as mixed or as mild variants. From this vantage point *contentment*, if one takes note of its different connotations in everyday usage, can be understood, as Descartes understood it, as a species either of *joy* or of *desire*.

Again, when one thinks of the complex emotional states, like *jealousy, humility, embarrassment,* etc., our analysis of the component parts and of their varying intensities will determine into which "basic" category we place each such complex emotion. In this context, *jealousy* may be represented by a vector integrating its three ingredients (*hate* toward a rival, *sorrow* at anticipated loss of a love object, and *desire* for the object). One can see immediately that there are hundreds of varieties of jealousy, each reflecting some particular balance among those three ingredients. Although Descartes grouped *jealousy* primarily under *desire*, one can readily envision instances where the hatred-of-the-rival component is predominant. This would tempt us to reclassify *jealousy* as a species of *hatred*. Here I think humility (itself a complicated emotion) would force us to conclude that a more flexible approach is necessary in relation to *jealousy*, no one component of which is always found in the ascendancy.

Our discovery that the most recent contributions to the taxonomy of emotions — namely, the elegant monographs of de Rivera and Dahl — were so closely prefigured in the *Passiones* stirs in us a mixture of Descartes' own primary passions: *admiration* at the philosopher's genius, *joy* at stumbling upon so modern a treatise from three centuries back, and *sadness* that Descartes' wisdom had, within this realm of the emotions, for so long lain neglected.

References

Alexander, F. G. and S. T. Selesnick (1966), *The History of Psychiatry*, Harper and Row, New York.

Dahl, H. (1978), A new psychoanalytic model of motivation, *Psychoanal. Contemp. Thought*, 1, 373–408.

Dahl, H. and B. Stengel, (1978), A classification of emotion words, *Psychoanal. Contemp. Thought*, 1, 269–312.

de Rivera, J. (1977), A structural theory of emotions, *Psychol. Issues: Monograph 40*, International Universities Press, New York.

Descartes, R. (1650), *Passiones Animae*, Elsevier, Amsterdam.

Freud, S. (1895), *A Project for a Scientific Psychology, Standard Edition, Vol. 1*, The Hogarth Press, London.

Freud, S. (1916), *Introductory Lectures on Psychoanalysis, Standard Edition, Vol. XX*, The Horgarth Press, London.

James, W. (1890), *The Principles of Psychology*, Henry Holt and Company, New York.

Kernberg, O. F. (1976), *Object Relations Theory in Clinical Psychoanalysis*, J. Aronson, New York.

Mac Lean, P. D. (1967), The brain in relation to empathy and medical education, *J. Nerv. Ment. Dis.*, 144, 374–382.

Rado, S. (1956), *Psychoanalysis of Behavior*, Grune and Stratton, New York.

Senault, J. F. (1671), *On the Use of the Passions*, Paris.

Vives, J. L. (1524), *Introductio ad Sapientiam (Introduction to Wisdom)*, with Introduction by M. L. Tobriner, Ed., Teacher's College Press, New York City, 1968.

Vives, J. L. (1531), *De Tradendis Disciplinis*, Translated with an Introduction by F. Cordasco, Rowan and Littlefield, Totowa, New Jersey, 1971, p. 84.

THREE

Core Processes In
The Organization
Of Emotions

PETER H. KNAPP

INTRODUCTION

Emotions comprise a vast area of inquiry. It is beset with verbal pitfalls, since so much about emotions is unverbalizable; it is logically treacherous, since they span so many differing frames of reference.

Two groups of questions can be distinguished: those at the level of phenomenological description, which are essentially psychological, and those at the level of motivational mechanism, which are more psychoanalytical, ultimately perhaps neuropsychological.

At the phenomenological level, some deceptively simple questions have to do with definition. What are the key factors which characterize experiences and behaviors we call emotional? Some of these features are (1) a kind of *vividness* and immediacy; (2) a connection to bodily, especially *visceral,* processes; (3) an *urgency* or imperiousness; (4) a *quantitative range,* from faint traces to massive and intense reactions; (5) a tendency to *persist,* to flow and ebb relatively slowly; (6) the appearance of *parallel and simultaneous aspects* rather than only exclusive and single ones; (7) relatively *stereotyped expressive patterns,* many of which are shared with other animals.

At the phenomenological level we also face problems of classification. Numerous schemes have attempted to identify basic emotions and to trace their modes of combination into more complex

Supported in part by grants from The American Psychoanalytic Association and The Boston Psychoanalytic Society and Institute.

configurations. The early scheme of A. Shand (1914) was a pioneering venture in this direction. Two recent efforts in classification, by Plutchik (1962) and by Tomkins (1962), will be stressed later in this paper. Here it is only worth noting that so far no classificatory scheme has had undisputed success.

At the level of motivational mechanism additional questions arise. Many of them are distinctively psychoanalytic. What is the relationship of emotion to defensive and adaptive tactics and strategies and, in particular, to the vicissitudes of consciousness? The layering of emotions, their "taming" and "desomatization," as Schur puts it (1966), and their use as protective signals have been noted by many analysts, in work thoroughly summarized by Rapaport (1953). Such observations suggest that the multiplicity and often simultaneity of emotional manifestations are far from random but rather constitute an intricately organized field.

At times a central emotional theme seems to emerge through layers of symbolic disguise or distortion, showing us what we believe a subject "really" feels. Freud remarked on this tendency in what is still a most provocative discussion of affect, Chapter VI of *The Interpretation of Dreams* (1953); but he noted that we often encounter an opposite pattern, namely, one emotion replacing and protecting against another.

Psychoanalysis has also tried to discern relationships between surface elements and deeper determining processes. Such an attempt has involved theories not only of emotion but of underlying motivational or drive states. Psychoanalytic views have characterized emotions as the result sometimes of "discharge," sometimes of conflict between drives. Although either a "discharge" or a "conflict" theory alone leaves many features unexplained, the two together encompass a large number of emotional phenomena. However, questions are only pushed deeper, into the nature of human drives themselves. A simple instinctual dichotomy of libidinal and aggressive drives has obscured the nature of "reactive motives," to use French's term (1970). These stem principally from anxiety and depression, and play crucial roles in emotional life. Freud's original formulation of instinct as "a concept on the frontier between the mental and the somatic" (1957), no less than his earlier view of emotions as "discharge into the interior of the body" (1956), continues to raise fundamental neuropsychological and psychosomatic issues. These remain lively in discussions of the nature of emotions, which inevitably focus on the interface between brain and periphery and between mind and body.

The present paper proposes a model made up of a combination of certain core processes. The model contains three major components, each of which has been part of previous partial explanatory theories of emotion. By core is meant an aggregate of underlying mechanisms which contribute to generating emotions. These mechanisms are formulated in psychological terms and are intended to have independent psychological validity, but they are homologous with current knowledge of brain function. Thus what is proposed is a neuropsychological model.

The notion of a tripartite transactional model derives ultimately from Wundt, a pioneer in modern experimental psychology (cf. Boring, 1950). Wundt was himself still dominated by the notion of distinct "faculties" in psychological life; but he initiated the experimental study of many aspects of behavior, including emotion. He saw emotion as having three major dimensions: pain/pleasure, excitement/calm, tension/relaxation. These three dimensions actually are congruent with another way of classifying essential emotional phenomena, namely, along an axis of input-central processing–output.

In a more general sense we can distinguish (a) on the side of input, *sensory apperception;* the term apperception (rather than perception or registration) is intended to indicate — after Webster — "understanding something perceived in terms of previous experience"; in the emotional sphere the further connotation is one of hedonic evaluation; (b) *central processing;* this refers to the general activation or deactivation of emotional elements; (c) *expressive mobilization,* which immediately prepares for and accompanies agonistic/fearful or sensuous encounters with the environment. These three elements, their components and their transactional relationship to one another, constitute the core model. Figure I is a diagrammatic representation of the model. Each component will be discussed separately, and then some remarks will be made about their relationship to one another and to other processes relevant to emotions.

SENSORY APPERCEPTION – HEDONIC EVALUATION

Pleasure and pain were crucial concepts in Freud's thinking and have run through many psychoanalytic conceptualizations about emotion, although in an unsystematic way. As sensory qualities they contribute to many of the characteristic features of emotion

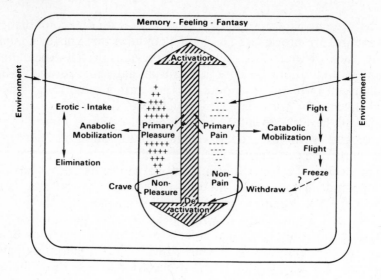

Fig. I. Emotion: Neuropsychologic core.

which we have already identified at the phenomenological level. Hedonic tone contributes to the vividness of emotion, although at the same time pleasurable and painful sensations can be elusive, even ineffable. As we shall see later, neither pain nor pleasure are invariant, unitary sensations. Motivationally both contribute to the imperiousness of emotion. The pleasure principle, in Freud's terminology, rules during childhood and the adult must acquire strength and sophistication to overrule it. Avoidance of pain is by the same token a major motivating factor for defensive and adaptive effort.

Along with the vividness and imperious nature of pain and pleasure goes a sense of their being rooted in the body. Many of the bodily connections are now well known. Some are of particular importance for psychological theory. When painful stimulation ascends to central areas in the thalamus and adjacent areas, an integral consequence is sympathetic nervous system discharge, spreading out to the periphery of the body (Melzak and Wall, 1965). There is thus an immutable linkage between primary painful apperception and an agonistic/fearful response. Similarly, pleasurable stimulation, including that from drugs like the opiates, has invariant visceral concomitants, strongly sensuous, often frankly erotic. Discoveries by Olds (1955, 1958) of neuroanatomical loci governing physiologically distinct, intense pleasurable reactions on the one hand and painful, aversive reactions on the other hand, have lent further impetus to spelling out the neuropsychology of pain and pleasure. Undoubtedly, urges to achieve pleasurable consummation lie behind many behaviors we call emotional. On the dysphoric side the appetitive structure is less clear. The relationship of anxiety to other types of unpleasurable affect, which it seems to pervade and in some ways dominate, is particularly confused.

Figure I shows incoming stimuli reaching centers for pain and pleasure. A cautionary note must be sounded from the neurophysiologic viewpoint. Apperception of pain and pleasure is not a purely reflex matter. Incoming stimuli are regulated and filtered by numerous gating mechanisms, as described by Melzak and Wall (1965). These may attenuate painful stimuli at the periphery. That capacity may account for some of the widespread effects observable in acupuncture. In addition there are undoubtedly central processes which match incoming stimuli with past memories and which focus attention on or away from them. Such complex activity — summarized in Figure I by a thin layer labeled Memory-Feeling-Fantasy — may be invoked in procedures such as hypnosis, which the careful work of Hilgard (1975), along with others, has shown can substantially affect apperception of pain.

Thus primary painful and pleasurable apperception is intimately linked not only to expressive systems, but to systems concerned with arousal and the regulation of tension. Through them positive or negative feedback can accentuate or attenuate hedonic evaluation. A clear avenue is open for the entrance of symbolic systems. It is not clear to what extent inner symbolic factors can *initiate* pleasure or pain *de novo.* Vivid experiences during dreaming provide evidence that they can, although dreams also show an opposite capacity, to detach the dreamer from primary hedonic sensations, particularly painful ones, by distortion and disguise and thus diminish their power to interfere with sleep.

Let us examine further the phenomenological diversity of pain and pleasure. The pain of depression is not like that of a toothache, though the two may overlap. The pleasure of relaxing after a period of stress is not like that of sexual stimulation. Part of the difference results from associated processes of arousal and specific expressive mobilization. However, some of it stems from crucial differences in the quality of experience. Pain and pleasure that are *"primary,"* involving specific neurophysiological reinforcement systems, must be differentiated from pain and pleasure that are *secondary,* coming to some extent from absence of the opposite primary state. Acute lack of pleasurable satisfaction, as in boredom, or even hunger, constitutes a kind of pain. Relaxation, escape from painful stimulation, constitutes a kind of pleasure.

We therefore have a fourfold hedonic *sub*model. It includes primary (neurophysiologically reinforcing) pleasure and secondary pleasure (non-pain), as well as primary (neurophysiologically aversive) pain and secondary pain (non-pleasure). Clearly such a model represents only the merest beginning of an hedonic calculus. A number of psychoanalytic observers, in particular Krystal (1974, 1978), have traced the ways in which pleasure of one or another sort may become associatively linked to affective processes such as anxiety ordinarily thought to be distressing, so as to create subtle and paradoxical quasiaddictive patterns of "attachment to painful feeling," in a phrase from Valenstein (1973). We will return to this complexity of emotional experience later when we consider its symbolic elaboration.

ACTIVATION–DEACTIVATION

The view that activation or arousal (to use a term with more of a feeling connotation) plays a central role in emotion has been argued by a number of workers, chiefly Lindsley (1957). At times proponents have tended to equate emotions with some kind of unidimensional state of growing arousal. Excitement and its potential for flooding the individual is important in Freud's original thoughts about the stimulus barrier (1920). Observations on children have emphasized the role of arousal, potentially progressing to excitement, and the need to master it as crucial in the course of development.

Closer scrutiny suggests a variety of different sorts of excitement, for example, pleasurable elation, or painful panic. Aggressive or erotic impulses and their expressive manifestations may be mixed with arousal. Readily available positive feedback channels exist between pain, pleasure, and activating processes. The latter stimulate memories, images, and fantasies, which stimulate additional hedonic responses and still further arousal. This state of affairs is indicated in Figure I.

Control mechanisms restraining such mounting states of excitement are imperfectly understood. Tension, once activated, may focus on key aspects of the external or internal world, on organized plans for, or finally on the execution of, actions. Such measures serve to limit the emotional buildup, to channel it by progressively more narrow activation of certain elements, while others are in some way inhibited. At times we see sudden switching to states of massive deactivation. The switch from eroticized excitement to lassitude and sleep following sexual consummation is one prototype. Its culmination, characterized by actual physiological elimination in male ejaculation, may have facilitated our use of the term "discharge" as a metaphor (cf. Knapp, 1967). Other, still more sudden, switching may be observed — for example, the sudden "freezing" in states of fear withdrawal. Such shifts may be crucial to Engel's seminal concept of conservation.

It is important to note that there are various types of activation. Selective accentuation may involve the motor sphere, racing thoughts, or pressure of speech. The same is true of deactivation or inhibition. This may vary from momentary arrest of function to massive inhibition by "countercathectic" accentuation of tonic, restraining impulses, as in the inhibited state of obsessive and many depressive individuals. We must take account of the reciprocal, automatic inhibition of one system by activation of another. In the emotional sphere most psychological functions reflect what is true throughout the nervous system, namely, a balance between excitement and inhibition. For this reason it may be difficult to know whether a given bit of behavior represents actual activation or release of deactivation.

For the most part, we have till now tried to describe these processes in terms consistent with psychological observation. In many areas we can see parallel lines of evidence spelling out the actual role of neurophysiologic or neurochemical processes to produce activation or deactivation and their behavioral consequences. The stages of sleep and particularly of dreaming are obvious examples. In REM sleep, as Hobson (1977) and others have shown, there is selective inhibition of external perception and at the same time a diffuse electroencephalographic pattern of low-voltage fast "arousal" along with specific excitation of visual pathways and the production of vivid, internally generated experiences, which are often exquisitely emotional.

A leading theory of the basic defect in schizophrenia also centers around the notion of diffuse arousal. At least for "pure" schizophrenia, compelling evidence exists that this type of excitation leads to a flooding of consciousness with stimuli so that discrimination of outer and inner environment, of self from other, becomes jeopardized. This "arousal theory" has been elaborated by Mirsky and Kornetsky (1969); it fits with current hypotheses about hyperactive biogenic amine systems in the brain and the postulated blocking action of these by neuroleptic drugs.

The acute arousal of schizophrenia exemplifies what is intended by the term emotional/motivational "core." Even though intense, such arousal may not lead to what is generally identified as intense emotion. Massive deactivation may overlay and dominate the clinical picture, as in the motor and expressive inhibition of catatonia. Or there may be more partial surface inhibition, resulting in flat, inappropriate affect, even during the phase of schizophrenic turmoil. At times, emotional manifestations may appear but be overshadowed by cognitive disruption or by enactment of primitive instinctual impulses. At other times, of course, intense emotion may be reported in retrospect. Rarely, it may be overt, flooding the patient almost uncontrollably with a sense of horror, or panic, or exaltation and bliss. Then the usually unstructured and silent processes involved in activation recruit emotionally tinged imagery and memories. These interact with and amplify hedonic apperception; they also interact with the third type of core process in our model, namely, mobilization for environmental interchange.

EXPRESSIVE MOBILIZATION

Here we came closer to traditional emotion. This component of the model designates processes that initiate and precede the expression of crucial instinctive behavior. They include characteristic patterns of motor–expressive display. These in turn intermingle with stereotyped neurovegetative and endocrine responses, which are, at least potentially, capable of quantitative measurement.

The best known, and in ways the simplest, of such processes are those concerned with agonistic–fearful environmental interaction. These are the flight–fight reactions clarified by Cannon (1920) ("F" processes in Figure II). Their motor-expressive patterns, such as clenched teeth, tense muscles, and scowling, are accompanied by manifestations related to sympathetic nervous activity — sweating, dry mouth, piloerection, and tremor. Cannon's unifying theory of the adaptive importance of the sympathetic nervous system was extended by Hess (1957), who traced its organizing neurophysiology to the hypothalamus in what he called ergotrophic centers, and also by Selye (1975), who linked short-term adrenal medullary responses to secretion from the adrenal cortex, having more long-lasting effects, thus backing up or sustaining what came to be thought of as a general reaction to stress.

Oversimplification, which so often follows major discoveries, plagued subsequent investigations. Often emotion became equated with these "stress" reactions or even with the purely physiological aspects of sympathoadrenal activity. In 1954, Engel called for a new physiology of emotions, to extend beyond the response patterns elucidated by Cannon and Selye. However, at times even he seemed to propose an oversimple polarity, advancing the concept of a "conservation withdrawal response" as a polar opposite of anxious aggressive mobilization. Other investigators, such as Benson (1975), have seen "relaxation" as this kind of polar vector-opposing stress.

The model proposed here would encompass withdrawal and relaxation as exemplars of intensified deactivation, having high adaptive value; but it would insist upon the complexity of core interacting elements, both within the flight–fight sphere and between it and other core components. Although flight and fight reactions resemble each other, they also differ in important ways, as Plutchik (1962) and others have remarked. Some of these ways are behavioral. Anger impels the individual toward the source of distress, fear impels him away from it. There are obviously a host of other subjective and objective differences. Moreover, their hedonic linkages differ. Fear is immutably linked with pain, psychologically and also, as we have noted, physiologically. Rage is more ambiguous; it is generally evaluated as distressing, but often, at its height, it combines with covert, if not overt, tinges of primary pleasure.

Fear responses are complicated further: usually they are accompanied by urges and impulses to flee, with all their motor representations; at other times, these appear to be replaced by an inhibitory "freezing" and withdrawal, even though the cardiovascular response associated with anxiety may persist. We observe a form of behavioral switching whereby primary fearful responses suddenly invoke a partial adaptive deactivation.

At the biological level, similar ambiguities remain. The specific physiologic dimensions of anger and fear are unclear. Peripheral hormonal mediating systems, catecholamines and their receptors, form an intricate array of substances. For example, alpha and beta adrenergic systems are clearly separable; the latter seem more closely associated with anxiety and increases in heart rate and blood pressure. However, the exact psychological correlates of alpha or beta stimulation, or blockade, are still unknown.

These "F" systems also bear a contrapuntal relationship to a second class of system, designated in this model as "E" systems. These are in some ways still more complex. Physiologically, they are related to the parasympathetic nervous system. Cannon noted that this system lacks the homogeneity and capacity for massive discharge of the sympathoadrenal system. He saw discrete parasympathetic components as responsible for "housekeeping" functions (1920). A more general characterization is that they have to do with sensuous interactions and interchange with the environment. One form of such interchange is, broadly speaking, erotic, involving intaking, prolonging, oral and sexual aspects, libidinal in the widest sense. Another kind has to do with elimination. Hence, the designation of "E" systems. Elsewhere (1967a,b), I have argued that the notion of elimination should be widened. Building on Rado's concept of riddance (1956), we can see it encompassing a variety of ways of purging the individual of unwanted substances and sensations. It also includes the curbing of undesirable or excessive appetite and the accompanying excitement in both psychological and physiological spheres. Thus, oral impulses are curbed by satiety and disgust. Other libidinal impulses are curbed by shame. Even sorrow — the visceral expression of which is weeping, a parasympathetically mediated function — may belong in this family of processes having to do with purging and curbing. A speculation is that these "E" processes may govern the crucial surveillance and purging carried out by some parts of the immune systems.

Secondary pain, or displeasure, thus accompanies these eliminative processes. Again, we encounter difficulties in the hedonic calculus. This kind of distress often has a bittersweet quality, and it may involve intricate reversals. Satiety, for example, replaces hunger, in a relatively sudden shift accompanied by feelings of repleteness. These have an ambiguous hedonic tone. They may be subtle signals, occurring well in advance of gastric sensations that are painful in any primary sense. Possibly, they have a learned component which adaptively anticipates actual excessive intake and its harmful physiologic consequences. Stunkard (1975) argues that satiety is a learned phenomenon by which the organism gains a progressive mastery over its environment.

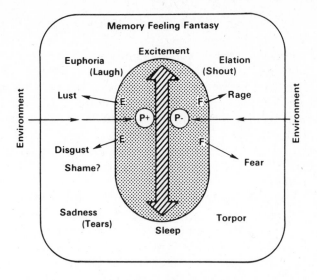

Fig. II. Other–self: General model.

CORE TRANSACTIONS AND WIDER ASPECTS OF EMOTION

The components of the model having to do with expressive mobilization were introduced — to repeat — as being "closer" to emotion. Neither an erotic nor a destructive urge by itself, any more than its visceral concomitants alone, constitutes emotional experience in the full sense of that term. The latter results from the interplay between hedonic evaluation and the quasiobligatory mobilization to respond, modified by activation and deactivation of wider elements, memories, anticipations, fantasies, and plans. Emotions result from reverberating adaptive equilibria of core components. Some of these patterns have been mentioned already. A more formal depiction of them appears in Figure II. Essentially, this represents an expansion of the layer designated "memory feeling fantasy" surrounding the postulated core.

At times, a single core element with all its visceromotor concomitants and ideational trappings — for instance, rage — may dominate the emotional field, often proceeding toward culmination in expression and action. Then we speak of "discharge" although what we mean is actually a restabilization of the emotional field.

Such relatively "pure" states, eight in number, are shown in Figure II. They are euphoria, lust, disgust, sadness, torpor, fear, rage, and elation. Incidentally, the status of shame is left ambiguous. An argument suggesting its intrinsic relationship with sorrow and disgust is presented elsewhere (1967a,b). The model also depicts extreme states of excitement and their opposite, withdrawal into sleep. As mentioned earlier, both of these, taken by themselves, lack the hedonic and expressive aspects of full emotional experience.

Tomkins (1962) advanced the view that there were six basic emotions: surprise, joy, sorrow, disgust, fear, and anger. Ekman (1972) has found empirical evidence that these emotions have characteristic facial expressions recognizable across many cultures. There is a high degree of correspondence between the Tompkins-Ekman classification and the "feeling layer" proposed here.

A model of emotion must have the capacity to go beyond any such list of basic affects to richer and subtler states. At many times more than one element may be present, exhibiting the parallel and simultaneous character of emotional manifestations which we have already mentioned. This proposed model allows not only for switching from one dominant element to another, but also for the persistence of several elements at one time. Persistence may be not harmonious but rather the start of conflict, leading to a crescendo of unresolved feeling — for example, rage and erotic need in competition with each other. Such competition may be further experienced as inner threat and lead to mounting anxiety.

A different configuration may result from the blending of various simultaneous elements into complex complementary states: rage and greed may combine in envy, or longing, sadness and inhibition in states of boredom. Plutchik (1962) particularly stressed the mixing of emotions, using the analogy of a color chart. He too proposed a basic grouping of emotions, somewhat similar to those proposed in this and Tompkins' theory.

However, the present model differs from both those of Plutchik and Tomkins in seeing emotions, not as primary motivators themselves which implicitly, or in the case of Tompkins, explicitly, stand in contrast to "drives." Rather, it tries to use a psychoanalytic theoretical perspective to do what psychoanalysis itself has not succeeded in doing, namely, to trace the relationship of emotions to the instinctive foundations of behavior. At the same time, it tries to avoid certain difficulties of psychoanalytic theory. These have to do with the postulation of independent instinctual energy, and with unresolved questions as to how such energy is transformed into "discharge cathexes" or "tamed" to result in signal affects. The present model suggests that the basic components — hedonic, activational, expressive — are shared with the rest of the animal kingdom; are identifiable subjectively while also having correspondence to equally identifiable neurophysiologic systems; and interact to produce the phenomena we call emotions. The core alone includes some of the phenomena that have been identified as instinctual drives. The combination of erotic and eliminative processes, regulated by pleasure and pain, provides for an interface with more purely physiologic drive states described in neurophysiologic terms, such as factors regulating salt, or water intake, or other metabolic activities.

Clearly, much more detailed argument and evidence would be needed to trace the relationship between the emotional/motivational core proposed here, on the one hand, to current neurophysiological knowledge, and, on the other hand, to psychoanalytic propositions. This paper can deal with only one further aspect, the uniquely human relationship of this "core" to fantasy and felt experience, that is, the quasicognitive aspects of emotion.

The first statement that should be made is that this model is dynamic, not static. It portrays an adaptive organism constantly adjusting itself to and attempting to master the environment. It is thus related to a world of key other persons, originally and persistently. Incoming stimuli, however discrete and immediate their sensory character, are evaluated as evidence of the nature of the impact of the relevant world. Automatic activation of responses betrays intent toward that world. That is, an individual prepares to move toward and take in, or to eliminate, or to attack, or to flee from a part of the human environment.

In the sense that this model goes beyond affect *per se* to an instinctive core, this is only another way of stating what Freud said originally in his theory of instincts, namely, that each of them has an aim and an object. This model, unlike the early psychoanalytic models, sees not a machine being powered by some inner, instinctual fuel, but, rather, an organism with primitive adaptive mechanisms, shared with animal forebears, constantly experiencing and adapting to an environment, chiefly an environment of fellow organisms.

The primal motivational mechanisms of hedonic evaluation and expressive mobilization are accompanied by dimly emerging cognitive processes having to do with memory and anticipation, which become activated or deactivated by feedback relationships between the incoming stimuli and the responses they evoke. Such cognitive processes are present in the infant and in his mammalian progenitors. As this early cognitive potential unfolds, the infant organism ceases to live in constant flux. He begins to develop abstract schemata, in the Piagetian sense, which classify and order experience so as to produce the beginnings of vague images of the world and the self. These lend experience constancy and predictability. Core elements, aided by learning, develop repetitive patterns. A good-other + secure-self, along with affectionate urges, may develop; or a bad-other + distressed-self along with anxious or aggressive urges.

Developmental phases can be categorized more precisely. In the earliest phase schemata are rudimentary. Hedonic evaluation automatically activates urges for expression and action. Because of this I have spoken of a "schemactive core." The phase refers to schemata which are automatically associated with action; it indicates the adaptive automaticity whereby hedonic reactions lead to programs for action. One form of action is, of course, thought. Seen in its core beginnings, this kind of model may be of value in addressing certain artificial splits that take place later in our conceptualizations, such as the split between mind and body.

An additional feature marking the earliest phase of schemactive core patterns is the failure to clearly distinguish self from other. We must postulate that the infant experiences a kind of Otherself, a unit formed by a personal outer world, having hedonic influence, and a Self, influenced by and stirred toward action. Separation within this unity into a world composed of subject and object is a later development, a point made by Von Bertenlanffy (1964). We must postulate that this early, unified, quasireflexive mode of experiencing corresponds to Piaget's sensori-motor phase. It is scarcely necessary to stress how much this phase is dominated by motivational/emotional features.

A second phase follows. In it there is the beginning of the uniquely himan capacity for symbolization. Images and memories start to be laid down. These become organized around Otherself clusters of good and bad worlds, along with derivative, increasingly complex, representations of these. Mother becomes equated with a house, a blanket, a familiar warm scene, or with warmth itself. Personal experience contributes to the range of derivates. We know the plasticity and also the confusion of the child's world as this symbolic process unfolds. Once more, it has been richly documented by Piaget in his discussion of preoperational thought.

I have used the term idiosymbolic activity to characterize the type of mentation developed in this phase. Naturally, such mentation continues throughout life. It tends to be holistic, using nondiscursive or, in Langer's term, presentational symbolism. But, as a system of symbolic reference, it allows an individual to contemplate the world without needing to fly into immediate action. Each individual accumulates his idiosymbolic store of memories, like a motion picture reel of almost endless length. This type of storage and potential recall is what Tulving (1972) and Cofer (1976) call episodic memory.

The important aspect of such idiosymbolic mentation is that it remains in intimate contact with the schemactive core. It is activated by and activates the core processes of hedonic evaluation and expressive mobilization.

The final developmental phase is, of course, the emergence of discursive symbolic thought. This corresponds to Piaget's stages of concrete operations and, finally, formal operations. It encompasses the wide range of linguistic and other cognitive activities which we know as the major part of conscious thought. It comes to dominate our lives because of its high adaptive value, although it functions constantly in conjunction with persisting idiosymbolic inner experience. At times, such inner experience becomes outer creation, in triumphs of aesthetic activity, heavily tinged with the emotion to which idiosymbolic processes remain connected. Discursive thought involves what Tulving (1975) calls semantic memory, a capacity to name, categorize, and otherwise deal with the world and with past experience in precise, publicly shared terms.

Figure III represents a different view of the core and superordinate elements. It emphasizes the organization of hedonic evaluation and motivational striving into "Otherself" repertoires. By way of connection with more advanced mentation, there is constant reverberating interchange between the neuropsychologic core and higher processes responsible for idiosymbolic memory. More advanced processes, still "higher," aided by focused attention and additional cognitive operations, including semantic memory, serve as an organizing focus, like a spotlight, for consciousness, enabling an individual to sort out aspects of the outer world in order better to act in it. The spotlight may even turn upon the organism itself and focus, with its advanced cognitive skills, upon inner, idiosymbolic life. For the most part, however, during waking life, idiosymbolic experience remains as a penumbra, a "ground" against which the conscious "figure" is displayed.

For the present discussion, I would emphasize three further points. First is one already mentioned, namely, that idiosymbolic processes are the elements originally activated by and activating the emotional core. It is a reasonable hypothesis that this relationship is maintained throughout life. Personal memory and nondiscursive imagery stir feeling. Consider the difference between two five-word sentences: "I'll flag down a cab," and "The flag is still waving." Both involve the concept of undulating movement. However, "flag" in the former sentence is a subordinate semantic marker, designating an action, which is the underlying linguistic focus. In the latter sentence, "flag" serves as a symbol, invoking an image rich in connotations which sets emotions stirring, however varied or muted these may be. The idiosymbolic image, even though in the background of discourse, serves as a persistent mediator between cognitive (secondary process) activity and core, emotionally tinged responses.

A second point follows from the first. Acquisition of rudimentary ability to symbolize has, as we have noted, adaptive value. The child sees classes of stimuli, A gesture stands for an attitude. He develops clusters of responses. A gesture stands for a series of actions. As psychic life grows more complicated, one learns to delay and to deceive oneself. A gesture may be misinterpreted as comforting rather than threatening, in order to avoid distressing implications and the responses these invoke. One sees the world as benign rather than devastating. Similarly, one learns to manipulate expressive mobilizations and the actions they are instigating. One mobilizes affectionate, submissive attitudes to avoid the dangers that might follow aggressive mobilization. Thus, defensive strategy alters apperception, managing pain and pleasure with what game theorists call a minimax principle. Defensive strategy uses similar minimaxation — if we may use the term — in mobilizing responses.

Discursive thought and language can themselves be part of such strategies, ways of flattening or avoiding the richness of idiosymbolic imagery and associated affect. But, if affect can be connected with appropriate idiosymbolic experience, it can cut through defensive maneuvers and dissect out the true impact and intent in schemactive operations. Such is the task of psychotherapy.

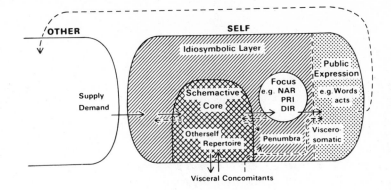

Fig. III. Emotion: Core + "feeling layer."

An example may clarify. Quite some years ago I had a dream. It was very simple: a group of students were sitting in a room looking at a friend and colleague of mine, George C. He was sitting alone, weeping copiously. Just that silent detached scene. I promptly forgot the dream. Only that evening did I recall it, when my sister phoned me to remind me of the fact that this was an important date — which I had also forgotten. It was the 10th anniversary of our mother's sudden, tragic death.

Without going into many of the deeper motives for forgetting, we can readily arrive at a translation of the central preconscious meaning of this dream. In point of fact, that task was performed by a master. A day or so later I happened to be with a distinguished visitor to Boston, the late Bertram Lewin. I told him this example of dreaming activity. With characteristic wit he made a summary interpretation: "Let George do it."

To summarize this example in terms of the previous discussion, we see (a) a schemactive core involving a painful Otherself state and the urge to weep; (b) the idiosymbolic dream image of a weeping other person; (c) the discursive, potentially therapeutic interpretation, "Let George do it."

A further, tangential observation is important: Many individuals with powerful core conflicts and potentially explosive emotions may develop highly effective strategies for avoiding contact with idiosymbolic inner life. My own experience with psychosomatic patients indicates that many, though not all of them, have this type of character. It is important to probe them skillfully with the discursive, but affectively tuned, instrument of psychotherapy. If one does so, one finds a wealth of near-overwhelming emotions.

This bears on current concepts subsumed under the term *alexithymia,* as developed chiefly by Sifneos (1973). The term refers to an alleged block — some feel a perhaps physiological and irreversible one — between consciousness and inner feelings and fantasies, thought to be a prominent feature of patients with psychosomatic disorders and possibly some other groups. In my opinion the term describes habitual defensive stances of many, not all, such patients. It does not refer to an immutable inability for them to gain contact with their emotions, but rather, their use of massive denial, avoidance and externalization. We need firm data about the presence and frequency of so-called alexithymic features, as well as about their deeper structure and ways we can deal with them. My own clinical experience suggests that usually they are understandable and treatable within a psychoanalytic frame of reference similar to that proposed here. This, I believe, is particularly true of psychosomatic patients.

A third and final point has to do with hemispheric specialization and emotion. There is now compelling evidence that allocation of tasks, according to cortical and subcortical prewired potential, directs the elaboration and perhaps storage of different sorts of information. It seems likely that nondiscursive, idiosymbolic imagery and personal episodic memory (cf. Cofer, 1976; Tulving, 1976) are preferentially handled by the nondominant (usually right) hemisphere. By contrast, discursive operations, and probably semantic memory and cognitive rules, may be elaborated by the dominant (usually left) hemisphere. That would explain the blunting of emotion caused by tissue damage to the right hemisphere, described by Geschwind (1974).

Such specialization does not, incidentally, mean that emotion is "located" in the right hemisphere. It means that certain symbolic activities, which play an important role in triggering and reverberating with core processes and thus in elaborating emotional activity in humans, may be preferentially organized by the right hemisphere.

What we call emotion goes well beyond such cortical activity. It depends upon a number of core processes. These are related neuropsychologically to sub-cortical brain structures, bilaterally located, and to their sensory, autonomic and endocrine connections, which are diffusely distributed throughout the body.

The core model proposed here offers a conceptual bridge between these physiological and neurophysiological elements and the phenomena observable by psychology and by psychoanalysis in the sphere of emotion.

References

Benson, H. (1975), *The Relaxation Response*, Morrow, New York.

Boring, E. G. (1950), *History of Experimental Psychology*, 2nd ed., Appleton Century Crofts, New York.

Cannon, W. B. (1920), *Bodily Changes in Pain, Hunger, Fear, and Rage*, 2nd ed., Appleton, New York.

Cofer, C. N. (1976), in C. N. Cofer (Ed.), *An Historical Perspective in the Structure of Human Memory*, W. H. Freeman, San Francisco.

Engel, G. L. (1954), Selection of clinical material in psychosomatic medicine: The need for a new physiology, *Psychosom. Med.*, **16**, 368.

Engel, G. L. (1968), The psychoanalytic approach to psychosomatic medicine, in J. Marmon (Ed.), *Modern Psychoanalysis: New Directions and Perspectives*, Basic Books, New York.

Ekman, P., W. V. Friesen, and P. Ellsworth (1972), *Emotion in the Human Face*, Pergamon, New York.

French, T. M. (1970), *Psychoanalytic Interpretations (Selected Papers)*, Quadrayle Books, Chicago.

Freud, S. (1953), *The Interpretation of Dreams, Standard Edition*, Vol. V, Hogarth Press, London, pp. 460–487.

Freud, S. (1956), *Formulations Regarding the Two Principles of Mental Functioning, Standard Edition*, Vol. XII, Hogarth Press, London, p. 215.

Freud, S. (1957), *Instincts and Their Vicissitudes, Standard Edition*, Vol. XIV, Hogarth Press, London, pp. 111-140.

Freud, S. (1957), *Beyond the Pleasure Principle, Standard Edition*, Vol. XVIII, Hogarth Press, London.

Geschwind, N. (1974), The development of the brain and the evolution of language, in *Selected Papers on Language and the Brain*, D. Reidel, Boston.

Hess, W. R. (1957), *The Functional Organization of the Hypothalamus*, Grune & Stratton, New York.

Hilgard, E. and J. Hilgard (1975), *Hypnosis in Relief of Pain*, W. Kaufman, Los Altos, Cal.

Hobson, J. A. and R. W. McCarley (1977), The brain as a dream state generator: An activation-synthesis hypothesis of the dream process, *Am. J. Psychiatry*, **13**, 1335-1348.

Knapp, P. H. (1967), Some riddles of riddance: Relationships between eliminative processes and emotion, *Arch. Gen. Psychiatry*, **16**, 586-602.

Knapp, P. H. (1967), Purging and curbing: An inquiry into disgust, satiety and shame, *J. Nerv. Ment. Dis.*, **144**, 514-534.

Krystal, H. (1974), The genetic development of affects and affect regression, *Ann. Psychoanal.*, **2**, 98-126.

Krystal, H. (1978), Aspects of affect theory, *Bull. Menninger Clin.*, **41**, 1-26.

Lindsley, D. B. (1957), Psychophysiology and motivation, in M. R. Jones (Ed.), *Nebraska Symposium on Motivation*, University of Nebraska Press, pp. 44-104.

Melzack, R. and P. Wall (1965), Pain mechanisms: A new theory, *Science*, **150**, 971-979.

Mirsky, A. F. and C. Kornetsky (1959), The effect of centrally-acting drugs on attention, in *Neuropsychopharmacology, A Review of Progress, 1957-67* (Public Health Service Publication No. 1836), U.S. Government Printing Office, Washington, D.C.

Plutchik, R. (1962), *The Emotions: Facts, Theories, and a New Model*, Random House, New York.

Rado, S. (1956), An adaptational view of sexual behavior, in *Psychoanalysis and Behavior: Collected Papers*, Grune & Stratton, New York.

Rapaport, D. (1953), On the psychoanalytic theory of affects, *Int. J. Psychoanal.*, **34**, 177-198.

Schur, M. (1953), in R. M. Lowenstein (Ed.), *The Ego Anxiety in Drives, Affects, Behavior*, International Universities Press, New York.

Selye, H. (1975), *The Physiology and Pathology of Exposure to Stress*, Montreal Acta.

Shand, A. (1914), *The Foundations of Character*, Macmillan, London.

Sifneos, P. (1973), The prevalence of "alexithymic" characteristics in psychosomatic patients, *Psychother. Psychosom.*, **22**, 255-262.

Stunkard, A. J. (1975), Satiety in a conditioned reflex, *Psychosom. Med.*, **37**, 383-387.

Tomkins, S. (1962), *Affect Imagery Consciousness, 1 and 2*, Springer, New York.

Tulving, E. (1972), Episodic and semantic memory, in E. Tulving and W. Donaldson (Eds.), *Organization of Memory*, Academic Press, New York.

Valenstein, A. F. (1973), On attachment to painful feelings, *Psychoanal. Study Child*, **28**, 365-392.

Von Bertenlanffy, L. (1964), The mind body problem: A new view, *Psychosom. Med.*, **26**, 29-45.

PART TWO

Developmental Aspects Of Affect

FOUR

The Origins Of
Affect—Normal And
Pathological

CLARICE J. KESTENBAUM

INTRODUCTION

I am going to attempt to describe the origins of affect, normal
and pathological, with a particular focus on the affects categorized
as pleasurable. Selecting one developmental aspect implies that a
dualism exists between affect and cognition, soma and psyche. Let
us assume for a moment that such a dichotomy could exist —
that affect could indeed be teased out of the total personality and
examined in isolation. Imagine a world inhabited by human beings
whose cognitive functions are otherwise intact but who lack
human feelings. Such a world was depicted in the science fiction
film, "Invasion of the Body Snatchers." Humanoid figures which
sprouted from seedlings attached themselves by weblike tendrils
to sleeping humans. The physical attributes of the people were
slowly sucked out of them, feeding the monsters who began to
resemble their hosts down to the last birthmark. Leaving behind
a desiccated shell, the phenocopy awoke in place of the original,
who seemingly went about his daily business. Family and friends
noted that something was wrong. The people looked the same
but the expression was different; emotion was absent and the
eyes were blank. There was no anger! no remorse! no passion!
no love! Living in those terms became meaningless, a mockery of
life.
   The study of emotional behavior, beginning with Plato and

Presented at the 23rd Winter Meeting of The American Academy of Psychoanalysis,
New York City, December 2, 1979.

73

Aristotle, has been confounded for centuries by the problem of definition. What is an emotion, an affect, a mood; how do they affect the way one behaves or conceptualizes the universe?

Affect and *emotion* are words which are often used synonymously. Webster (1958) defines emotion (from Latin *emovere,* "to move out") as "strong, generalized feeling; psychical excitement; any of various reactions with both psychical and physical manifestations."

Mood is defined as a "particular state of mind or feeling, humor, or temper"; it encompasses a range broader than the other two terms and emphasizes the pervading quality of the feeling over a period of time. It is a transient as opposed to a permanent characteristic generally acknowledged as *temperament.*

Hippocrates described those ingredients which contributed to an individual's "temperament" as consisting of the four humors: blood, phlegm, bile (choler), and black bile. In ancient and medieval psychology the mental disposition of an individual was determined by the relative proportion of these bodily fluids; thus behavioral characteristics were considered to be constitutionally determined. The sanguine individual was warm, passionate, optimistic; the phlegmatic person, sluggish and apathetic. The angry and irritable choleric character stood in sharp contrast to the melancholic soul who would still, most likely, fit a diagnostic description of DSM III.

Descartes, in the 17th century, suggested that six primitive emotions — admiration, love, hate, desire, joy, and sadness — combined to produce those introspective feelings called emotion. The soul, he maintained, contained animal spirits which, via the sense organs and nerves, created an impression on the pineal gland (!), producing a "passion."

It was Darwin, of course, who set the stage for all subsequent formulations with his theory of evolution. In *The Expression of Emotions in Man and Animal* (1872), he pointed to the continuity between men and other species. Action, he wrote, was the biologically significant aspect of emotion within a framework of environmental stimulation.

Modern theories of emotional behavior, while deeply rooted in an evolutionary past, branched into seemingly divergent directions.

The last decade, however, has brought together many such diverse theories into a more integrated conceptual framework. Although I am not suggesting that we have at the present time a single, all-inclusive theory of affects [although Izard (1972) and Pribram (1969) come close], I feel we are beginning to bridge gaps in knowledge between hitherto unrelated disciplines.

There are over 100 extant theories of emotion. Most, if not all of them, agree on certain basic principles: that emotion is a biological "given," that it is adaptive, serves as the "motor" and "motivator" behind behavior, and is necessary for species survival. Fundamental theoretical differences involve the age-old "nature versus nurture" question of what is learned, what is innate, and how large an aspect does heredity play in organizing human behavior.

I am going to discuss briefly the concept of emotional behavior using three separate but interrelated systems: emotion as action; emotion as cognition; and emotion as communication.

EMOTION AS ACTION

William James (1890) considered that emotions *are* our perception of bodily changes and that sensations originated from the afferent feedback resulting from our action.

The great wave of behaviorist theories originating from Watson's work (1929) placed emphasis on behavior rather than on internal states and feelings.

Stimulus–response, classical, and operant conditioning theories emerged which are based on the premise that an organism tends to repeat a pleasurable activity and avoid those which produce pain. The perception of the stimulus even from within is, of course, an integral part of the theory. Cannon (1915, 1927) was the first of the "emergency" theorists to set the cornerstone for the science of neurophysiology. Cannon maintained that the thalamus, when aroused, was responsible for the quality of emotion perceived. Papez (1937) also developed his theories from a neurophysiological basis. Simply stated, his theory maintained that emotion implies both specific action and subjective feeling, and depends on the connections between the cerebral hemispheres and the hypothalamus. Subsequent investigation by MacLean (1945) has led to a generalized theory of the functions of the limbic system. Anatomical loci (viz., the amygdala) have been found to control self-preservative behavior where fear and rage are concerned, mediated by the sympathetic nervous system. In contrast, the septal region of the limbic system generates species-preservative pleasurable behaviors such as social and genital contact and "mothering" activities which are parasympathetically mediated. Another outgrowth of the "emotion as action" theories constitutes the psychosomatic studies of Engel (1960) and Alexander (1950), who developed the theory that emotional responses may not always be consciously perceived but may have unconscious determinants as well. Endocrine and neurohormonal studies reveal that individuals behave and perceive the world differently under different hormonal conditions. [Cf. Benedek (1952); Schildkraut (1965).]

EMOTION AS COGNITION

The group of cognitive psychologists (Lazarus, 1968; Ruckmick, 1936; Schacter, 1964) have addressed themselves to the subjective meaning of a personal experience. They deal with the phenomenological aspect of an emotion and those internal and external cues which help us identify and label our emotional states. Schacter (1964, 1970) contends that there may be very little physiological differentiation between emotional states, and that labeling such states is a cognitive function. His experimental subjects after adrenaline injection behaved differently from controls if they were told exactly what to expect from the drug and differently from controls who were given placebos.

Leventhal (1974) also noted that a person's expectations are important determinants of his emotional state. Ideas alone − noxious memories, for example − can increase heart rate and cause flushing and palpitations. One of the goals of psychoanalytic therapy is, in fact, to help a patient become aware of his subjective states, discriminate between them, and report them verbally.

The language of emotion has been studied extensively by Davitz (1969), who was concerned with the private meaning of emotional terms. Davitz' main propositions were as follows: "(1) Emotion is partly concerned with private (experienced) events − a clear, phenomenological, subjective viewpoint. (2) Emotion embraces specific states which are labelled, and each label refers to experiences about which there is reasonable common ground within a culture. (3) The language of emotion reflects experiences but is also directly influenced by linguistic considerations; people make mistakes in their descriptions of emotions, and, in fact, learn to label the emotion from the situation. (4) Definitions of emotional states fall into four dimensions of emotional experience: activation, relatedness, hedonic tone, and competence. (5) Labelling emotion depends on experience. Any change in experience will change the label and the state. (6) Emotional states come about from stimuli which are psychologically relevant to the four dimensions of emotional meaning" (in Strongman, 1978, p. 225).

Davitz has illustrated the subtle differences between the various states subsumed under any of the four categories. Pleasure, for example, (a hedonic tone) can be replaced by the terms joy, gladness, enjoyment, delight, glee, cheer, felicity, bliss, rapture, or ecstasy, depending upon the word that best describes a particular emotional state.

A second group of cognitive psychologists suggests that appraisals are the basis of cognitive analysis of emotion. Arnold (1960) maintained that appraisal complements perception, is instantaneous, and produces a tendency for action. A new experience is evaluated in terms of past experiences; thus memory is a basis for appraisals. Affect-laden memories may continually distort our judgment. In the absence of harmful stimuli affects may be purely cognitive, involving no direct action. Cognitive appraisals can change a simple reflex action if the motivation to do so is great enough (cf. Arieti, 1970).

To illustrate this point, I will describe an individual under two different social circumstances. In the first instance, a man dining out alone picks up a plate the waiter failed to mention was "hot out of the oven" and immediately drops it on the floor while cursing at the waiter. The following night the same man is dining out with a woman he wishes to impress. The same waiter brings the hot plate and again the man inadvertently takes it, but this time he endures the pain, gently sets down the plate, and saves his invectives for another day.

It is a short step from the study of cognitive phenomena to cortical theories of perception. The split-brain and lateralization studies (Bogen and Gazzaniga, 1965), with implication of the "right brain" in Gestalt theories of perception, are an area recently under investigation. Neuropsychological studies have demonstrated serious alterations of perception and judgment in individuals with cortical pathology (Flor-Henry, 1979).

The third group of cognitive psychologists are often phenomenological philosophers and are more concerned with the mind than the body (Ryle, 1948; Sartre, 1948). They have produced interesting theories of individual experience which are more germane to the understanding of art and philosophy than to science, since their underlying hypotheses are difficult to test. They have made important contributions, nonetheless, to the understanding of emotion as a cognitive experience.

EMOTION AS COMMUNICATION

The group of psychologists that views emotion chiefly in terms of its communicative components is a diverse lot; it includes, along with cognitive psychologists, ethologists, psycholinguists, anthropologists, and social psychologists.

Tomkins (1962) and Izard (1972) have been the chief proponents of a theory that affects are reflected, for the most part, by facial responses. Facial expression is the signal for revealing feelings nonverbally and communicating them to others.

Izard feels that affect can be fully understood only by viewing personality as a process of communication within a social environment. Tomkins lists the primary affects revealed by facial expression as interest (excitement), enjoyment (joy), surprise (startle), distress (anguish), disgust (contempt), anger (rage), shame (humiliation), and fear (terror).

Izard (1972) has, moreover, reviewed a number of cross-cultural studies that show agreement in the recognition of emotion by facial expression in Europe, Asia, and Africa.

The study of expressive behavior takes us full circle to Darwin's original treatise on expression of emotion in man and animals and to the work of modern ethologists. Eibl-Eibesfeldt (1970) has recorded a variety of animal signaling systems. He noted behaviors that establish contact, such as courtship behavior, and those that serve as warning signals, such as ritualized attack behavior. He has attempted to address the questions of whether these phylogenetic adaptations pertain to man, and whether there are instinctive behavior patterns "built in" to the human species as there are for lower animals. He observed that a number of movements develop in every member of a given species in the same way, even if it is deprived of the opportunity to learn the patterns by trial and error or imitation. The genetically stored information is given the term, "fixed action patterns."

Phylogenetic adaptations are found, according to the ethologists, in the form of specific learning dispositions. These are special mechanisms, evolution of which insures that an animal will learn the "right thing at the right time." Imprinting, for example, is a species-specific attachment behavior in birds that resulted in the observation that the object to which an animal is exposed during the critical period (32–36 hours) is the one to which it becomes most strongly attached (Lorenz, 1952). It is questionable how significant to human development is the concept of the critical period, which has undergone a great deal of adaptive modification. Eibl-Eibesfeldt, in his work with red squirrels, attempted to tease out innate from learned behavior. In squirrels the pattern for burying nuts is as follows: (a) the squirrel, in order to hide the nut, carries it to the ground and scratches a hole; (b) deposits the nut; (c) tamps the nut with his snout; (d) covers over the nut; (e) packs it down.

In an experiment eighteen baby squirrels were raised in a wire mesh cage and fed only liquids. At two-and-a-half months, when presented with nuts in the earth, five performed the act perfectly. Thirteen, without available dirt, completed the sequence as well. Opening the nuts was another story. Twenty-three mature squirrels had been deprived of nuts from infancy. At six months they were given nuts for the first time. None were skillful and struggled with 10 to 20 nuts until the act could be completed in two minutes. In other words, they had to practice. They could still perform the act but without grace or skill. It is an interesting observation that animal play does not seem to be merely immature behavior, but rather a practicing for adult life. Play imitating hunting, fighting, and flight behavior is observed in all young animals. Dogs at play, for example, demonstrate a strong inhibition against biting, wagging their tails during an "attack."

Harlow (1966), whose work with rhesus monkeys needs no elaboration, has presented a detailed account of the maternal affectional system. Harlow questioned that the infant's "love" for the mother is learned through the association of the mother's face and body when hunger and thirst are alleviated. He believes that the infant monkey has an *instinctive* need to cling and that it will cling to a terry cloth dummy even when food is provided by a wire dummy monkey. He noted maternal behaviors as well, and divided them into three definite stages: (1) attachment and protection; (2) ambivalence (maternal punishment at four to five months; (3) rejection. He noted in stage 1 the enormous importance of intimate contact clinging. An infant rhesus monkey, for instance, raised in isolation, developed bizarre, self-clutching, rocking behavior. When presented to a normal adoptive mother, the infant gave her no "feedback" and did not cling, clasp, or attempt to contact her in other ways. When the isolation-raised monkey became a mother (after much effort in attempting to impregnate her, for she did not present herself for mounting), she abused her own infant mercilessly. She was unable to respond to her infant's signals. Thus we see the subtle interplay of instinctual and learned behavior as it is transmitted from one generation to another.

Instinctive behavior is not inherited. What is inherited is a potential to develop certain sorts of behavioral systems. From the signaling systems of animals a second system evolved — language. The inborn potential for language and symbolization is, of course, the particualr adaptation that distinguishes man from animals. "Its influence," stated Humboldt (1905), "extends over everything man thinks or feels, decides or achieves. It transforms the world into a possession of the mind" (p. 11). It is possible for one individual to transmit his emotional experience to another, replete with physiological manifestations, by words alone. The capacity for empathy, and imagination based on early affect-laden memories, are involved as well.

In order to illustrate this point I shall present a hypothetical situation involving two men, whom I shall designate A and B. The two are on an African safari when a lion suddenly escapes from his makeshift cage 100 yards away. Both men experience an increased heart rate and sweating palms. A reaches for his gun, but quickly perceives that the lion is a fair distance away, and that others are attempting to control him; thus he grabs his movie camera instead of the gun. B, however, begins to shout and gesticulate, drops his gun and runs. Several months later A is showing the film to his young son, who is deeply impressed. A recalls the event without the original physiological sequelae, feels a surge of pride in his achievement, and even sells the movie to a documentary film club. B is awakening nights in cold sweats from frightening nightmares. His son, who heard the story of his father's narrow escape, is also having scary dreams, is afraid to go to the zoo, and cries more often.

Although the son of A had never seen a lion, he wants to grow up to be a famous lion tamer, while the son of B, who likewise never saw a lion, is fearful of growing up at all.

THE PSYCHOANALYTIC APPROACH TO THE
STUDY OF EMOTION

I would now like to discuss another model for personality and character formation, less easy to test but far broader in scope than those under discussion thus far: the psychoanalytic model.

The classical psychoanalytic theory of emotions, or affects, the term most employed in the psychoanalytic literature, draws from both biological origins in terms of the concept of the instinctual drives (libido and aggression) and at the same time attempts to deal with a hypothetical "mental" model. For Freud the concepts of tension reduction and transformation of energy were fundamental. He explained hysterical symptoms as the consequence of increased tension resulting from undischarged or accumulated affect (1894), a theory later revised in favor of the concept of anxiety as a "signal" of danger (1926).

Freud separated the affect from its associated ideational content. By following the independent development of these two fundamental components of symptoms, he could demonstrate how conflict over repressed wishes was transformed into various mental phenomena. Freud stated that in mental functions there is "a quota of affect . . . which is capable of increase, diminution, displacement and discharge . . . which spreads over the memory-traces of ideas as an electric charge is spread over the body" (1894, p. 60). Furthermore, the theory states, increase in tension leads to unpleasure and decrease in tension to diminution of unpleasure until homeostasis is reached.

Rapaport (1942) attempted to address the problems inherent in a psychoanalytic theory of affects. "An incoming percept initiates an unconscious process which mobilizes unconscious instinctual energies; if no free pathway is open for these energies (conflict) they find discharges through channels other than voluntary motility; these discharge processes — 'emotional expression' and 'emotions felt' — may occur simultaneously or may succeed one another or may occur alone . . ." (p. 37).

Emotions, which could be experienced as overwhelming and disorganizing if intense, are "handled" via the various mental mechanisms postulated, in other words, defenses. The developing individual learns how to avoid being overwhelmed by the discharge of energy, according to the theory, and to use it as a signal of impending danger.

Brenner (1974), addressing himself to the separation of affect and idea, attempted to redefine affect as a complex mental phenomenon which includes sensations of pleasure and unpleasure, together with thoughts, memories, wishes, and fears. He noted that affect is a sensation of pleasure, unpleasure, or both, plus the ideas associated with that sensation.

Rado had long been aware of the two distinct aspects of emotional states, which he termed *"the psychodynamic awareness* process and the *physiologic* reporting process." In 1954 he wrote, "since we need an operational hypothesis . . . I have assumed that the psychodynamic awareness process and the physiologic reporting process are exactly synchronous and exactly cogruent" (p. 287).

Arlow (1969), in discussing precursors of affect, concluded that these are sensations of pleasure or unpleasure connected with drive tension and drive discharge. He believes they constitute the undifferentiated matrix from which affects later in life develop when ideas become associated with these sensations. The critical memories, traumata, and fantasies serve to determine the nature of the individual's affective life. He maintains, furthermore, that unconscious fantasy activity establishes the mental set against which the data of sensory registration are selectively perceived, inhibited, disregarded, or transformed. The present is misperceived in terms of the past.

In searching for the roots of "pleasure," the concept of libidinal zones evolved. One of the most fascinating aspects of Freud's hypothesis regarding mental functioning was his clinical observation that, contrary to popular belief, children had a highly charged sexual life (1905). The normal maturatural phases, he postulated, were oral, anal, and phallic, and during each phase the appropriate organ was "cathected with libido." In other words, the phase-specific sensory zone produced intense pleasure when stimulated. From memory traces or stored impressions, Freud believed, a body-ego, derived from body sensations, developed a mental projection of the surface of the body. In explaining the earliest experience of satisfaction, Freud (1894) used the example of an infantile experience of hunger: the infant is hungry, has an unpleasurable sensation, screams, and is subsequently fed; the unpleasure is removed; he is "satisfied." The removal of "unpleasure" from an endogenous stimulus releases tension, and homeostasis is achieved; a memory trace of the initial state of "unpleasure" and the subsequent "pleasure" is thus recorded. Freud deemed the infant peacefully nursing at the mother's breast the prototype for all subsequent human bliss.

Post-Freudian ego psychologists such as Hartmann, Kris, and Loewenstein (1946), while noting the importance of the theory of instinctual drives and mechanisms of defense, attempted to emphasize a different set of mental processes. Hartmann observed that "perception, intention, thinking, memory, . . . the motor developmental phases of grasping, crawling, walking, the maturation and learning processes implicit in all of these," take place in the absence of instinctual conflicts. In fact, he concluded, they comprise a "conflict-free" ego sphere. Ives Hendricks in 1942 proposed a third instinctual drive he considered to be as important for survival as libido and aggression — an *instinct to master* which, he argued, yields primary pleasure quite apart from the sensory value of the activity.

THE MOTHER–CHILD PAIR

It is now evident that we cannot discuss the origins of emotional expression and feeling in the infant without consideration of the human being to whom he will become attached and through whose help he will first come to know his ever-expanding universe and ultimately himself — his mother.

Let us assume that we are dealing with a biologically healthy, full-term baby, well endowed genetically from a healthy set of parents (and grandparents) who anticipated his birth with pleasure. Although early bonds can be formed with fathers, adoptive mothers and other caretakers, for the moment I am going to speak of the most conventional pair, the good-enough mother and the good-enough baby (Winnicott, 1960). This platonic ideal of a mother is in her late twenties or early thirties, has had a good relationship with her own mother and a sense of herself as a competent human being. She was euphoric during the pregnancy, proud of her very visible achievement. Her relationship with her husband became even closer than before. The delivery was uncomplicated and the mother was allowed to hold her infant immediately after the birth. Powerful feelings of joy and love for the infant were almost instantaneous during the "sensitive" period of initial bonding. He was everything she had dreamed of and more — the fact that she had secretly hoped for a girl slipped from her mind the moment she was presented with a son (Kestenbaum et al., 1979).

In turning our attention now to the infant, I would like to note that our views of the newborn have greatly changed because of infant research findings during the past two decades. Earlier researchers believed that the infant was a helpless, totally dependent creature delivered into a world he could only perceive as chaotic. His reflex activity, of course, helped him fulfill physiological functions. When he wasn't sleeping or nursing, his random movements indicated some degree of unpleasant sensation which could call the mother to him. Sensations we would consider pleasurable were not yet perceived as such.

Recent research on very young infants has demonstrated that although the infant is dependent upon the caretaker for his most basic needs — nourishment and protection — he is far from helpless. In fact he is fully equipped at birth with a large repertoire of reflexes — actually behavior patterns — all serving to help bind him to the mothering figure.

Bowlby (1969) speaks of these reflexes as "built in" attachment systems in the same way the ethologists speak of fixed action patterns, innate responses upon which subsequent behavior is organized. For example, the healthy full-term infant can suck vigorously; it has been demonstrated experimentally that within hours he has learned to control the rate of the flow (Marquis, 1958). He can grasp and cling, follow with his eyes, cry, and, within a few weeks, smile.

Brazelton (1961) reported that an infant can see at birth and will follow a moving hand approximately a foot away. Within a few days the infant will focus on moving objects with sharp contours and seems to prefer, above all other patterns, the human face (Fantz, 1961; Spitz, 1955). He can discriminate a photograph from a real object (Bower, 1972). The infant responds to the high-pitched voice that mothers use intuitively when speaking to their infants, a voice which happens to "fit" the infant's sensitive auditory perception of speech in the high-frequency range (Lang, 1972; Sandor, 1975). The baby clearly needs the warmth of the mother's body, the touching, caressing, fondling, the sound of her voice, and the gazing at her face. The mother needs him, too, "for the mother–child relationship is . . . a symbiosis involving two people in which both are enveloped in an exclusive, mutually satisfying world. Each comes to know the other's rhythms in a wordless communication which flows from one to the other. The mother becomes acutely sensitive, tuned in to the baby's needs. It is well known that a woman who can sleep through police sirens . . . may awaken the moment her infant whimpers" (Kestenbaum, 1973, p. 8).

The powerful effects of the infant on the caretaker have been carefully investigated by researchers such as M. Lewis (1974), Brazelton (1963), and Robson (1967). Robson has suggested that mutual gaze during nursing, for example, is one of the most powerful "innate releasers" of maternal caretaking responses.

The microanalysis of filmed mother–infant interactions of Stern (1974) have demonstrated that in this first "dance" of life, the infant sets the pace, initiates and terminates the gaze; the mother "follows the lead" and learns to adapt her behavior to the needs and tempo of the child.

Another phenomenon of the early "oral" period is mutual smiling. At six to eight weeks the infant smiles at a number of stimuli — sounds, mobiles, and faces, for example. By 12 weeks the baby and mother begin to exchange smiles directly in response to one another, the first true sign of socialization. "Nothing elicits warmer, more protective, loving feelings in the adult caretaker than the smile. The baby smiles; the mother smiles back . . . (reinforcing his smiling, for even blind babies smile) and a circle of intensifying feelings of intimacy is set in motion. The early reciprocal and synchronous play that characterizes human relatedness in the first months has been investigated extensively by David Schecter (1972). The first game all babies delight in, peek-a-boo, is, he notes, the first mutually responsive communication with a love object (Kleeman, 1967). The child can evoke a social response even when he is not hungry or wet. This positively stimulating playful pattern of response is produced in relation to another human being (Kestenbaum, 1973, p. 10).

The early bond is fragile, yet powerful, and determines the manner in which the child is destined to relate to those around him. A child's trust or his suspicions, warmth toward others or hostility are, on the whole, to be understood as outgrowths of the success or failure of this developmental phase.

At the same time that the mutually shared joy inherent in the human bond is developing, a second kind of pleasurable emotion is beginning to emerge — the joy of mastery and the feeling of competence (Bruner, 1973). Piaget noted that in the first two years of life (which he termed the "sensory-motor period"), the ever-increasing ability to "do" takes precedence over all other activities (1954). In learning to coordinate his early reflex activities (e.g. sucking, grasping), the infant learns that what he did at first "for its own sake," such as kicking his foot, will now cause a change in the environment. The infant begins to repeat behavior in order to produce a result. He kicks his foot now, for example, so that the mobile on the crib rail will move. He soon learns that what he does can produce a desirable result. The pleasure derived from stimulation of his body as well as the pleasure-in-mastery play is obvious in his facial movements, gestures, and vocal utterances. He needs the reinforcement — the feedback — from the mother to encourage and help him in his efforts to "do it himself." Using her as a model, he imitates her behavior, her gestures, her facial expressions. When he attempts to feed himself or crawl upstairs, he needs her to return the spoon which he playfully dropped from the high chair. He learns, moreover, that when he does attempt to climb the stairs, she will be there as long as necessary to protect him from falling down. The intuitively good-enough mother will sing to the child, speak in soft tones; she will imitate his babbling sounds and change them into words. She will use her voice to caress and comfort and interpret his world to him, even though she knows he doesn't yet understand a word she is saying. She will do this until he has acquired word symbols of his own. Early language play is as pleasurable as sensory-motor play and needs encouragement and reinforcement so that language expression is optimal.

I have spoken thus far of the "good-enough" mother and the "good-enough" baby without taking into account the importance of what Escalona (1968) calls the mother–child "fit." Individual differences at birth have been found to have profound influences on early experience. As Korner (1974) notes, "by confronting his caretaker with differences in organismic organization, the infant contributes heavily to the unfolding of the mother–infant relationship and to the kind of mothering he will require. Some of the differences may contain the seeds of the variations in style with which different children will approach and master some of the developmental milestones" (p. 51). There are, for instance, quantitative differences in oral drive manifestations (sucking, hand–mouth behavior, and self-comfort activities). In her research with full-term, healthy, three-day-old infants, Korner noted highly significant differences in behavior. Using Wolff's classifications of the infant's state (regular sleep; irregular sleep, with or without REM activity; drowsiness; alert inactivity; waking activity; crying), she observed differences in crying and irritability levels. How frequently and how long infants cry and how "soothable" they are differs remarkably from one to another and is characteristic of the infant's particular "personality" (Bennett, 1971). The active, crying baby, moreover, will initiate interaction more frequently than the placid baby. Brazelton has pointed out that extreme irritability and inconsolableness on the infant's part can have a devastating effect on the mother. Those infants with a narrow range of states, he noted, later demonstrated atypical development. Most babies learn to shut out noxious stimuli (too much light, noise, or external activity). Very sensitive babies tend to become overwhelmed with overstimulation unless the mother serves as a shield and tension-reducing agent (Bergman and Escalona, 1949).

Mothers soon learn what their babies' cries mean and what comforting techniques their babies prefer. Some mothers have learned that holding certain infants upright so that the babies can gaze downward quiets them more than lap-rocking. Recent experiments regarding vestibular stimulation (Korner, 1974) demonstrated that, indeed, bright-eyed scanning and visual alertness followed the act of holding the infant in an upright position. Mothers who are particularly tuned in to the special signaling characteristics of their infants help them develop feelings of security and ultimately of mastery. If the baby fits the mother's expectations the result is a harmonious interaction, but if by chance the two are on different wavelengths, tension and turmoil can result. Escalona, along with Thomas and Chess (1968), reminds us that temperament is inborn (shades of Hippocrates!), not the result of environmental influences which subsequently *shape* the personality; the mother must adapt herself to her particular infant's style so that smooth synchronous interaction can continue despite temperamental differences between the two participants.

THE DEVELOPMENT OF PATHOLOGICAL AFFECTS

The Diseases of Nonattachment

I have described the origins of pleasurable emotions in normal infants in the mother–child bond. When pathological affects develop, one has to examine the bonding process and ascertain first and foremost whether such an attachment was ever made or whether such an attachment was made and subsequently ruptured. There are a multiplicity of reasons for nonattachment. Selma Fraiberg (1967) believes that there are some striking parallels between Harlow's primate studies and human studies of certain aberrant patterns in early childhood, which she calls "the diseases of non-attachment." The distinguishing characteristic of such children is their joylessness, their inability to form human bonds. In the absence of human ties, a conscience cannot be formed, nor the qualities of self-observation and self-criticism.

These children are often found in institutions and slums; many have been victims of child abuse — cumulative trauma — and have been shuffled from foster home to foster home. In school these youngsters are noted to be humorless and driven, with impairment of intellectual function; they lack impulse control. When seen in agencies and child guidance clinics, they are called unreachable because they cannot form a transference to the therapist. Prognosis is usually considered poor.

A second group of joyless children has been able to form meager attachments, which have been characterized by frequent separations or losses. Never able to rely on a stable adult, they defend themselves against further loss by keeping all emotions "under wraps"; they appear suspicious and guarded. These are the future hollow men and women Fraiberg writes about, leftovers of society, unwanted and unattached.

There is another group of children who have been unable to form close and trusting bonds as the result of inadequate maternal care. The mother, who is too psychotic, too depressed, or too exhausted to respond appropriately to her infant's signals, is unable to participate in joyful interaction with him. Unless there is someone else in the environment with whom to interact, the infant soon stops crying, smiling, or gesticulating for attention. He simply stops trying and a pattern of learned hopelessness is set into motion.

Finally there is a large group of pathological conditions that prevent appropriate attachment, not because of traumatic external events or inadequate maternal care, but because the infant is born with central nervous system impairment. Rado (1954) believed that anhedonia was a major component of the schizophrenic genotype. The condition may be severe, as with autistic children, or mild as in the case of atypical or borderline children (Ekstein, 1954). Most mothers of such children feel a sense of rejection from the lack of body molding, eye contact, or smiling. Many mothers who are "good-enough" with "good-enough" infants are unable to give the necessary extra effort to these damaged children who need more than the usual care. Such children are usually flooded by excitement they cannot understand. They have difficulty distinguishing anger from fear, frustration from sadness, and they need someone to help identify their own subjective feelings and correct their distortions. Other disturbed children make attachments but are unable to separate themselves from their mothers. The seemingly driven quality of their activity, often mistaken for gaiety, is a poor substitute for true joyfulness.

Childhood Depression

In the recent past, psychiatric opinion regarding depression in childhood was that it was practically nonexistent. If a child had experienced a loss, for example, he tended to defend against the feelings engendered by the loss by acting up in school, fighting, clowning, denying the event in every possible way. Since adult depression is characterized by motor retardation, insomnia, and often profound feelings of guilt, children who did not display these symptoms were not considered to be clinically depressed. In recent years, a number of workers have presented the view that depression in children exists and is expressed in a variety of ways: negative self-image, withdrawal, overdependence on parents, tantrums, and tearfulness. Anthony and Scott (1967) noted that the difference between child and adult depression stems from the child's inability to describe his affective state, incomplete development of the superego, and absence of a consistent sense of himself. They felt that some children had a constitutional predisposition to depression, a position also held by Cytryn and McKnew (1972).

Recent studies of the children of parents with affective disorder, including several studies of children who were adopted away at birth (Cadoret, 1978; Mendlewicz and Rainer, 1977), point to a strong hereditary factor. Environmental influences, however, have been found to enhance or diminish the likelihood of a vulnerable child's developing the illness.

DISCUSSION AND OVERVIEW

I have attempted to examine various hypotheses concerning the origins of human emotion and have presented a bewildering array of theories. Which one is correct? One could look at the problem in two ways: either we are dealing with the proverbial blind man and the elephant, in which case it depends on which portion of the emotional apparatus we find under our examination, or we are dealing with the well-known rabbi of Shalom Aleichem. In settling a dispute between a quarreling husband and wife, the rabbi told each one that he was right. When a discerning rabbinical student questioned how indeed both parties could be right, the rabbi answered, "Yes, that is a good question! You also are right!"

Each theory represents a particular viewpoint and provides a particular frame of reference; the correctness of the answers depends upon the questions asked. With an intangible such as "emotion" we must deal in models and metaphors. When studying the products of emotion, we can measure electrophysiological charges and urinary catecholamines. When studying the philosophy of emotion, we speak of the wellspring of life − élan vital and love. It is a superfluous exercise, in my opinion, to ask whether we "love" with the id or the ego, the hypothalamus or limbic lobe. It is important to understand the various models, use the ones which apply to the particular question at hand, and not mix metaphors.

In the light of recent knowledge I would like to reexamine some former assumptions. The metapsychology of pleasurable affects, which postulates that increased tension results in unpleasure and a decrease in tension to a state akin to pleasure, is not justified. Jacobson (1953) pointed out that certain pleasurable affects can occur under conditions of *increased* tension or drive as in sexual orgasms; moreover, as Knapp (1963) has noted, the idea that emotional reactions may result from direct excitation independent of conflict is supported by "neurophysiological self-stimulation studies with reward and punishment centers" (p. 8). Rado came to similar conclusions 25 years earlier.

Arlow (1977) questions the usefulness of those studies which define the nature and quality of affective experience in terms of "the rate, the rhythm, patterns, or quantity of energic discharge as well as in terms of fusion or defusion of instinctual drives." Such theories, he feels, "cannot be substantiated by reference to clinical experience." Knapp further notes that the concept of psychic energy is being replaced by many modern theorists by the ethological conception of instinctual drives as inherent, neurologically organized patterns of behavior. The second point I would like to emphasize deals with this concept, originally discovered by Darwin. We have a heritage of inborn, species-specific adaptive mechanisms according to which subsequent behavior is organized. These mechanisms serve to protect us during life as well as preserve the generations that follow us.

In past decades the infant-watchers in the nursery did not have at their disposal today's sophisticated instruments for measuring infant responses to stimuli. They could observe seemingly random gross movement in response to a variety of stimuli, particularly noxious ones. They did not measure R.E.M. sleep, cardiac acceleration during stress and deceleration during quiet attention, or galvanic skin response. They believed that at first only painful stimuli were experienced and perceived in some manner, and that as percepts led to concepts and memory, the infant learned through repeated experience to attach to the need-satisfying mother. We know how significant learning is, even in the animal world, and that infants can and do learn from the first few days of life. I agree with Bowlby's formulation, however, that the infant's reflexive repertoire — crying, clinging, sucking, following with the eyes, and subsequently smiling — is made up of innate attachment mechanisms which activate the mother's responses in the service of protection and care. Under the loving care of a good-enough mother, the world is first *perceived* as safe and loving, then *understood* as such when language acquisition enables the child to translate his feelings into words. *Thus pleasurable affects are innate and have their roots in the attachment system;* the nature of early mother–child bond sets the background mood for subsequent unconscious fantasies.

A second source of pleasure is also innate: the drive for mastery, achievement, and activity. Animal studies and Piaget's observations give us conclusive evidence. Thus the infant has within him the capacity for two kinds of pleasure, as exemplified in the grasp reflex. He is born "holding on"; with practice he can learn how to "let go." Both can lead to the sense of enjoyment and comfort (satisfaction, well-being, intimacy, solace) and the joys of action (seeking, learning, competing, creating) that are every child's birthright (Kolb, 1979).

My last point concerns the pursuit of pleasure. Although the capacity for pleasure is inborn, society shapes the form the pleasurable activity will take. One can encourage a society of comfort-seeking lotus eaters or a society of work-oriented superachievers. (There was, I understand, no lack of joy in Sparta.) When a civilization moves too far in one direction, subsequent generations seem to restore the balance.

In conclusion, I would like to emphasize that emotions are at the very core of life, the prime mover and chief motivator; that happiness should not have to be pursued — it is ours to begin with and we should treasure it so that we can transmit to our children a sense of joy in living.

References

Alexander, F. (1950), *Psychosomatic Medicine. Its Principles and Applications,* Norton, New York.

Anthony, E. J. and P. C. Scott, Manic depressive psychosis in children, *Brit. J. Child Psychol. Psychiatry,* 1, 53-72.

Arieti, S. (1970), Cognition and feeling, in *Feeling and Emotion,* M. B. Arnold, Ed., Academic Press, New York, London, pp. 135-143.

Arlow, J. A. (1969), Unconscious fantasy and disturbances of conscious experience, *Psychoanal. Q.,* 38, 1-27.

Arlow, J. (1977), Affects and the psychoanalytic situation, *Int. J. Psychoanal.,* 58, 157-170.

Arnold, M. B. (1960), *Emotion and Personality* (2 vols.), Columbia University Press, New York.

Benedek, T. (1952), *Studies in Psychosomatic Medicine: The Psychosexual Function in Women,* Ronald Press, New York.

Bennett, S. (1971), Infant-caretaker interactions, *J. Am. Acad. Child Psychiatry,* 10, 321-335.

Bergman, P. and S. K. Escalona (1949), Unusual sensitivities in very young children, *Psa. Study Child,* 3-4, 333-352.

Bogen, J. E. and M. S. Gazzaniga (1965), Cerebral commissurotomy in man: Minor hemisphere dominance for certain visuo-spatial functions, *J. Neuro-Surg.,* 23, 394-399.

Bowlby, J. (1969) (1973), *Attachment and Loss,* Vols. 1 and 2, Basic Books, New York.

Bower, T. G. R. (1972), Object perception in infants, *Perception,* 1, 15-30.

Brazelton, T. B. (1961), The psychophysiologic reactions in the neonate. I. The value of observation of the neonate, *J. Pediatr.,* 58, 508-512.

Brazelton, T. B. (1963), The early mother-infant adjustment, *Pediatrics,* 32, 931-938.

Brenner, C. (1974), On the nature and development of affects: A unified theory, *Psychoanal. Q.*, **43**, 532-566.

Bruner, J. S. (1973), Organization of early skilled action, *Child Dev.*, **44**, 1-11.

Cadoret, E. J. (1978), Evidence for genetic inheritance of primary affective disorder in adoptees, *Am. J. Psychiatry*, **135**, 463-466.

Cannon, W. B. (1929), *Bodily Changes in Panic, Hunger, Fear, and Rage*, 2nd ed., Appleton-Century, New York.

Cannon, W. B. (1927), The James-Lange theory of emotion; a critical examination and an alternative theory, *Am. J. Psychol.*, **39**, 106-124.

Cytryn, L. and D. McKnew (1972), Proposed classification of childhood depression, *Am. J. Psychiatry*, **129**, 63-69.

Darwin, C. (1872), *The Expression of Emotions in Man and Animal*, Philosophical Library, New York, 1955.

Davitz, J. R. (1969), *The Language of Emotion*, Academic, New York, London.

Eibl-Eibesfeldt, I. (1970), *Ethology – The Biology of Behavior*, Holt, Rinehart and Winston, New York, London.

Ekstein, R. (1954), Observations on the psychology of borderline and psychotic children, *Psychoanal. Study Child*, **9**, 344-369.

Engel, G. L. (1960), A unified concept of health and disease, *Perspec. Biol. Med.*, **3**, 459.

Escalona, S. (1968), *The Roots of Individuality: Normal Patterns of Development in Infancy*, Aldine, Chicago.

Fantz, R. L. (1961), The origin of form perception, *Sci. Am.*, **204**, 66-72.

Flor-Henry, P. (1979), On certain aspects of the localization of the cerebral systems regulating and determining emotion, *Biol. Psychiatry*, **14**, 677-698.

Fraiberg, S. (1967), The origins of human bonds, *Commentary*, December, 47-57.

Freud, S. (1894), *The Neuro-psychoses of Defense, Standard Edition, Vol. 3*, Hogarth Press, London, p. 60.

Freud, S. (1905), *Three Essays on the Theory of Sexuality, Standard Edition, Vol. 7*, Hogarth Press, London.

Freud, S. (1926), *Inhibitions, Symptoms and Anxiety, Standard Edition, Vol. 30*, Hogarth Press, London.

Harlow, H. and M. H. Harlow (1966), Learning to love, *Am. Sci.*, **54**, 244-272.

Hartman, H., E. Kris, and R. M. Loewenstein (1946), Comments on the formation of psychic structure, *Psychoanal. Study Child*, **2**, 11-38.

Hendrick I. (1942), Instinct and the ego during infancy, *Psychoanal. Q.*, **11**, 35-38.

Izard, C. E. (1972), *The Face of Emotion*, Appleton-Century-Crofts, New York.

Jacobson, E. (1953), The affects and their pleasure-unpleasure qualities in relation to psychic discharge processes, in *Drives, Affects, and Behavior*, R. M. Lowenstein, Ed., International University Press, New York.

James, W. (1950), *The Principles of Psychology*, Dover, New York.

Kestenbaum, C. J. (1973), Introduction, in *The Emerging Child*, P. Brusiloff and M. J. Witenberg, Eds., Jason Aronson, New York, pp. 15-33.

Kestenbaum, C. J., S. Underwood, I. Kochen, and E. Gottlieb (1979), The maternal attitudes and adaptation scale, paper presented at the 26th Annual Meeting of the American Academy of Child Psychiatry, Atlanta, October 26.

Klaus, M. H., R. Jerauld, N. C. Kreger, W. McAlpine, M. Steffa, and J. H. Kennell (1972), Maternal attachment, the importance of the first post partum days, *N. Engl. J. Med.*, **286**, 460-463.

Kleeman, J. A. (1967), The peek-a-boo game: Part I: Its origins, meanings, and related phenomena in the first year, *Psa. Study of the Child*, **22**, 239-273.

Knapp, P. (1963), in *Expression of the Emotions in Man*, Peter H. Knapp, Ed., International Universities Press, New York.

Kolb, L. C. (1980), Reconceptualization of Ego functions — The assertive sets or sublimated traits (unpublished).

Korner, A. F. (1974), Individual differences, at birth — Implications for child-care practices, in *The Infant at Risk*, D. Bergsma, Ed., Intercontinental Medical Book Corp., New York, pp. 51-60.

Lang, R. (1972), *Birth Book*, Genesis Press, Los Angeles.

Lazarus, R. S. (1968), Emotions and adaptation: Conceptual and empirical relations, in *Nebraska Symposium on Motivation*, W. J. Arnold, Ed., University of Nebraska Press, Lincoln.

Leventhal, H. (1974), Emotions: A basic problem for social psychology, in *Social Psychology: Classic and Contemporary Integrations*, C. Nemeth, Ed., Rand-McNally, Chicago, pp. 1-51.

Lewis, M. and S. Lee-Painter (1974), An interactional approach to the mother infant dyad, in *The Effect of the Infant on its Caregiver: The Origins of Behavior*, Vol. 1, M. Lewis and L. Rosenblum, Eds., Wiley, New York.

Lorenz, K. Z. (1952), *King Solomon's Ring*, Methuen, London.

MacLean, P. D. (1945), The limbic system and its hippocampal formation: Studies in animals and their possible application to man, *J. Neurosurg.*, **II**, 29-44.

Marquis, D. P. (1941), Learning in the neonate. The modification of behavior under three feeding schedules. *J. Exp. Psychol.*, **29**, 263-282.

Mendlewicz, J. and J. A. Rainer (1977), Adoption study supporting genetic transmission in manic-depressive illness, *Nature*, **268**, 327-329.

Papez, J. W. (1937), A proposed mechanism of emotions, *Arch. Neurol. Psychiatry,* **38,** 725-743.

Piaget, J. (1954), *The Construction of Reality in the Child,* Basic Books, New York.

Rado, S. (1956), Hedonic control, action self and the depressive spell, in *Psychoanalysis of Behavior,* Grune and Stratton, New York, London, pp. 286-311.

Rado, S. (1962), Schizotypal organization: Preliminary report on a clinical study of schizophrenia, in *Psychoanalysis of Behavior,* Grune and Stratton, New York, London, pp. 1-10.

Rapaport, D. (1942), *Emotions and Memory,* Williams and Wilkins, Baltimore.

Robson, K. S. (1967), The role of eye-to-eye contact in maternal-infant attachment, *J. Child Psychol. Psychiatry,* **8,** 13-25.

Ruckmick, C. A. (1936), *The Psychology of Feeling and Emotion,* McGraw-Hill, New York.

Ryle, G. (1948), *The Concept of Mind,* Hutchinson, London.

Sander, L. W., G. Stechler, P. Burns, and H. Julia (1970), Early mother-infant interaction and 24-hour patterns of activity and sleep, *J. Am. Acad. Child Psychiatry,* **9,** 103-123.

Sartre, J.-P. (1948), *The Emotions: Outline of a Theory,* Philosophical Library, New York.

Schacter, S. (1964), The interaction of cognitive and physiological determinants of emotional state, in *Advances in Experimental Social Psychology,* Vol. 1, L. Berkowitz, Ed., Academic Press, New York, pp. 49-80.

Schacter, S. (1970), The assumption of identity and peripheralist–centralist controversies in motivation and emotion, in *Feelings and Emotion, The Loyola Symposium,* M. B. Arnold, Ed., Academic Press, New York, London.

Schecter, D. (1972), On the emergence of human relatedness, in *Interpersonal Explorations in Psychoanalysis,* E. Witenberg, Ed., Basic Books, New York.

Schildkraut, J. J. (1965), The catecholamine hypothesis of affective disorders: A review of supporting evidence, *Am. J. Psychiatry,* **122,** 509-522.

Spitz, R. A. (1957), *No and Yes on the Genesis of Human Communication,* International Universities Press, New York.

Stern, D. N. (1974), The mother and infant at play — The dyadic interaction involving "facial, vocal, and gaze behavior," in *The Effect of the Infant on its Caregiver. The Origins of Behavior,* Vol. 1, M. Lewis and L. A. Rosenblum, Eds., Wiley, New York.

Strongman, K. T. (1978), *The Psychology of Emotion,* Wiley, New York.

Thomas, A., S. Chess, and H. G. Birch (1968), *Temperament and Behavior Disorders in Children,* New York University Press, New York.

Tomkins, S. S. (1962), *Affect, Imagery Consciousness. II. The Positive Affects,* Springer, New York.

Von Humboldt, W. (1971), in *Psycholinguistics – An Introduction to Research and Theory,* H. Hurmann, Ed., Springer, New York, Heidelberg, 11th ed.

Watson, J. B. (1929), *Psychology from the Standpoint of a Behaviourist,* 3rd ed., Lippincott, Philadelphia, London.

Webster's New International Dictionary (1962), World Publications, Cleveland, New York.

Winnicott, D. W. (1965), The theory of the parent-infant relationship, in *The Maturational Process and the Facilitating Environment,* International Universities Press, New York, pp. 37-55.

FIVE

Early
Emotion

STEPHEN L. BENNETT

Sorting out the meaning of emotions in young children is difficult. The earlier we look, the more we must rely on intuitive guesses. For example, the concept of depression in children can be challenged by the question of whether despair is experienced if it cannot be articulated. A bright and verbal little boy might not state his sadness directly. The reason we would feel he is depressed could be based on his mournful expression, his grimaces and sad stories he might tell us of being abandoned and alone. The inferences made follow from what we imagine we would feel if we looked like that and saw the world that way. Such speculations increase manyfold as we approach early childhood, when words are available only from the caretaker, and the infant's communicative and expressive behaviors are just beginning.

When we look for emotion in infancy, we often see what we expect – innocence or emptiness or primitive urgency. Let me describe the interpretations of two researchers looking for the earliest evidence of emotion because we must make sense out of the same data. Darwin, in the 1840's, kept a diary on the behavior of his son, Doddy. There he describes his surprise at the humor appreciated by a 3- or 4-month-old when peek-a-boo was played, but he felt he understood it when he remembered how very early puppies and kittens begin to play (1877). St. Augustine, in the fifth century, looked at infants, noted the smile during sleep, and wondered what this could tell us about the nature of God (1961).

Well, then, what shall we look for? Although man's animal nature and God may be a more worthy search, it can be hoped that a consideration of the early expressions of emotional ex-

A shorter version of this paper was presented at the 23rd Winter Meeting of The American Academy of Psychoanalysis, December 2, 1979, as part of the panel on Normal and Pathological Development of Affect in Children.

change within the infant/mother pair during normal and pathological development can provide us with some ideas that may help
us in our therapeutic efforts.

The approach here will be to take a broad view and cover each
of the three areas one may find when considering emotion as described by Knapp (1963). These are: private states of experience,
the physiological processes that accompany these states, and the
expressive behavior that permits communication about these
states and processes to the environment. However, this will be a
highly selective look, with emphasis placed on those aspects of
emotion that can be turned to practical clinical use. We will examine this, not in the infant alone, but within the context of the
infant/mother dyad. This approach to early emotion is powerful,
not just because we add an adult, but because caretaker and infant
each show unique expressive behavior in the presence of the
other, and together take on a unity that transcends separateness.

NORMAL EMOTIONAL DEVELOPMENT
IN INFANCY

Maternal Emotions and Fantasies

The beginnings — the mythic roots — of the infant's emotions
are to be found in the mother's experience, her fantasies of what
it means to have and to be a baby — especially in her inner representation of herself as a baby with her own mother. Clinical
experience with the issues of early infancy supports the view that
one of the most powerful influences is the mother's remembered
relationship with her own mother. One destructive representation,
described by Fraiberg et al. (1975) as a ghost in the nursery, pulls
upon the mother's affective experiences of her own damaged
childhood, continuing on as a malign influence until exorcised.
But we must evoke the good ghosts as well, the figures of positive
identification. Margaret Lawrence draws upon ego strengths
during her treatment of families, especially the positive models
that go back many generations (1975). I can think of one family
in treatment where the picture of the dead grandmother on the
wall of a bare apartment took on almost a living presence when we
discussed the names of the children and traditions of child-rearing.
Advice and discussion is often only vaguely helpful, but pulling

upon the image of an old, good mother can be powerful in its force.

The REM Smile

The infant brings into the world a number of tricks and talents, including a central nervous system organized to spill out a flow of states, and a regular sequence of sleep and wakefulness. It is of interest that neurophysiological maturity, as evidenced by increasing NREM sleep time during the first year, has been linked to mother/infant interaction (Rathbun, 1979). One curiosity during REM sleep is the existence of a variety of facial expressions, such as grimaces, smiles, frowns, and looks of astonishment. These also occur during a special phase of drowsiness when REM's take place. This drowsy REM is unique to the first two months. The infant's eyes are open, but often glassy, and there are smiles and sucking (Emde et al., 1976). Oftentimes, the infant is considered to be awake, and this attracts the caretaker. This behavior often passes for emotion. Why should we not call it such? We can argue that it is, especially if the caretaker consistently interprets it so. However, what would turn us away is that the state underpinning it is not one which we would link with later emotionality.

The Alert State

One state — alertness — appears to be a fertile ground for the emotions. It is characterized by wide-openness and brightness of the eyes, and the infant's ability to visually fix and follow objects and to orient to the direction of sound. Although present only 10% of the time during the first weeks, this state has the powerful consequence of being seen by the mother as the counterpart of what in adults would be conscious awareness (Wolff, 1965). The infant enters the world revved up and alert, and encounters the mother when she also is in a highly aroused state. This joint capacity and interest in making visual contact is, as Klaus et al. (1972) point out, one of the most powerful mechanisms of bonding.

It is during alertness that the infant is capable of producing his most mature behaviors. In fact, especially during the first months, the study of emotional expression is an exercise in patience, waiting, and ingenuity in producing an aroused alertness.

The most effective technique for obtaining it is playful interaction with the infant. Restated concretely, if you do not get involved, the early expressions of emotion will not appear. Not only does this play stimulate affectual behavior, but it draws us in close so we can see the subtle facial displays. You can provoke big, gummy smiles across the aisle on a bus from a 4-month-old on the mother's lap. Not so in the first weeks, when the infant's focal distance is 8/9 inches. The very action of close-in positioning of the face required to produce an emotional response puts you where you are best able to read it.

Early Facial Expressions

The infant in the first days and months offers subtle and varied facial expressions which appear to play a role in early communicative and affectual exchanges. These have been described by Stechler and Latz (1966), Bennett (1971), Beebe (1973), and Trevarthan (1977). Certainly those observers who stress the fast and rhythmic tempo of early interaction comment on this expressive versatility (Brazelton, 1976; Stern, 1974b). Nevertheless, the literature in the past has considered the infant as possessing only a few crude primary expressions, with the smile receiving almost exclusive emphasis. However, the smile is only one, perhaps the most vivid, in a repertoire of infant facial displays.

The positive expressions of the first weeks are powerfully appealing. One highly evocative piece of facial behavior is a curling and rising of the mid-upper lip which may expand into cupping. This can occur in coordination with an intense gaze, eye crinkling, and cheek contouring and puffing. There are mouth movements allied to sucking which, although affectually neutral, convey approach and withdrawal. To get a feel for the impact of these expressions, imagine yourself 8 inches directly in front of a significant person who widens his or her eyes, bends forward, mouth open, lips pursed or pouting, with little tongue thrusts, a tension and quiver of the body, and a cooing and moaning vocalization.

Maternal Perception of Infant Characteristics

How do these early expressions function within the mother/infant interplay? That they convey meaning to the caretaker, serving as social signals has been examined in a systematic way by

Emde et al. (1978a). Now let us see what role they may play in the mother's elaboration upon the fantasies already present. If caretakers are observed during play and chores, there is offered, through chatter and banter, and especially in the soothing and scolding words, the construction of a consistent story. Out of this emerges an infant "personality." What cues are picked up? Certainly striking physical characteristics, but also the rhythms of sleep and wakefulness, especially the characteristics of the organization of alertness, as Korner (1973) has described. Using a physiognomic approach, caretakers read faces, especially their expressions, and interpret them as full-blown emotions and character. Baby nurses and most mothers are unified as to what theoretical view of infancy they subscribe to, in that they are Kleinians in the sense that they attribute to the newborn qualities of sexuality, rage, greed, and sophisticated object ties. It is out of these fantasies, the imagined beginnings of a unique individual, that caretakers create the framework within which subtle engagements can be made. If there are no stories or fantasies, there is little "personality," and the care offered can only be rigid and routine (Bennett, 1971).

Infant-Elicited Maternal Behavior

Let us move on now to more secure ground and look at some of the things that caretakers actually do when around babies. Most dramatic is the exaggeration of the mother's facial expressions when she sees her baby. As Stern (1974b) has described, these facial displays are extended in space and time, and repetitious in their occurrence. The mother does not use her full range of expressions, but rather offers a limited few that are enough to initiate, maintain, and terminate the interplay with the infant. Maternal vocalizations share these exaggerated qualities, as is heard in the sing-song rhythms of baby talk. Gaze between infant and mother is prolonged to a degree which, if repeated in the subway, would bring on erotic or aggressive consequences we might not be prepared for. These facial, vocal and visual behaviors occur in integrated units as sharply demarcated packages which, in their repetition and exaggeration, may be programmed to fit the infant's timing and ability to process information. Also, these discrete bursts of maternal behavior provide a highly ordered stimulus world for infants, a constant beat of visual and vocal stimulation, offered again and again, not only in the same form, but with the same timing. Whether voice or movement, the temporal pattern is the same for all sensory channels (Stern et al., 1977). Thus, while a few histrionic giggles or smiles offered to the infant are not interesting, the time-and-again rhythms that provide the structure of emotion and communication are.

Mother/Infant Play

In the free play that occurs at 3–4 months, we can see both maternal and infant abilities blossom in a lively, often joyous, give and take. The mother, by using the repertoire we have described, engages the infant and maintains the play. Mutual pleasure is the joint goal (Stern, 1974a). The mother's principal task can be considered to be this regulation of incoming social stimulation, and she herself is the major source of it. She must repeat familiar themes, prevent overload, but also provide enough variation to maintain interest. This incoming stimulation is closely allied to internal arousal in that the behaviors used to regulate one have consequences for the other. The mother is regulating the infant's arousal, maintaining it at a mid-range wherein the most mature communicative and expressive behaviors appear (Beebe and Stern, 1977).

Infant Self-Regulation of Arousal

The 3–4-month-old infant serves also as gatekeeper to the perceptual world. At this time, his visual-motor apparatus has reached functional maturity so that in games depending upon deft eye and head movements, the infant performs with the adult as an equal. Not only is the infant able to gate, sort, and regulate social stimulation, but also as a consequence modulates his own internal arousal. When excitement reaches a high pitch or the incoming situation is adverse, the infant can turn off by shutting the eyes, swinging away the head, going limp, or crying. There are accompanying expressions of wariness, coyness, sobering, frowning, and grimacing. A mother/infant pair described by Beebe and Stern (1977) illustrates this control dramatically. The mother's head movements had a looming quality and in hundreds of tries, she was not able to make direct eye contact because of the infant's ability to avoid her. The 3–4-month-old infant possesses "veto power" over the mother's attempts to engage. This control is not just a crude turning off, but a virtuoso and rapid-fire dodging. The other direction of eye contact is head-on engagement with the mother, wherein the infant is highly aroused, and the expressions are intensely positive. The infant can maintain this by deft turns back and forth. Of equal interest, however, is the infant's ability to follow the mother over a 180° arc with an accompanying wide range of movements and expressions. This interplay is made up of behaviors less than a half-second in duration, a "split-second" world, one which would not be entirely in the mother's conscious awareness (Beebe and Stern, 1977).

Infant Schemata

The infant's twists and turns can be seen as defensive, not just in the loose sense of guarding and adjusting, but in the strict sense of a defense as protection against internal events. Beebe and Stern (1977) describe also a spectrum of engagement and disengagement behaviors ranging from direct contact to turning away. This is made up of clusters of the infant's behaviors, especially his head position, gaze and facial expression, internal arousal, perception of the mother's behavior, and the sequence and timing of the interaction with the mother. It is out of these action schemes that the affectively charged internal representations of the infant in interaction with the mother are formed.

Play as the Spirit of the Relationship

We have looked at the micromomentary events of play — emotion as displayed by expressive behavior — but we should pay attention to the mother's patter and her verbal projections in response to the baby's reactions. These reveal a fantasy being played out as well as the affectual theme. As Call and Marschak (1966) write, "since they [games] develop spontaneously between mother and infant, they can be regarded as a precipitant, a condensation, or the essence of that relationship." Fraiberg (1974) enlarges our clinical view by her description of games as "a valuable diagnostic instrument for assessment of infant-parent relationships." Adults in play with infants can express the entire range of feelings, from sadness and sensuality to tenderness and rage. These games also have a defensive function in that they can help defuse the parent's conflictual emotions.

Early Infant-Mother Communication

Comments on early emotion and preverbal communicative exchanges tend to be the same. Two themes are developed, which need not be in opposition. One emphasis is on the infant as pre-wired so as to be able to communicate with humans (Bruner, 1977; Trevathan, 1977). For example, infant gaze patterns have the same timing as that of an adult's speech during a dialogue (Jaffe et al., 1973). The other theme is that the mother reads into infant behavior one part of a dialogue and replies as if this had communicative and emotional meaning. This is not just low-level adultomorphosing; rather it provides, because the mother sets it up this way — out of awareness — the rhythm and grammar of language and emotion.

Imitation

An important issue concerns how soon the infant is able to imitate the mother's expressions and feelings. Whatever the answer to that may be, it is clear that mothers are constant mimics, and most of what babies do is played back by the mother (Pawlby, 1977). Here is one mechanism for contagion or infection of feeling. It illustrates Winicott's (1967) mystic comment that the baby sees himself when he looks at the mother because what she looks like is related to what she sees in the infant.

Simultaneous Communication

For the most part, we have stressed the alternating he-said, she-said interaction. However, during play sessions, mother and infant make sounds simultaneously twice as often as they do in an alternating pattern. In talk, as in mutual gaze, mother and infant spend a lot of time doing things together. In 3–4-month-old infants, there appears to be a parallel emergence of two separate dyadic modes of vocal communication which continue on through life. The alternating pattern leads to the adult dialogue, with its transmission of symbolic information. The simultaneous pattern is seen during high levels of arousal — either positive or negative — and is seen later in life during periods of intense emotion, as in the murmurs of love, growls of anger, or cheering during a game. Here is a vehicle for emotional communication concerning the moment-by-moment interpersonal relationship (Stern et al., 1975).

Early Emotions

We may question just what it is that we call "infant emotion." Putting aside the inclination to say that it has been there all along, inside the mother's head, we may feel that it is to be found (at three to four months) in the infant–mother system we have been examining. I offer this as an emotional rather than a logical conclusion. It feels right, in that at a time when we are likely to become involved clinically, there is present a richly intricate infant–mother affectual organization. Certainly this system will undergo many changes, and there are affectual constellations in various stages of development, with some, such as anger and fear, requiring a season or more before they are formed and functional. Sroufe (1979) has described (in a clear and detailed essay) the levels of emotional development, and the ontogenesis of the specific affect systems.

One concept of early emotions that has been given too much attention is that they have a preemptory quality. That a cry or a smile is compelling and possesses crude survival value is clear enough. However, the data appearing over the past decade demonstrate that these signals are only the extremes of a wide range of subtle and rapid-fire expressive behaviors.

PATHOLOGICAL EMOTIONAL DEVELOPMENT

Let us now look at deviant development and the ideas that follow concerning emotion. Most of us use, for a quick evaluation of an infant, our feel for the richness and versatility of expressive behavior. The words we all use — animation, liveliness, vivacity, vitality, and joie de vivre — mean the same thing: that the infant is really alive. The lack of this affective quality is demonstrated, as Provence (1978) describes, when the infant's "range of expressed feelings is narrow, if they lack vividness and intensity, if they do not show up in his actions, and if he shows us only a few compared with other infants of his age."

Deprivation

We are most likely to have had clinical experiences with the consequences of deprivation. Provence and Lipton (1962) have observed in the institutional infant a blandness and barrenness of the affective repertoire and the absence of play. Also, they describe the first and most dramatic indication of improvement, besides weight gain, to be the animation of the infant's face, replacing the frozen, flat deadness of before. We are most likely to have observed, within a general clinic population, the evidences of deprivation in the varieties of failure to thrive and in the clear and borderline cases of neglect and abuse. But we must consider more than the simple absence of stimulation and wonder about skewed and faulty interaction and even overstimulation.

Uncomplicated deprivation does still exist, unfortunately. One recent experience I had with this occurred during the observation of a group of babies in a nursery awaiting placement. What strikes me now was the incredible experiment that had been set up by the institution. This was the determination of the minimum involvement necessary to produce weight gain — a quick and efficient pushing in of food — but not enough to permit any animation. Facial expressions, except for cries and some mechanical smiles, were rare. The nursery was filled was fat, dead-faced babies.

Congenital Esophageal Atresia

One problem in appraising other causes of disordered emotional development is that deprivation is often part of them. It is only during the last few years that there has been a realization that the specific deficits resulting from blindness, deafness, and Down's Syndrome also affect in a profound way the mother–infant relationship, and hence result in skewed and deficient stimulation. Many of the therapeutic efforts have to do not only with finding alternate sensory channels so as to make up for the specific deficit, but also with providing an adequate and tuned-in level of stimulation.

Dowling (1977), in his study of seven infants with esophageal atresia — Monica being one of them — has made a thoughtful effort to distinguish the effect of deprivation from the absence of a normal oral experience. Those children who did not receive sham feedings showed a complex psychological picture which included impoverishment of affective expression. Although they resembled (in many ways) institutional children, there were differences. Later on, for example, they showed strong attachments to their parents rather than the shallow relationships of children raised in institutions. This important study shows that the lack of one specific early experience — orality — has a profound influence on emotional development and human relationships.

Blindness

The particular impact of the blind infant on the caretaker has been described by Fraiberg (1974). Missing is the resonance of mood that occurs with the sighted infant. This follows from the absence in the blind infant of several elements in the repertoire of expressive language. There is, to use her phrase, the absence of "eye language." As we have already considered, wide-open, intent eyes are the most powerful mode of greeting and communication. Missing, also, is the "smile language." At 1½ to 2½ months, blind infants show the same irregular smiling to touch and voice as do sighted infants, but by 2½-3 months, the mother's voice will not regularly elicit a smile. The blind infant's smile is inconstant, less frequent, and mute compared with that of the sighted infant (Fraiberg, 1971). Between the extremes of cries and lukewarm smiles, there is an absence of differentiated facial signs. This does not mean, at least in the beginning, that the affective states usually assumed from these expressions are lacking. Mood and emotion were observed to be communicated by a richly expressive "hand language" which, if read, opened up communication.

Deafness

Detailed data concerning the emotional development of deaf infants are not available at present. A recent study by Galenson et al. (1979) considered, that the later disturbances found in deaf children, as with the blind, may have as much to do with the impairment of the mother–child relationship as with the sensory deficit. One specific finding was that the affective attachments of deaf children raised by deaf parents were shallow.

Infant Abuse

Abused infants and abusing adults provide the opportunity to examine feelings gone wild. Gaensbauer and Sands (1979) have described the personality traits of abused children — although, at 6–36 months, they are older than those we have looked at here — which, they believe, contribute to their abuse and neglect. They feel that within the caretaker–infant pair, the infant sends by means of his expressive behavior "affective messages" which parents use to organize their behavior toward the infant. Their study demonstrated the variety of potent signals – here negative – infants can offer. This, then, is an answer to the question, "So what if a baby does some odd things with his face?": certain parents react to these cues with rage and violence. The distortions coming from the infant include affective withdrawal, shallowness, and negative affective communications. These disagreeable behaviors then play into the characteristics of abusing parents, as described by Green (1976). The parents rely on the child to gratify their own dependency needs, but these infants, are not likely to be cute and do not offer much. Also, there is a tendency towards projection of negative feelings by the parents. For example, an infant's eye aversion could be interpreted as a rejection by the parents, the same as had been done to them, and the infant then would be the target of rage.

Down's Syndrome

Infants with Down's Syndrome offer the chance to study the relationship between cognitive and emotional development (Cytryn, 1975). Cicchetti and Sroufe (1978) describe that early laughter and other emotional expressions can predict cognitive development in the second year better than early mental tests. Here is research support for our use of guesses based on the infant's emotional organization.

There is an early lack of clarity in the affective signaling of Down's infants, which has an impact on the mother–infant relationship (Emde et al., 1978b). This finding has a direct bearing on the therapeutic programs designed to remedy the lack of stimulation that can ensue.

Caretaker–Infant Mismatch

The study of the major pathological syndromes and sensory defects of infancy, although offering important research and therapeutic ideas, nevertheless covers only a small portion of the difficulties occurring between infant and caretaker. There is a large range of less dramatic and serious difficulties that represent a mismatch or faulty connection between members of the infant–caretaker pair. For example, in the normal infant and mother described by Beebe and Stern (1977) (in the section, "Infant Self-Regulation of Arousal"), it is possible to imagine that the mother's looming intrusions and the infant's dodging avoidance with grimaces could continue to the point that this interaction became fixed and mutually distressing. Even for an experienced observer, what was going on may not, at first, be clear, but what would be evident was that the emotion hanging in the air was anger and frustration, and, perhaps later, apathy. Unfortunately, unless there is a failure to gain weight, such unhappiness is usually ignored by pediatricians. It is only during the last few years, with the awareness of such interactional difficulties and the emergence of infant psychiatry, that such issues could be evaluated and corrected.

THE AFFECTIVE THEMES OF THERAPY

Until recently, most programs that attempted to work with young infants stressed motor and cognitive issues, and although parents were often involved, this has not been a major issue. One example of an affect- and parent-centered approach is the impressive program for the severely and multiply handicapped infant sponsored by the Developmental Disability Center of the Louisiana State University Medical Center. Haslett and her coworkers (1979) describe their rigorous attention to affective development and their primary emphasis on training the parents to do the actual therapeutic work with their infants.

However, big projects pose special problems and have their unique populations. Our interest here is in the solo practitioner, such as the child psychiatrist in his office and the resident doing ward consultation. They are not likely to have teams of observers, special testing, videotapes, or frame-by-frame analysis. How can we evaluate this intricate system without elaborate support? One thought, to an idea of Stern's (1979), is that both baby and mother are the most sensitive machines available for evaluating each other. But how can we read this equipment, with its split-second interplay that is almost out of awareness? One way is to go beyond ordinary attention to feelings and fantasies and engage in freewheeling adultomorphizing. The tough-minded research literature warns against this (Emde et al., 1976, 1978). However, not to use these empathic elaborations is crippling. Here, in this consideration of feelings, we come into our own. Ferholt (1979) tangles with this issue in his description of the families of psycho-physiologic dwarfs. Within a day after the child's separation from or reunion with the family, there is a shift in growth hormone. No test available now, or group of tests, is able to catch the intense and specific power of these families. What is available is the observer's empathic sense of malignant craziness that is not felt at any other time.

Following the dominant emotional theme is a sturdy principle of child therapy and this will serve us as well with the infant–mother pair. One of the first statements and still the richest description of deft and delicate attention to a child's emotions is to be found in Berta Bornstein's classic description of the analysis of Frankie, starting at age 5½ (Bornstein, 1949). At a time when not much was being said about emotions beyond the crude power of fear and rage, she described her approach to the analysis of defenses through the awareness and interpretation of affects. Although this technique is called defense analysis, perhaps because of the interest then in ego psychology, it could as well be called affect analysis.

The process of therapeutic change in the mother–infant system follows from our description of normal and pathological development. Much of the practical and routine work done with infants and mothers involves provision of support and structure. Help with Welfare, arrangement for a homemaker or infant day care, although they seem to be concrete and straightforward acts, reveal a complex implicit assumption, which is that the infant–mother pair is phylogenetically programmed for developmental progression given that stability is obtained from external support.

The next order of therapy goes beyond the self-correction possible with external support. This involves learning and is a complex process that involves behaviors a fraction of a second in duration. Examples would be the modification of a maternal head movement so it was no longer looming, and the development of sustained physical play that made full contact with a blind child. Stern (1974a) points out that mothers are capable of rapid readjustments in their games and interaction if they are in conflict-free areas. Caretakers learn when their successful interactions are emphasized and responded to positively with something like, "Did you see how your baby smiled when you did that?" These quick shifts touch the affectively charged representations of mother–infant that are positive. However, such rapid learning is not possible when the areas involve conflictual issues and touch negatively charged mother–infant representations. The therapeutic approach required in such situations is the intensive and complex involvement with all areas of the life of mother–infant described by Fraiberg and her associates (1975), but most particularly with feelings and fantasies.

We have come full circle from the influence of maternal affects and fantasies on infant development to a detailed description of mother–infant expressive and communicative behavior, the role of emotionally charged memories in therapeutic change, and finally the use of the therapist's own feelings as a guide and for assessment.

References

Beebe, B. (1973), Ontogeny of positive affect in the third and fourth month of life of an infant; unpublished doctoral dissertation.

Beebe, B. and D. N. Stern (1977), Engagement-disengagement and early object experiences, in *Communicative Structures and Psychic Structures,* Freedman and Grand, Eds., Plenum, New York, pp. 35-55.

Bennett, S. L. (1971), Infant-caretaker interactions, *J. Am. Acad. Child Psychiatry,* **10**, 321-335.

Bornstein, B. (1949), The analysis of a phobic child: Some problems of theory and technique in child analysis, in *Psychoanalytic Study of the Child,* International Press, New York, Vols. 3-4, pp. 181-226.

Brazelton, T. B. (1971), *Neonatal Behavioral Assessment Scale (Clinics in Developmental Medicine, No. 50),* Heinemann, Lippincott, London, Philadelphia.

Brazelton, T. B. (1976), Early parent-infant reciprocity, in *The Family – Can It Be Saved?,* Vaughn and Brazelton, Eds., Year Book, Chicago, pp. 133-141.

Bruner, J. S. (1977), Early social interaction and language aquisition, in *Studies in Mother-Infant Interaction,* H. R. Schaffer, Ed., Academic Press, New York, pp. 177-202.

Call, J. and M. Marschak (1966), Styles and games in infancy, *J. Am. Acad. Child Psychiatry,* **5**, 193-209.

Cicchetti, D. and L. A. Sroufe (1978), An organizational view of affect: Illustration from the study of Down's Syndrome Infants, in *The Development of Affect,* M. Lewis and L. A. Rosenbaum, Eds., Plenum, New York, pp. 309-350.

Cytryn, L. (1975), Studies of behavior in children with Down's syndrome, in *Explorations in Child Psychiatry,* J. Anthony, Ed., Plenum, New York, pp. 271-285.

Darwin, C. (1877), A biographical sketch of an infant, *Mind,* **2,** 285-294.

Dowling, S. (1977), Seven infants with esophageal atresia: A developmental study, in *The Psychoanalytic Study of the Child,* Yale University Press, New Haven, Vol. 32, pp. 156-215.

Emde, R., T. Gaensbauer, and R. Harmon (1976), *Emotional Expression in Infancy, A Biobehavioral Study, Psychological Issues,* International Universities Press, New York.

Emde, R., D. H. Kingman, J. H. Reich, and T. D. Wade (1978a), Emotional expression in infancy: I. Initial studies of social signaling and an emergent model, in *The Development of Affect,* M. Lewis and L. A. Rosenblum, Eds., Plenum, New York, pp. 125-148.

Emde, R. N., E. L. Katz, and J. K. Thorpe (1978b), The expression of emotion in infancy: II. Early deviations in Down's Syndrome, in *The Development of Affect,* M. Lewis and L. A. Rosenbaum, Eds., Plenum, New York, pp. 351-360.

Ferholt, J. (1979), Personal communication.

Fraiberg, S. (1971), "Smiling and stranger reaction in blind infants, in *The Exceptional Infant,* Vol. 2, Brunner/Mazle, New York, pp. 110-127.

Fraiberg, S. (1974a), The clinical dimensions of baby games, *J. Am. Acad. Child Psychiatry,* **13,** 202-220.

Fraiberg, S. (1974b), Blind infants and their mothers: An examination of the sign system, in *The Effect of the Infant on Its Caregiver,* M. Lewis and L. A. Rosenbaum, Eds., Wiley, New York, pp. 215-232.

Fraiberg, S., E. Adelson, and V. Shapiro (1975), Ghosts in the nursery: A psychoanalytic approach to the problems of impaired infant-mother relationships, *J. Am. Acad. Child Psychiatry,* **14,** 387-421.

Gaensbauer, T. J. and K. Sands (1979), Distorted affective communications in abused/neglected infants and their potential impact on caretakers, *J. Am. Acad. Child Psychiatry,* **18,** 236-250.

Galenson, E., R. Miller, E. Kaplan, and A. Rothstein (1979), Assessment of development in the deaf child, *J. Am. Acad. Child Psychiatry,* **18,** 128-142.

Green, A. H. (1976), A psychodynamic approach to the study and treatment of child-abusing parents, *J. Am. Acad. Child Psychiatry,* **15,** 414-429.

Haslett, N. R., D. B. Bolding, J. A. Harris, and H. Chin-Chin (1979), Workshop: The development of a parent training curriculum for affective development in the severely and multiply handicapped infant, Meeting of the American Academy of Child Psychiatry, Atlanta, October 27, 1979.

Jaffe, J., D. N. Stern, and J. C. Peery (1973), Conversational coupling of gaze behavior in prelinguistic human development, *J. Psycholinguist. Res.,* **2,** 321-330.

Klaus, M., R. Jerauld, N. Kreger, W. McAlpine, M. Steffa, and J. Kennell (1972), Maternal attachment: Importance of the first post-partum days, *N. Engl. J. Med.*, **286**, 460–463.

Knapp, P. (1963), Introduction: Emotional expression – past and present, in *Expression of the Emotions in Man*, P. Knapp, Ed., International Universities Press, New York, pp. 3–19.

Korner, A. (1973), The effect of the infant's state, level of arousal, sex and ontogenic stage on the caretaker, in *The Effect of the Infant on Its Caregiver*, M. Lewis and L. A. Rosenbaum, Eds., Wiley, New York, pp. 105–121.

Lawrence, M. (1975), *Young Inner-City Families: The Development of Ego Strength Under Stress*, Behavioral Publications.

Pawlby, S. (1977), Imitative interaction, in *Studies in Mother-Infant Interaction*, H. R. Schaeffer, Ed., Academic, New York, pp. 203–224.

Provence, S. (1978), A clinician's view of affect development in infancy, in *The Development of Affect*, M. Lewis and L. A. Rosenblum, Eds., Plenum, New York, pp. 293–307.

Provence, S. and R. Lipton (1962), *Infants in Institutions*, International Universities Press, New York.

Rathbun, J. (1979), The relationship of mother-infant interactive patterns and sleep patterns in two month old infants, paper presented at the American Academy of Child Psychiatry, Atlanta, October 26, 1979.

Saint Augustine (1961), *Confessions*, Penguin, New York, Book I, Sec. 6.

Sroufe, A. F. (1979), Socioemotional development, in *Handbook of Infant Development*, J. Osofsky, Ed., Wiley, New York, pp. 462–516.

Stechler, G. and E. Latz (1966), Some observations on attention and arousal in the human infant, *J. Am. Acad. Child Psychiatry*, **5**, 517–525.

Stern, D. (1974a), The goal and structure of mother-infant play, *J. Am. Acad. Child Psychiatry*, **13**, 402–421.

Stern, D. (1974b), Mother and infant at play: The dyadic interaction involving facial, vocal, and gaze behaviors, in *The Effect of the Infant on Its Caretaker*, M. Lewis and L. A. Rosenbaum, Eds., Wiley, New York, pp. 187–213.

Stern, D. (1979), Panel: Perspectives on assessment and prediction in infancy, The American Academy of Child Psychiatry, Atlanta, October 28, 1979.

Stern, D. and B. Beebe (1977), Engagement-disengagement and early object experiences, in *Communicative Structures and Psychic Structures*, N. Freedman and S. Grand, Eds., Plenum, New York.

Stern, D. N., J. Jaffe, B. Beebe, and S. L. Bennett (1975), Vocalizing in unison and in alternation: Two modes of communication within the mother-infant dyad, *Ann. N. Y. Acad. Sci.*, **263**, 89–100.

Stern, D. N., B. Beebe, J. Jaffe, and S. L. Bennett (1977), The infant's stimulus world during social interaction, in *Studies in Mother-Infant Interaction,* H. R. Schaffer, Ed., Academic, New York, pp. 177-202.

Trevarthan, C. (1977), Descriptive analysis of infant communicative behavior, in *Studies in Mother-Infant Interaction,* H. R. Schaffer, Ed., Academic, New York, pp. 227-270.

Winicott, D. W. (1967), Mirror-role of mother and family in child development, in *The Predicament of The Family,* P. Lomas, Ed., International Universities Press, New York, pp. 26-33.

Wolff, P. (1965), The development of attention in young infants, *Ann. N. Y. Acad. Sci.,* **118**, 815-830.

SIX

Early Developmental
Roots Of
Anxiety

DAVID E. SCHECTER

Anxiety can be defined as the ego's reaction to or anticipation of danger (Freud, 1926). When the ego is overwhelmed or disorganized by the reaction to the danger situation we refer to the quality and quantity of anxiety as traumatic. By contrast, *signal anxiety* is a smaller dose of tension in anticipation of the danger situation, signifying "danger ahead." From a developmental point of view, it would make sense to refer to signal anxiety only when the ego has begun to develop the function of anticipation or foresight at around three to four months of age.

There are several areas that contribute to the individual's predisposition to anxiety: hereditary–constitutional factors, prenatal conditions, the birth experience itself, and early postnatal experience. However, at this point in our knowledge we know too little about the contribution of each of these areas to postulate anything beyond the general likelihood of their positive contribution to the predisposition and threshold to anxiety.

Benjamin (1963) notes a critical period in the infant at three to four weeks of age, when there is a rapid change in neurophysiologic maturation, especially in the area of "plugging in" of sensory modalities to central nervous system experience. There is EEG evidence of neurophysiologic change at this time. The mother must function as part of the infant's stimulus barrier, or protective shield, in order that he not be overwhelmed by the new connections of sensory experience from within and without. The variability in the adequacy of parenting in this critical period is

This paper was first given at The American Academy of Psychoanalysis on November 30, 1979.

probably another factor in the variability of predisposition to anxiety later on.

Benjamin describes a "fear of the strange" developing around four months of age. This includes strange sounds and sights while the infant is not able at the same time to see mother's face. This takes place at a stage in the infant's development when there is specific attention to facial expression. The infant can respond with negative affect — i.e. early anxiety — to even a frown on mother's face. Thus, mother's "forbidding gestures" (Sullivan, 1953) induce anxiety in the infant, a fact of great developmental and clinical importance. Other changes in mother's appearance — a new hat, hair curlers, sunglasses — will also induce "strange-mother" anxiety. My view on this form of anxiety is that it is due to the "perceptual dissonance" (Sandler, 1977) between the familiar and strange factors in mother who is thus *both* familiar and strange (Schecter, 1974). There is in these phenomena a combination of both stranger and separation anxiety.

STRANGER ANXIETY

Let us now turn to the dramatic phenomenon of *infantile stranger anxiety* proper, which can begin between five and eight months and which has been called the "eight-month anxiety" by Spitz (1950). Both Spitz and Freud (1926) explained the phenomenon of stranger anxiety as being based on the experience of mother's absence — the presentation of the strange face gestalt when the familiar mother gestalt is expected. (We use the term "mother" to stand for "parenting one" since we now know that separation anxiety from father can be equally significant.)

Phenomenologically, the infant's reaction to the stranger's face runs the range of behaviors from no apparent reaction, to sobering of the infant's face, expressions of mild apprehension, or wide-eyed staring, a freezing (inhibition) of motor and expressive behavior, aversion of visual gaze, clinging, quivering of lips to outright screaming and panic behavior. Indelibly imprinted on my memory is a young toddler who froze upon the appearance of strangers, in an uncomfortable crouched position, for 20 minutes before he began to loosen up and become mobile.

Benjamin, in contrast to Freud and Spitz, described some intriguing differences between separation anxiety and stranger anxiety. Though stranger and separation anxiety are related dynamically and correlate positively, statistically there are babies who demonstrate high separation anxiety and low stranger anxiety as well as vice versa. Stranger anxiety can occur whether or not mother is present, whereas separation anxiety occurs in the absence of mother whether or not anyone else is present. Also, the average and peak times of onset are different for each type of anxiety, occurring somewhat earlier for stranger anxiety. We assume with Benjamin that stranger anxiety, though sharing a common root with separation anxiety — fear of object loss — has in addition a *relatively independent source of anxiety based on the infant's fear of the strange,* which is observable even earlier than the anxious response to the stranger per se. For example, the three-to-four month old may become apprehensive with strange objects or sounds or when he is handled in an unfamiliar manner.

An apprehensive response may also be aroused in the young infant by altering an anticipated gestalt pattern through the addition of unfamiliar elements or by the omission of some apparently crucial familiar element. For example, we have noted that for some infants the visual presentation of a smiling, nodding adult face without the accustomed accompanying vocalizations may evoke an anxious expression. When vocalizations are added the infants relax and smile, giving the impression of closure of the anticipated familiar gestalt. In a similar vein, humming or a falsetto voice excluding the visual presentation of the adult face could produce fearful reactions (Benjamin, 1963).*

The expression around the adult's eyes seems to be of particular importance to the infant, and this fits in with Wolff's (1963) observation of the infant's tendency to search out the eye area and make eye-to-eye contact before smiling at the face presentation. All these signs of increasing perceptual discrimination of alterations of facial gestalt, including the discrimination of adult nega-

---

*We have also noted that to both the face mask and the stranger the infant may be alternately sober, then apprehensive, smiling, and apprehensive once more. He may respond with apprehension to a variety of alterations of the facial gestalt such as placing pads over the eyes, the forbidding expression of a frown with vertical (as against horizontal) forehead creasing (Spitz, 1965) or with changes in mother's appearance.

tive affect expressions, predate and constitute the precursors to the appearance of infantile stranger anxiety in Benjamin's sense.*

From observation one can describe a range of experience in the infant from "strange" to "novel" to "familiar." If the infant is secure on mother's knee he may react to the strange toy as if it were merely novel and proceed to explore it. For this to happen mother is sometimes required to give the new toy her "magic blessing" by handling it, thus transforming the strange-forbidden into the novel-exciting in the sense that the child now handles the toy with curiosity. In a parallel way in psychoanalytic therapy the analyst through his mediation helps transform a frightening, strange area of experience into one that is now open to exploration with the curiosity characteristic of pursuit of the novel.

ANXIETY BY CONTAGION

It now becomes possible to understand the relationship between stranger anxiety and *that form of anxiety that is induced in the infant by the anxiety of the mothering one.* Sullivan (1953) refers to the as-yet unknown mechanism which mediates the interpersonal induction of anxiety as "empathic linkage"; Escalona (1953) refers to the process with the felicitous word, "contagion." We are all familiar with the contagion of affects from clinical work and observation of normal families. It is our speculation that when mother is anxious or distressed she appears as *both familiar and strange to her infant.* We know that by six to seven months the infant has clearly come to discriminate mother (or father) from less familiar persons. We see this from the great eagerness of his smiling response to her at this time as well as his beginning separation protest. We assume that he has a positively endowed memory of a gestalt experience of mother, including her facial and vocal physiognomy, as well as the quality of her touch and probably body scent. We would speculate that the child through repeated pleasurable experiences anticipates seeing, hearing, and feeling the familiar "good mother" and is shocked, frightened and baffled when the strange elements of her anxiety — facial

*Wells Goodrich (personal communication) has suggested that there may be a value in considering two types of stranger anxiety. One would be based on the stranger reaction before object constancy has been achieved. The second would occur after the achievement of object constancy, which would afford a more secure base from which the stranger is experienced.

frown, tight lips, and vocal alterations — are all presented simultaneously with her recognizably familiar elements. Dan Stern's (1971) work on the "ballet" of eye-to-eye contact and aversion suggests a further mechanism by which anxiety is induced in the infant by the mothering one. I would speculate that observation would reveal a distinct change in the interpersonal rhythm and "choreography" in the area of eye-to-eye contact when mother is anxious. The loss of smooth, familiar visual rhythm would disrupt the euphoric quality of the relationship and contribute to the induction of anxiety.

SEPARATION ANXIETY — THE BASIC HUMAN ANXIETY

Separation anxiety is the basic anxiety of infancy and remains a fundamental anxiety throughout life. In childhood and adulthood separation anxiety becomes transformed into a fear of abandonment, an almost universal fear which is available to psychoanalytic inquiry. Whereas in the early months the infant may react with negative affect upon separation from any caretaker, by seven or eight months the anxiety reaction is specific to the parent to whom the baby is most significantly attached. A not uncommon finding is strong protest with crying and distress when mother leaves the room even if the child is left in the presence of a familiar person. A young mother I see in therapy describes a heart-rending daily departure for work to the accompaniment of the wailing of her infant, left in the care of a familiar babysitter. Through the use of empathic observation the observer notes the protest, rage, and fear expressed by the baby in the separation reaction. There is peak separation anxiety around eleven to twelve months and then again at eighteen months, lasting, in lessening degree, often until age three years, when object constancy becomes more consolidated (Mahler et al., 1975).

Bowlby (1973) describes three important stages in the separation reaction. First there is angry, anxious *protest* in which the infant seems to be demanding the return of the disappearing mother.* (Interestingly, there is no separation anxiety expressed when the baby takes the initiative to leave mother. However, there is frequent checking back visually to assure him that mother is

---

*This is an example of the adaptational value of the expression of anxiety.

still available.) A second stage of the separation reaction, if separation is prolonged, is described by Bowlby as *despair*. The infant looks despondent, in grief and mourning, and may even regress in his ego functioning, e.g., a child who has been toilet trained may regress to wetting himself during this stage.* The third stage of a prolonged separation is described as *detachment*. The child is no longer manifestly anxious, angry, or despondent during this phase; however, he may actually avert his gaze from mother upon their reunion. Theoretically, the detachment defenses are crucial in understanding the development of *characterologic detachment*, which is seen not only in the schizoid character but as part of the defensive structure of a patient who may bear any diagnostic label (Schecter, 1978). Detachment is a protective defense against the painful affects of separation and also serves to withdraw the child or patient from a state of attachment to a significant figure.

The intensity of attachment, and of separation anxiety, is heightened by illness, fatigue, fear, a strange environment, a recent separation, or following a period of increased social stimulation, for example, by a doting relative.

Although Freud did not use the concept of separation anxiety as the fundamental human anxiety, he did state (1926) that missing someone who is loved is the key to the understanding of anxiety. We wholeheartedly agree with this latter position. A later development in the fear of object loss (separation anxiety) is the anxiety that is triggered by the *loss of love*. This form of anxiety is so important that it will be considered separately from separation anxiety even though it can be regarded as part of a continuum of the separation reaction.

Aggressive feelings toward the beloved object-person serve to increase separation anxiety. Since angry, aggressive feelings are evoked upon separation, the makings of a vicious circle exist: separation – aggression – fear of abandonment – further anger, and so on. We have to consider the fact that angry, aggressive feelings can be projected onto the parent, after which a cycle of persecutory anxiety is set up. The child comes to feel abandoned because he feels hated by mother. We are now in a situation of "bad-mother" and "bad-me," a situation that can only be terminated upon the tender reunion of parent and child. However, probably starting from the second half of the first

---

*It needs to be emphasized that prolonged separation or loss of love leads to anaclitic depression (Spitz, 1946).

year, the infant begins to symbolize a "bad-mother" and a "bad-me" which become internalized objects or personifications characterized by structural constancy. This phase represents the end of the "Garden of Eden" bliss between mother and child. Concurrently, differentiation of self and mother proceeds apace during the individuation–separation phase (Mahler et al., 1975). Here we have the beginning splits of self as subject and object and, as object, the child begins to feel observed, evaluated and potentially ashamed. The experience of shame includes the anticipation of or reaction to the danger situation in which the child is failing a standard or ideal set up for him — a standard that will soon be internalized. Since shame involves the reaction to or anticipation of a danger situation, we can refer to the affect as *shame anxiety,* which is often accompanied by the dread of abandonment. Shame anxiety is so fundamental that it can affect *how* the self evolves — under constant scrutiny from within or without as against under relatively spontaneous conditions.

By the same token, when the child feels he has transgressed a forbidden boundary, he feels "bad" and experiences *guilt anxiety.* This occurs after the taboo area has been internalized by the child. Later on both of these forms of anxiety can be classified as *superego anxieties.* Both anxieties can be accompanied by a plummeting self-esteem that in itself can evoke severe anxiety.

It must be remembered that anxiety is highly contagious, so that if mother suffers high separation anxiety, she will induce anxiety in the infant around separation situations. This phenomenon is observable early in life and comes to the fore when the child separates regularly as in going to nursery school, kindergarten, etc.

There are also more subtle forms of separation anxiety. One example is found in the underresponsive mother who may be quite depressed or detached so that the infant experiences periodic breaks in the "refueling dialogue" (Sandler, 1977) that normally goes on in the healthy parent–child relationship. This form of deprivation surfaces frequently in analysis when the patient feels a lack of empathic responsiveness by the analyst.

In the older child — from age four years onwards — there develops the ultimate separation anxiety, namely, the fear of death. Once the child cognitively evolves the concept of eternity, i.e., "forever," he becomes prone to thoughts and fears about the death of those who are close to him as well as the notion of his own mortality. Life is never again the same for him once he is captured by the sense of its finitude. Developmentally this marks the beginning of what has been referred to as existential anxiety.

ANXIETY THROUGH LOSS OF LOVE AND SECURITY

In a healthy mother–child relationship there is a two-way flow of loving behaviors, a musical conversation, smiling faces, various forms of touch, cuddling, cooing, soothing, etc. These loving behaviors are available when the child needs them and this need is empathically sensed by the parent. However, if the parent is depressed or disapproving, the loving behaviors will be withheld or even replaced by a scolding voice or a frowning face. This experience of loss of love signals a danger situation for the child and hence he experiences anxiety. He cannot then count on a loving "refueling dialogue" and he symbolizes this situation as bad — "bad me" and "bad mother." Moreover, since the loving and soothing behaviors act as a kind of antianxiety protection, their withdrawal renders the infant vulnerable to experiencing anxiety from whatever source without the loving protective barrier.

Love to the infant means the security of empathic responsiveness to his needs by the mothering one. *

Sullivan (1953) puts it this way: "The tension called out in the mothering one by the manifest needs of the infant we call *tenderness* and a generic group of tensions in the infant, the relief of which requires cooperation by the person who acts in the mothering role, can be called *need for tenderness.*" Winnicott (1965) uses the term "holding" to denote the total "environment provision" offered by the mothering one. "The infant exists only because of maternal care, together with which it forms a unit." [Cf. Mahler's (1975) symbiotic unit.] Winnicott goes on to describe how the infant develops means for doing without actual care. "This is accomplished through the accumulation of memories of care . . . with the development of confidence in the environ-

---

*When this empathic responsiveness becomes internalized by the child, we have the beginnings of that structure we call the Loving Superego (Schafer, 1960; Schecter, 1979).

Paul Lippmann (personal communication) points out that the infant's *active* loving *of* the parenting one tends to be neglected in discussions of the infant's need for love *from* the parent.

ment" [cf. Erikson's (1950) Basic Trust]. Further, Winnicott's holding environment has as its main function "the reduction to a minimum of impingements to which the infant must react with resultant annihilation of personal being. . ." (p. 47). Winnicott sees anxiety in early infancy as related to the threat of annihilation, by which he means the cessation of the "continuity of being" caused by "reactions" forced by impingements on the infant. I agree with Winnicott's view that it is through *identification* of herself with her infant that the mother knows "what the infant feels like and so is able to provide almost exactly what the infant needs in the way of holding and in the provision of an environment generally."

I quote these authors in part to show that love, security and holding have very specific meaning to the infant and the loss of love can signal a major calamity for the infant. We can only mention here the security function of transitional objects (Winnicott, 1958) in maintaining security without the direct participation of the mothering one.

THE ANXIETY GRADIENT AND THE SELF-SYSTEM OF H. S. SULLIVAN

Sullivan (1953) describes learning by the "anxiety gradient" as learning to discriminate increasing from diminishing anxiety, with alteration of activity in the direction of the latter. I would suggest that one of the major ways that the child experiences loss-of-love anxiety is through the disapproval patterns of the parents — which is not to suggest that this is pathologic. To quote Sullivan (1953): "This is the great way of learning in infancy and later in childhood by the grading of anxieties so that the infant learns to chart his course by mild forbidding gestures or by mild states of worry, concern or disapproval mixed with some degree of anxiety on the part of the mothering one. The infant plays . . . the old game of getting hotter or colder, in charting a selection of behavioral units which are not attended by an increase in anxiety." Sullivan reminds us that anxiety is responsible in a basic sense for a great deal of what comes to the psychiatrist for attention. Although anxiety is not the motor of interpersonal relationships, "it more or less directs the course of their development."

Severe anxiety, unlike the anxiety gradient, is like a blow on the head. It causes confusion and little opportunity for recall or learning. It is connected with uncanny feeling and the beginning personification of *not-me* which is experienced in nightmares or in the waking life of someone suffering from a severe schizophrenic episode. To quote Sullivan (1953): "The not-me is a gradually evolving personification of an always relatively primitive character that is organized in unusually simple signs in the parataxic mode of experience and made up of poorly grasped aspects of living which will presently be regarded as "dreadful" and which will still later be differentiated into incidents which are attended by awe, horror, loathing or dread." These are the uncanny *not-me* affects usually associated with intense forbidding gestures on the part of the mothering one.

By contrast, "*good-me* is the beginning personification which organizes experience in which satisfactions have been enhanced by rewarding increments of tenderness, which come to the infant because the mothering one is pleased with the way things are going." "Good-me" is the ordinary topic of discussion about "I." It should be noted that the pursuit of the good-me is not only in the service of adaptation but also of conformity. In this sense we can see how this pursuit in later infancy and later life can lead toward the structuring of the "false self" (Winnicott, 1965), a course that may be utterly required for the psychological survival of the child.

Bad-me is the beginning personification which organizes experience in which increasing degrees of anxiety are associated with behavior involving the mothering one. "Bad-me is based on the increasing gradient of anxiety and that in turn is dependent on the observation, if misinterpretation, of the infant's behavior by someone who can induce anxiety."

The dynamism of the *self-system* is purely a product of interpersonal experience arising from the general pursuit of satisfaction. The self-system is an antianxiety system — not the whole self — which functions as a compass to steer the infant away from experiences of increasing anxiety and toward maximum euphoria. The pursuit of "good-me" is maintained just as the moving away from "bad-me" is simultaneously pursued. Sullivan refers to the self-system as coming into being in late infancy as an organization of experience which will ultimately be "of nothing less than stupendous importance in the personality." The self-system gives the infant a structure through which it is possible to live with the socializing parenting person. Sullivan goes on to say, "The self-system is thus an organization of educative experience called into being by the necessity to avoid or minimize anxiety" (p. 165). This in turn frees the infant to pursue his needs for satisfaction since anxiety is a vector that pulls 180 degrees in the opposite direction from the pursuit of satisfactions. In fact, Sullivan implies that the self-system, with all its unfortunate consequences, comes into being "and can be said to have as its goal the securing of necessary satisfaction without incurring much anxiety." The self-system — in some degree parallel to Freud's ego defenses — is at the same time the principal obstacle to favorable change in the personality. Sullivan points out that there can be inculcated in the growing personification of "bad-me" and "not-me" "disastrous distortions" which will manifest themselves in the subsequent development of personality and with which the project of therapy will have to come to grips.

The self-system cannot necessarily contain a continuous flooding of anxiety that may be coming from the parenting ones. In other words there are limits to the success of the self-system's task of avoiding anxiety. With the failure of containment of anxiety by the self-system, mechanisms of defense are called forth to protect the infant from the raw experience of continuing anxiety. Two rather extreme defenses that Sullivan refers to are apathy and somnolent detachment, defenses for which the infant has to pay a high price, including severe constriction of his personality growth. If these defenses have to be in service frequently the infant will develop what I have called character detachment (Schecter, 1978), the extreme of which would be schizoid detachment.

DISCUSSION

We can look at each form of infantile anxiety as constituting the beginning of a "development line" (cf. A. Freud, 1965) that runs through childhood into adulthood. By this we do not have in mind a simplistic, one-to-one, causal relationship between anxiety experience in infancy and that of childhood and adulthood. Important structuralization of the ego and its defensive system occurs not only in infancy but in later developmental stages as well. These structures can modify or heal, in varying degree, the quality and quantity of anxiety experienced in infancy. Nevertheless the particular quality of, let us say, separation anxiety in infancy acts as an *organizer* for qualitatively similar anxieties in later developmental stages. Psychoanalytic reconstruction, as shaky an undertaking as it sometimes may be, reveals to us that significant separation or "loss of love" anxieties have developmental consequences.

Our clinical training alerts us to the importance of detailed history-taking in the psychoanalytic inquiry. It is not uncommon, for example, for an adult suffering specifically from fear of abandonment to have a significant history of marked separation reactions or "loss-of-love" anxiety. I have in mind a 25-year-old architect whom I have seen periodically since age seven and who suffered severely from separation anxiety that consciously baffled him. His early hospitalizations for repeated surgery involved anxieties of separation, of strangeness and strangers, and of body mutilation. Nevertheless, it is the separation aspect of his anxieties that can be followed like a red thread throughout his childhood, adolescence, and early adulthood. This developmental line, separation anxiety, has in part yielded to reconstruction in his analytic experience; it was a key without which his adult dread of abandonment could never have been understood. Similarly, his self-puzzling anxious reactions to strange new situations have been understood and largely worked through via the analysis of stranger and mutilation anxieties which also came to be organized early in life as separate developmental lines.

I would like to focus attention on the most neglected of developmental lines of anxiety, namely, that of stranger and strangeness anxiety. In a remarkably illuminating paper, A. M. Sandler (1977) describes a piece of psychoanalytic therapy with an adult woman related to the patient's fear of metabolizing anything new and strange in her self- and object-representations. Sandler emphasizes that the source of dissonance in self-image can be internal just as the source of dissonance (strangeness) can be external for object-representations. She states her hypothesis in the following way: "The child constantly and automatically also scans and has a dialogue with his own self to get refueling and affirmation through the perception of cues that his self is his old familiar self, that it is no stranger to him. . . ." The child may attempt to protect himself from danger in a strange situation "through action in which he alters himself which makes his self-representation more affirming, more reassuring." He may grossly distort his attitudes and behavior in order to avoid the dissonance and panic which accompanies simply being himself, by creating varieties of "false self." This is often done by idealization of the self as well as the object. To quote Sandler: "Mrs. B's [reaction] to my comments was a kind of almost reflex-like panic which forced her to deny any internal emotional stress and cling automatically to some concrete island of security, based on denial and negation and the preservation of me as the 'perfect' object." What was denied was any perception of the new and unfamiliar in the self, in the therapist, and in their relationship.* "Interpretations, however correct, aroused the danger that she might be faced with a strange and unfamiliar part of herself and of the object. . . ." She made strenuous efforts to dissociate strange, threatening and unwanted thoughts, wishes, and feelings from herself. With ongoing therapy the patient seemed to increasingly tolerate the dissonance of the strange.

When we think of Sandler's patient it becomes clear that much of what we call "resistance" in psychoanalytic therapy has to do with anxiety connected with the conscious discovery of strange, new, ego-alien aspects of the self, of significant object-persons and of their relationships. In this sense Sandler's description of her patient's fear of dissonance is the rule (resistance) rather than the exception in clinical psychoanalysis. A simple clinical illustration of the analysis of that which feels foreign is the analysis of aggressive and sadistic character tendencies in a person whose ideal self-image is one of gentleness and tenderness. Resistance often functions in the service of maintaining a sense of self-constancy and continuity, warding off a sense of discontinuity in one's identity.

The therapist's function in meeting such resistance parallels that of the mothering one of the child in some important ways. The therapist's gentle repetitions of the new and strange elements function as the "magic blessing" described earlier by the mother; the strange material is converted into the "merely" novel which can now potentially be faced with the zest of curiosity. The analyst represents the steady holding environment watching over the patient's struggle to look, together with the therapist, at the strange and ego-alien thoughts, wishes, and feelings which gradually can be accepted as part of the self-representation.

*By their very nature, transference and countertransference phenomena serve to make the therapeutic interactions feel familiar. The stranger analyst becomes the familiar parent. To the extent that transference expectations do not match the experience in the analysis, the latter comes to feel unfamiliar or even strange. The discrepancies of experience become material for analysis and clarify the nature of the transference.

Similarly, new elements can be looked at in the object-person who had often been idealized into perfection, and this includes transference figures. To see the self and other in their "suchness," e.g., without idealization, is an immensely liberating experience. One can now risk spontaneity and openness to the world because there is less stake in desperately maintaining an embedded familiar representation of self and other.

Change in therapy, as in life, involves the induction of anxiety that has to be endured in order for healthy development to proceed. The capacity to endure such anxiety is, of course, another variable that differs from person to person. The analyst offers a carefully titrated presentation of nonfamiliar aspects of the self so that the patient is not overwhelmed by the anxiety that is a necessary experience when nonfamiliar aspects of the self have to be metabolized.*

SUMMARY

Our purpose has been to consider the early developmental situations that constitute a danger and hence an anxiety for the infantile ego. We have taken as our definition of anxiety "the ego's reaction to or anticipation of danger." Several "developmental lines" of anxiety are described in some detail: Strangeness and stranger anxiety, anxiety by contagion, separation anxiety, and anxiety through loss of love or security. We have only mentioned the mutilation or castration anxieties, the fear of death, and the superego anxieties in the form of shame and guilt. From our study of anxiety we conclude that most types of early anxiety derive from some form of *disruption of a good "external" interpersonal relationship as well as of a good internal object relationship.*

The organization of experience by the anxiety gradient and the self-system (antianxiety system) is discussed as H. S. Sullivan's contribution to the understanding of the interpersonal and intrapsychic role of anxiety in infancy. The concept of "developmental line of anxiety" is presented and seen as an organizer of specific

---

*As a footnote to the concept of stranger anxiety we should make note of the widespread fear of the stranger and nonfamiliar as seen in racism and xenophobia in general. However, the Bible commands love for the stranger − not only for the neighbor − and explains this command by saying, "For you were sojourners in the land of Egypt" (Deut. 10:19) (Fromm, 1966).

forms of anxiety throughout the life cycle. The developmental line of stranger anxiety is discussed as an example of the application of developmental line anxiety to psychoanalytic theory and treatment.

References

Benjamin, J. (1963), Further comments on some developmental aspects of anxiety, in *Counterpoint*, New York University Press, New York.

Bowlby, J. (1973), *Attachment and Loss, Vol. 2, Separation*, Basic Books, New York.

Erikson, E. (1950), *Childhood and Society*, Norton, New York.

Escalona, S. (1953), Emotional development in the first year of life, in *Problems of Infancy and Childhood*, M. Senn, Ed., Josiah Macy Jr. Foundation, New York.

Freud, A. (1965), *Normality and Pathology of Childhood*, International Universities Press, New York.

Freud, S. (1926), *Inhibitions, Symptoms and Anxiety, Standard Edition*, Vol. 20, Hogarth, London.

Fromm, E. (1966), *Ye Shall Be as Gods*, Holt, Rinehart and Winston, New York, p. 83.

Mahler, M., F. Pine, and A. Bergman (1975), *The Psychological Birth of the Infant*, Basic Books, New York.

Sandler, A. M. (1977), Beyond eight month anxiety, *Int. J. Psychoanal.*, **58**, 195-207.

Schafer, R. (1960), The loving and beloved superego, *Psychoanalytic Study of the Child*, Vol. 15, International Universities Press, New York.

Schecter, D. (1978), Attachment, detachment, and psychoanalytic therapy, in *Interpersonal Psychoanalysis*, E. Witenberg, Ed., Gardner Press, New York.

Schecter, D. (1979), The loving and persecuting superego, *Contemp. Psychoanal.*, **15**, 361-379.

Spitz, R. (1946), Anaclitic depression, *The Psychoanalytic Study of a Child*, Vol. 2, International Universities Press, New York, pp. 313-342.

Spitz, R. A. (1950), Anxiety in infancy: A study of its manifestation in the first year of life, *Int. J. Psychoanal.*, **31**, 138-143.

Spitz, R. A. (1965), *The First Year of Life*, International Universities Press, New York.

Stern, D. (1971), A microanalysis of mother-infant interaction, *J. Am. Acad. Child Psychiatry*, **10**, 501-518.

Sullivan, H. S. (1953), *The Interpersonal Theory of Psychiatry*, Norton, New York.

Winnicott, D. (1958), Transitional objects and transitional phenomena, in *Collected Papers*, Tavistock, London.

Winnicott, D. (1965), Parent-infant relationship, in *The Maturational Processes and Facilitating Environment*, International Universities Press, New York.

SEVEN

A Developmental Approach To Depression In Childhood And Adolescence

JULES R. BEMPORAD

ARNOLD WILSON

INTRODUCTION

This paper attempts to offer some preliminary guidelines towards an understanding of depression-like states in children and adolescents, utilizing a predominantly developmental framework. In the years since Rie's (1966) comprehensive review of the literature on depression in childhood, numerous articles and an entire symposium (Annell, 1971) have appeared on the subject. Yet, despite this relative profusion of contributions (in contrast to the paucity of literature prior to the 1960s), there is still a good deal of disagreement as to the criteria for diagnosis, the childhood manifestations of depression, the underlying psychological mechanisms, and the possibility of the existence of a true depressive illness prior to puberty. In an effort to clarify the status of depression in childhood, the following points will receive special attention: the conceptualization of depression as a primary affect necessitating specific cognitive preconditions, the relationship of depression to loss, and the child's ability to experience, express, or defend against feelings of depression at various stages of development.

THE CONCEPT OF DEPRESSION

Until quite recently, the psychoanalytic position on childhood depression was clear and unanimous: it could not exist because the child did not have a sufficiently formulated superego, so that aggression could not be directed inward toward the ego. Rochlin (1959) made this point quite clearly, stating that since depression is, by definition, an inward deflection of anger, the psychic structures needed for such intrapsychic dynamics simply did not exist in the child. More recently Beres (1966) also expressed the belief that depression, as a superego phenomenon manifested by sustained guilt, is absent in children.

These objections to the possibility of depression in childhood have been criticized as a too heavy handed application of the psychodynamics of depression as originally intended for severely disturbed adults by Freud (1917) and Abraham (1924), which have gone through numerous alterations in the intervening years. However, even psychoanalysts who do not subscribe to the classical view of depression as a manifestation of retroflected aggression express grave doubts over the possibility of depression in childhood. For example, Rie (1966) notes that even the newer views of depression (such as Jacobson's, 1971), in which this affect is conceptualized as emerging from a disparity between the ego-ideal and actual self (resulting in a lowering of self-esteem), cannot really be applied to children since a stable self-representation still does not exist.

Yet, numerous clinical reports on childhood depression continue to appear. Poznanski and Zrull (1970), Cytryn and McKnew (1972), Weinberger et. al. (1973), and McConville et al. (1973) have described depressive syndromes in a good number of children. While the criteria for depression used by these authors may be disputed, it can no longer be doubted that depressive-like disorders do exist in children. This situation, in which theorists deny the possibility of depression in childhood while clinicians report such occurances, has prompted Mendelson to make the following strong statement: "It would seem that in no other area of the psychoanalytic literature on depressives are the theoretical papers so far removed from the observations that any clinician can make in the course of his daily practice" (p. 165).

Perhaps some aspects of this disparity between theoretical deduction and clinical observation may be resolved if a different view of depression is adopted. If depression is viewed as a primary affect (independent of complex intrasystemic conflicts or meta-psychological structures) that arises in specific, threatening situations, then its occurance in childhood may be more acceptable. Bibring (1953) has adopted this latter view, considering depression as a primary state of the ego which is evoked when the ego finds itself helpless to fulfill strongly held narcissistic aspirations. Later, Sandler and Joffee (1965) expanded Bibrings formulations, describing depression as a "psychobiological reaction" which is automatically experienced after a loss of a state of well being. These authors believe this is a more useful concept of depression, stating that: "If depression is viewed as an affect, if we allot to it the same conceptual status as anxiety, then much of the literature on depression in childhood (and this could be extended to adults) can be integrated in a meaningful way" (p. 90).

While this affect is briefly experienced by all adult individuals after a significant loss, according to Sandler and Joffee, only pre-disposed individuals go on to develop a clinical depressive episode. These latter individuals cannot fight off this painful feeling, have a history of capitulating under stress and a generally dependent personality structure. In any event, these authors believe that by postulating depression as a primary affective experience, they can justify its occurrence in childhood.

However, to classify this phenomenological state as a basic affect does not automatically mean that it can be experienced by individuals of all ages. Rather, it may be that the potentiality to experience certain affects depends on a cognitive understanding that is only possible after certain developmental accomplishments have been mastered. Therefore, a consideration of cognitive development must go hand-in-hand with any attempt to understand the ontogeny of affective behavior. This does not mean that the processes of understanding that give rise to specific emotions must be conscious, anymore than Piaget's cognitive schemata are postulated as being explicitly in awareness. Rather these schemata are unconscious systems of ideas that organize the understanding of experience and give it meaning and, thus, its emotional content.

This intertwining of cognitive and affective development has been described in detail by Arieti (1967) who postulates different hierarchical orders of emotions that arise during childhood as a result of cognitive advancement. These emotional states result from a differentiation of more primitive and global experiences in the course of development. With regard to depression, the precursors of this rather complex affect may be the general discomfort of the infant, the self-inhibition of the toddler, or the reaction of sadness of the older child to immediate environmental frustration or disappointment. Arieti conceives of development in a manner similar to Werner (1948) who defines this process as characterized by increasing differentiation and hierarchization. However, Arieti goes beyond Werner in speculating that certain cognitive achievements make the experience of certain affects possible. In turn, these new affects can further motivate cognitive processes. Just as young children cannot grasp the realities of the world as seen by the adult and therefore cannot experience the same emotion as adults, mature individuals, by virtue of their highly developed cognitive abilities, are motivated by higher feeling states than children.

Experimental studies by Kohlberg (1969) in the area of moral development and Loevinger (1976) in regard to overall ego development support the concept of the child's gradual accretion of abilities in an almost continuous fashion, with each stage blurring into the next. The salient point is that the cognitive processes of the child are developed by a series of incremental steps, and with these advances, changes in affective experience occurs. Anthony (1975) has recently summarized this position, linking affect to general development, in his work on childhood depression. He writes "It is possible to go further and suggest that depression itself undergoes development and that its characteristics are determined by parallel developments in symbolism, language, and logical operations" (p. 235).

If the view that considers depression in a primary affect which, however, necessitates certain cognitive capacities for it to be experienced, is adopted, then the problem of childhood depression becomes transformed. It is no longer a question of whether adultlike depression can occur in childhood but rather how the cognitive and affective limitations at various stages of development modify the experience and expression of emotions in general. Therefore, a fruitful approach to a theoretical discussion of childhood depression should focus on the inner cognitive capabilities of the child through development, although our knowledge of the internal world of the child is still very rudimentary.

DEPRESSION AND LOSS

Before proceeding to a tentative description of the varieties of depressive-like syndromes in childhood, a clarification of the precipitants of depression appears warranted. Traditionally, depression was seen as the reaction to the loss of an ambivalently loved object. This relation has been confirmed countless times, and still stands on empirical grounds, however, it may not account for all depressive episodes.

Originally, Abraham (1924) and Freud (1917) described melancholia as a regression to the oral stage, additionally hypothesizing that the depressive, by punishing himself, is actually expressing hostility toward an internalized object which has been established in the ego following an actual loss or disappointment in earlier years. Through the years, a number of difficulties with this formulation have arisen. The venting of anger outward did not necessarily relieve the depression. Self-recriminations, so crucial to this theory, were not always present. Finally, depression was found to arise from a consistently ungratifying way of life, without being precipitated by a loss. A further question was what the "loss" actually entailed for the depressed individual.

Thus, Sandler and Joffee (1965) carefully differentiate between the loss of an "object," per se, and the sense of well being that the lost object provides the individual. They conclude that depression is due to a loss of a "previous state of self" rather than the absence of an object in the environment. Safirstein and Kaufman (1966) have also expressed the opinion that depression is not simply a reaction to the loss of an external other

> "But that the loss is that of an idealized aspect of the depressed person. It is as if he constantly needs someone to tell him how great he is and when this no longer obtains, his sources of pride, satisfaction, and self-esteem are cut off and the state of depression sets in" (p. 230)

In a similar vein, Beck (1976) defines the depressed individual as one who perceives himself to be lacking some element or attribute (not necessarily an external other) that he considers essential for his happiness. It would appear that if an individual requires, or believes he requires, the continued relationship with another person as essential for his well being and happiness, then the loss of the relationship with that person may result in depression. If the individual believes he requires a certain status or certain prestigious position for his happiness, then the loss of this nonpersonal attribute may precipitate a depressive episode. Furthermore, some individuals may believe that they desperately need to obtain some personal goal, either in achievement or in relationship to others, and become depressed when they realize they will never achieve that all important goal.

Arieti (1962) has hypothesized that depression-prone adults have invested too much of their self-esteem in an external source which he termed the "dominant other," although this other need not be a flesh and blood individual, but may be an organization, social circle, etc. Jacobson (1971) has noted an excessive need for external reinforcement in depressed individuals. In addition, it has been speculated that depressed adults have been conditioned since childhood to respond to normal disappointments with a sense of paralysis, self-blame, and an extreme reliance on others to set things right. These characterological patterns transform the initial psychobiological reaction of depressive feelings, as described by Sandler and Joffee (1965), into a self-perpetuating clinical depression.

In these individuals, the affect of depression appears caused by the loss of what that other supplied to the depressed individual. Other cases may be the result of a growing awareness that goals necessary for self-esteem can never be achieved, no matter how hard one tries. What is relinquished in both instances is a needed state of self, of well being, of self-worth. Therefore, depression might be conceptualized as a response to a prolonged state of ungratifying existence, sustained by certain pathological cognitive constructs, which cannot be given up because of internal and external obstacles, and which ultimately leads to a sense of helplessness, hopelessness, and low self-regard. It is important to belabor this conceptual difference between depression as a loss of state of well being and depression as a reaction to an object loss because much of the literature on childhood depression deals with children who have suffered some sort of object loss, and the resulting behavior is automatically assumed to be depression whether or not there was any symptomology to justify such a diagnosis. Any reaction following a significant loss is postulated as a depressive equivalent,* almost to the point of absurdity, merely because theory states that depression should follow loss.

*The use of the term equivalent presents an additional conceptual problem. By citing another symptom as a depressive equivalent, it is not clear if (1) the child is defending against depression through the use of another symptom (a defensive equivalent), or (2) the symptom is a particular childhood form of depression resulting from psychological immaturity (a developmental equivalent), or (3) the symptom occurs where depression would be expected on theoretical grounds (a hypothetical equivalent). Finally, some authors describe equivalents as the predominant symptoms which are said to obscure an

Three published case reports of childhood depression may be used to differentiate between depression following the actual loss of a loved object, the loss of gratifying functions, and the inappropriate reaction to a psychological loss of a relationship which maintained a needed sense of self. Shambaugh (1961) has described a seven-year old boy who was in therapy when his mother passed away. The child did not appear depressed; rather, he exhibited hyperactivity, anger, and an increase of oral demands on the therapist. The boy also tried to take the mother's place in the family, but gave up this endeavor when his father remarried. Although the author deduced the presence of childhood depression on theoretical grounds (secondary to the loss of a love object), he frankly admitted surprise at the lack of depressive symptomatology. In contrast, Bierman, Silverstein, and Finesinger (1958) report the onset of a severe, almost adultlike depression in a six-year old boy who was forced to give up his usual satisfying activities because of illness. Two months after admission to the hospital for poliomyelitis, the boy demonstrated sad faces, cried easily, and turned his face to the wall when spoken to. The authors describe him as a "weakened, depressed child who has lost all hope." Since his mother visited him frequently, there was no question of object loss, but there was a very real loss of activities which were necessary for a sense of satisfaction and well being. Fortunately, there was an amelioration of the primary illness and the depression disappeared. The third case of childhood depression, which illustrates the loss of a pathologically needed relationship, occurred in a twelve-year old boy after his parents decided to adopt a ten-year old boy to be his companion (Anthony and Scott, 1960). This child suffered neither a loss of a love object nor the loss of gratifying activities, but is described by the authors as succumbing to depression as the result of an imagined loss of his favorite status with his mother. In this case, an unconscious cognitive distortion of events may be discerned. The 12-year old child exaggerated a mild narcissistic blow into an overwhelming loss which led to the depressive affect. The authors describe this

also demonstrable depression. In this case, the symptoms appear to be concomitant symptomatology and not true equivalents. In posing depressive equivalents, the logical connection between the alleged depressive affect and the equivalent symptom is largely theoretical. An unfortunate consequence is that the diagnostic status of childhood depression has been confused by the allotment of such a wide range of equivalents. Given our present limited knowledge of the inner life of children, it may seem appropriate to avoid usage of this concept at present.

patient as deriving a sense of omnipotence from being the "only fruit" of his mother's womb, the most precious thing in her world. He could not cope with the prospect of having to share his mother with another child. When hospitalized, he refused to see his mother, and on a second hospitalization, he complained that his mother had misinformed him about the origin of babies. Ten years later, the patient was hospitalized a fourth time with a manic-depressive psychosis.

These three separately published cases of childhood depression indicate that (1) depression need not follow an actual loss of a love object in a child if proper substitution is made possible or the child's day to day life is not severely disrupted, or if his sense of self-worth and gratification is not threatened, (2) a depression-like syndrome may follow the loss of only gratifying activities without object loss, and (3) in certain predisposed older children, depression results from a threat to a needed sense of self that a relationship supplies in a pathological manner. The child's cognitive conclusions, his beliefs about himself which are derived from experiences, are likely to play the most important role in the development of depressive affect. The role of object loss in depression becomes conditional on what the lost object has supplied for the individual.

DEPRESSION AND DEVELOPMENT

Specific prerequisites seem needed for the depressive affect to be experienced by adults. In adult depression, there does appear to be ceratin cognitive correlates, such as those postulated by Beck (1967), which accompany the depression and give it a characteristic experiential quality. Adults relate their present state of despair to a future that will be equally painful, showing an intellectual awareness of the continuity of time. The lowered estimation of self requires the ability to assess the self in a semi-objective manner. The feeling of guilt requires a previously established idea of responsibility for one's behavior. The adult also presents a sense of inhibition and helplessness to alter his situation (except perhaps by the manipulation of others), and this necessitates a previously established characterological defensive structure. These constituents of adult depression may well be beyond the cognitive capabilities of young children. It seems logical to conclude that the child might then experience, characteristically, different age appropriate forms of depression, depending upon the state of his cognitive maturity.

However, there are difficulties in attempting to demonstrate depression in children. One major problem is that children are very poor informants, so that some clinicians often have to infer depression from behavior rather than from verbal self-reports. This inference leads to difficulties in validation since there may be a tendency to project the investigator's own feelings onto the child, especially in the case of infants. Anna Freud (1953) has warned of this danger, noting that

"Some psychoanalysts credit the newborn already with complex mental processes, with a variety of affects which accompany the action of the various drives and, moreover, with complex reactions to these drives and affects, such as for instance guilt feelings" (p. 12).

Similarly, Buss and Plomlin (1975) conclude that there is a natural although mistaken tendency to assume that infants have the same range of emotions as older children and adults. It is highly questionable whether we can, at our present state of knowledge, correctly attribute adult affects to young children.

On the other hand, since children have difficulty verbalizing their feeling states, this limitation might tend towards the underreporting of specific mood disorders. A more crucial problem is that a preschool child may not be able to cognitively assess his own internal states and relate these states to external events. Young children may have "intuitive" reasons for their moods and not be able to grasp a causal relationship or a temporal sequence of their feelings. The young child's difficulty in being able to recognize, describe, and logically relate his feelings is further compounded by the finding that mood states in children are rarely sustained and rapidly shift with environmental stimuli. Finally, there is the problem that young children tend to act out their problems with overt behavioral symptoms rather than react to disappointments and frustrations with complex subjective states, distortion of self-images, and particular defense mechanisms. Thomas, Chess, and Birth (1969), in their longitudinal study of 141 children, found that there was a normal transition from action to ideation around the beginning of school age which reflected itself in both normal and disturbed children. In summary, the study of depression in childhood must acknowledge the difficulty of children to report or even recognize feelings. Similarly, investigators should be aware of the tendency to attribute adult feelings to children on the basis of the child's momentarily observable activity. With these warnings in mind, we will attempt to examine different developmental levels of the child, in order to determine what affective states are possible given the child's emotional and cognitive maturity at each level.

INFANCY

Syndromes which are suspected of being analagous to adult depression have been described in human infants by Spitz (1946), by Engel (1962), and by Harlow (1962) in monkeys. Spitz coined the term "anaclitic depression" to describe the infant's withdrawal into a state of apathy after separation from his mother. What seems unclear is whether the behavior Spitz observed was an infantile form of depression over an environmental loss or whether it was due to a persistent lack of stimulation over a prolonged period of time.

Spitz speculates that self-directed aggression plays an important part in anaclitic depression. The child, lacking an external love object who can absorb the normal flow of aggression and stimulate a neutralizing production of libido, turns this hostility against himself. This occurs despite the lack of a superego agency; in fact, it preserves the concept of self-directed aggression as the dynamic agent in depression, while bypassing the theoretical problem of how this aggression can become self-directed without recourse to a superego. Is the infant capable of directing aggression inward? Where is it received? Jacobson (1971) postulates an aggressive cathexis of the self-representation in adult depression, but it seems untenable to postulate a self-representation to a six-month old infant.

It is doubtful that an infant can demarcate a self or an other. It seems that there is enough reliable evidence in the developmental literature to conclude that an infant does not have any awareness of self, and to doubt any attribution of mentation to him. Piaget (1954), for instance, does not ascribe any representational thought to the child until he is 18 months old and begins to develop a capacity for mental imagery. It does seem reasonable to conclude, though, that deprivation of a mothering figure, without appropriate substitution during early infancy, produces not only a lack of source for well being, but also the lack of an important source of stimulation. Sandler and Joffee (1965) also assert that the clinical picture Spitz describes could be more profitably understood as a "basic psychobiological reaction to deprivation."

Benedek (1975) has been critical of attempts to attribute the affect of depression in infants. She asserts that depression necessitates an ambivalent object relationship. To Benedek, ambivalence is the primary root of depressive affect, and ambivalence can only occur after a love relationship is established. Prior to this stage of psychological development, the various types of withdrawal or retardation are assumed by Benedek, to be due to understimulation which prevents adequate maturation of ego functions.

The analogy between Spitz's anaclitic depression and adult depression is further weakened by the finding that similar infantile syndromes can be produced by a lack of cognitive stimulation (Dennis, 1957) nutritional deficiency (Malmquist, 1971), or organic deficiency diseases (Goldfand, 1947, cited by Sandler and Joffee, 1965). In Werner's (1948) terms, all of the infantile functions may by syncretically intermeshed at this age, and, therefore, any type of outside deprivation will influence all of the predifferentiated functions. Thus, to the infant, loss of the mother may be experienced in the same painful manner as a lack of stimulation or nourishment. It is possible that the similarity of the symptoms to adult depression which Spitz observed (lack of contact, apprehension, retardation of development, and loss of appetite), lead him to project adult affects onto the minds of infants. Until we know more about the mental life of infants, the conceptual status of anaclitic depression is unclear. At our present state of knowledge, this reaction may best be viewed as a result of the absence of appropriate stimulation, resulting in a lack of development, rather than depression. For example, Harlow (1962) found that most of the later deviations associated with maternal deprivation in infant monkeys could be prevented if these young monkeys had exposure to peers who supplied stimulation and contact. Separation from the mother, per se, therefore did not appear to be the crucial variable in causing later abnormalities. It may be more correct to classify these infantile reactions as "developmental deprivations," i.e., unpleasant, global experiences of the undeveloped psyche, precipitated by the absence of external stimulation which bears a tentative, unclear relationship to the later onset of depression.

In the depressionlike states of later infancy, as depicted by Engel (1956) and Bowlby (1960), it would seem that turning away from the world still represents a withdrawal from an ungratifying reality rather than depression. Bowlby (1960) describes how infants who experience separation will return from withdrawal and interact with strangers after a period of detachment. To Bowlby, this behavior is instinctively performed, a fully innate reaction. Engel (1956) postulates a basic "conservation-withdrawal" reaction as an instinctive prototype of helplessness and depression. This concept is based on observations of a damaged infant who in addition to being fed through a gastric fistula because of esophogeal atresia, was neglected by her mother during the first year of life. When seen by Engel, at age 15 months, the girl would react to strangers by withdrawal and detachment, falling into a state of sleep. Engel believed this is a basic biological pattern that underlies the later "giving up" syndrome of depression. However, he does not equate the infantile reaction with depression itself.

EARLY CHILDHOOD

Again, the pivotal concern at this age is if the cognitive capabilities of children are sufficiently mature to enable them to experience the affect of depression. The lack of clinical reports or depression in children of this age leads one to suspect that this capability has not yet been realized. Poznanski and Zrull (1970), in fact, in reviewing all of the records of the Outpatient Department of the Children's Hospital at the University of Michigan Medical Center, could find only one child younger than five years who could be considered to be displaying depressive symptoms. Even then, these authors were hesitant to make this diagnosis without a follow up evaluation two years later.

The toddler, as Mahler, Bergman, and Pine (1975) have described, now discovers that an entirely new repetoire of behaviors provides gratification. He delights in activity, in exploration, in locomotion, in doing rather than being done to. The child begins to individuate from the mother, using her as a sort of beacon to return to for "emotional refueling." The natural "oppositional" stage (Levy, 1955) occurs, and with it the child's initial testing of the will, or, as Erikson (1959) puts it, his autonomy. Fears, anxiety, and inhibitions seem conspicuously absent, as the child encounters his first taste of mastery over the external world.

Although the toddler bounces around, seemingly impervious to knocks and falls, seemingly immune to any depressive affect, this, nevertheless, is a time with potentially ominous indications for later affective psychopathology. The normal exuberance of the toddler that is so well documented in the literature may run contrary to the needs of the mother, so that the burgeoning, embryonic sense of self may be associated with fears of retaliation, loss of love, or of humiliation. To put it in Sullivan's terms, there may be a conflict between security needs and satisfaction needs.

At times, the child's exuberance may be so threatening to the parents that it is severely curtailed, and excessive punishment and restrictions may be administered. This is often accomplished through the use of a threat of abandonment or a withdrawal of love. Cohen et al. (1954) found that the mothers of future manic depressives preferred the passivity of the infancy stage to the willful behavior of the toddler period. As Erikson describes it, the child may be made to feel shame over his inclination for activity and to begin to doubt his own willfullness. In this way, the developmentally associated tasks of this age, the development of the assertiveness of the will, may be jeopardized. The child may be forced to surrender this asset in favor of a maintenance of maternal love and protection. A sense of self-inhibition and deferment to others may crystallize, which can become a passive dependence on others and a fear of personal fulfillment, as seen in adult depression.

The subtle sabotaging of the early emergence of the will appears most frequently in those homes in which the mother is depressed and cannot be bothered with the constant search of the child for novelty. In such families, there usually exists an atmosphere of gloom and a sense of impending disaster, where the joy of the child is looked upon as a bother and his maintenance an insurmountable undertaking. Although such children are threatened with the withdrawal or absence of love, they do not seem to lose the needed parent. Rather, they view reality as hostile and withholding, and they come to believe that parental nurturance will only be provided if they can maintain continual good behavior. Another situation observed is that of the mother who cannot tolerate the separation of the child and so devises tactics to bind the child into a continued dependency and immaturity. In such cases, love becomes a coin of manipulation, and threats of abandonment are used to mold the child's behavior into a desired pattern. What may then be communicated to the child is that his independence and tendency for free expression will be harmful to the needed parent.

When seen clinically, these children appear as little adults, lacking "spunk," and eager to please the grownups around them. They are prematurely earnest and serious, with a feeling that they must maintain tight control over their feelings and actions. Depending upon the parental mode of discipline, such children may also be whiny, clingy, and show early problems with separation, embryonic phobias, and hypochondriacal traits. There is a paradoxical dread of separation in conjunction with minimal satisfaction derived from actual contact with the mother. These children appear to have already substituted the pleasure of their parents for their own foreshadowing later pathological dependency.

Despite the unhappy picture that these children present, they cannot be called depressed without so stretching the meaning of the term as to render it clinically useless. Rather, these children are overly inhibited and "at risk" for later depression, as well as other psychopathology. These children do not yet generalize these patterns of inhibition, and have not yet fully internalized parental controls. Their behavior is flexible, responsive to environmental changes, rather than crystallized as self-perpetuating psychic processes. Their mood changes are extremely malleable, and can change tenor almost momentarily.

Children of this age still live from moment to moment, and it is doubtful if they conceive of existence in any sort of temporal continuum, so they cannot anticipate feelings of frustration or deprivation. They also do not generalize from one experience to another, instead treating each moment as if it was unique. Mahler (1966) notes that children of this age often tend to demonstrate symptoms only in the presence of their mother, and resume a natural childlike glee when the mother is not present. Children who display subdued behavior in the presence of a disordered parenting pattern may display autonomous, willful behavior at a daycare center, nursery school, or with other children. Thus, given the toddler's cognitive abilities, we can only say that depression may be prefigured by patterns of behavior which are established in early childhood in rudimentary forms, and which may be characterized as the beginning of inhibitions as a way of maintaining security.

MIDDLE CHILDHOOD

As the child approaches school age, longer periods of sadness or forlorness are evident. This sadness is observable in overt behaviors, for the child of this age is not yet capable of verbalizing his feelings with any great accuracy. However, he does have a plentiful fantasy life, as symbolic play now serves the child in working through and regulating conflicts and emotions, as the child plays through scenes that are borrowed from external reality but transformed by internal meanings. Here, we see an important cognitive tendency of these children, that of an age appropriate confusion of fantasy and reality, especially in regards to thoughts about oneself. There is, nevertheless, no cognitive capacity to sustain any consistent and continually low estimation of self. McConville (1973) found that children between the ages of 6–8 years were able to exhibit an almost pure feeling state of sadness, unaccompanied by conscious cognitive elements such as beliefs that one was bad or inferior. These children, then, may react to chronically frustrating or painful experiences with feeling states which automatically arise as a response to the environment. Internally generated self-depreciation is not yet possible.

Yet depreciation from others may still have a forceful impact on the child's affective state. Anna Freud (1960) notes similar phenomena when she states:

> "Neurotic symptom formation waits until the ego has divided itself off from the id, but does not need to wait until ego and superego have become two independent agencies. The first ego-id conflicts, and with them the first neurotic symptoms as conflict solutions, are produced with the ego under pressure from the environment, i.e., threatened not by guilt feelings arising internally from the superego, but by dangers arising from the object world such as loss of love, rejection, punishment" (p. 25).

Therefore, one would expect a sense of sadness to be found in those children whose environment blocks age appropriate gratification. However, this is still an immediately reactive state, the manifest sadness does not mean that a negative sense of self has been internalized and can be perpetuated independently of external situations. Also, the response is quite appropriate and does not rest on a distortion of external events as is seen in pathological depression. However, some cognitive internalization and generalization appears possible at this stage of development. One of these is the beginning of expectations that others will do similarly bad things to the child as do the parents. Self-demeaning does not take place, but the child can now generalize from past frustrations to other situations, leading them to suspect that others may harbor similar harmful attitudes.

Another cognitive transformation in this age group is the tendency to give up when disappointed. It is possible that this early fear of challenges results from yet earlier experiences in which attempts at mastery and competence were discouraged and thus failure was insured by the parents. Early inflated demands or early rejection by the parents may lead to a sense that the child cannot win and that to try is hopeless and leads only to unhappiness. What seems to be happening is that these children are given love and attention for activities which infantilize them, which undermines individuation and does not allow for self-gratification. As Sandler and Joffee (1965) put it:

"It not infrequently happens that the child's parents are in unconscious opposition to progressive individuation, and the influence of the parents may be perpetuated in their successor, the superego" (p. 94).

The clumsy attempts of the child to make sense out of parental rejection may lay the groundwork for a later negative self-image. These children will attempt to cope by behaving in ways which succeed in obtaining the needed love, and their natural inclinations thus become inhibited. Malmquist (1971) also describes this situation:

"A child may have meaning to a parent based primarily on a need to fulfill parental wishes or goals. Autonomy with respect to his own needs and wishes does not then develop. Instead of autonomy being promoted, the child is caught in a bind of guilt inducement if he resists, or lack of autonomy if he complies . . . a blurring of object boundaries results, leaving him with a residual need to accommodate to others' wishes" (p. 880).

Another type of depression in this age level occurs as a response to deprivation, to a lack of gratification in the environment. In this case, parents may be constantly rejecting of the child, especially if they are themselves depressed, or the child may contract a serious illness which precludes their attainment of gratification. These children's dysphoric response is quite appropriate as a response to a loss of well being, one which is often of a great magnitude. However, even under chronically frustrating circumstances (Bierman, Silverstein, and Finesinger, 1968), the mood state is reactive to the environment, and the sadness will probably be replaced by a more moderate affect if the deprivation is terminated.

This environmental reactivity, the presence of which makes the term dysphoria a more suitable characterization than depression, is in the main due to two characteristics of children of this age. First, they are still individuals of the moment, with an unsophisticated cognizance of past and future. Second, they will readily defend against any unpleasant affect. This trait is probably responsible for conditions described by some as "depressive equivalents" or "masked depression" (Cytryn and McKnew, 1972). These children display a remarkable adaptive capacity to forget about unpleasant events when these events are not in the child's immediate field of perception. Given a normal child's hedonism, it is clear why depressive like states are so infrequently described in this age group. The clinician should become concerned about pathological process at this age, if and when the denial of frustration becomes so excessive that it threatens to crystallize into a pathological defense, for example, as seen in adult hysterics.

In summary, middle childhood is a time in which prolonged unhappiness is possible in response to different types of environmental stress. Exposure to environmental deprivation and failure to individuate are the two chief forms of environmental stress discussed. These children are now exquisitely sensitive to feelings of rejection by the idealized parent, but the resultant moods are not readily maintained and respond to environmental changes. There is no evidence of feelings of guilt or lowered self-regard, but possible premorbid signs include an unusual preoccupation with making parents happy or the abnegation of personal satisfaction in order to obtain love and attention from the parents.

LATE CHILDHOOD

The child can now feel a sense of responsibility towards others, can comprehend and obey values and rules, and has a sense of self which is adequately separated from others. Judgements of peers and society come into play for the first time, and assume tremendous interest and importance. Yet, the child's beliefs and adaptational style are still the product of his former family life, and he will cope with frustration by employing mechanisms similar to those he used in his family. Children in late childhood, as in mid childhood, react to ungratifying circumstances with disappointment and sadness. However, an important difference arises in the transition from mid to late childhood. The child's cognitive apparatus is now developed to the point where it can sustain a more chronic depressionlike illness, which can evolve into a clinical depression.

The child, characterologically, is now well developed and adapts in a manner which is distinctively his own. For example, the child who was described in mid childhood as "giving up" in the face of frustration, upon reaching late childhood may now develop a sense of overwhelming loss coupled with shame and persistent doubts about his competence, self beliefs which will persist despite environmental changes.

In addition, the child has now crystallized a sense of self which can be dissociated from the effects of immediate experience and conceptualized as a seperated entity. The child can form a stable opinion of his own worth, an ability which, given the child's developmental immaturities, might result in self-depreciatory conclusions. As Erikson (1963) notes:

> "The child's danger, at this stage, lies in a sense of inadequacy and inferiority. If he despairs of his tools and skills or of his status among his tool partners, he may be discouraged from identification with them . . . . The child despairs of his equipment in the tool world and in anatomy, and considers himself doomed to mediocrity or inadequacy" (p. 260).

The child's ability to think logically and use logic to arrive at conclusions is another important cognitive development of this age. Affect is no longer a direct consequence of immediate experience, but is mediated by personal interpretive thought processes which produce the affective experience. Children of this age who disappoint or hurt their parents with their shortcomings may now conclude that the problem is their fault, and at the same time, they perceive that they are practically helpless to rectify the problem. They now react to the belief that they are unworthy rather than to the realisticly painful effect of rejection. Depression can no longer be considered to occur in the form of an immediate, stimulus bound sadness. This ability to form conclusions about oneself from experience may allow the affect of depression to perpetuate itself beyond immediate situations, since this affect is now linked to a view of the self.

Another result of the child's new ability to evaluate himself may be the hiding of feelings or tendencies of which he is ashamed. Often these are strivings for dependency which the child cannot accept. While the younger child may openly display clinging or regressive behaviors, the preteen child will not allow free expression of these tendencies. He begins to despise these aspects of himself, and this self-devaluation may further contribute to a feeling of worthlessness. This is a situation that is often remembered by adult depressives: that they were encouraged to be dependent on the parents and then belittled by the parents when dependency was openly expressed. As alluded to above, this conflict is resolved by a hiding of dependency feelings, the creation of an independent facade, but also the sense that one is weak and shameful.

Due to this cognitive leap in late childhood, the dysphoric state which the deprived child experiences may now be designated as "depression," in its customary sense. The child now bases his feelings on internal, logical conclusions about reality — that is, a stable system of ideas — rather than having feelings arise simply as a reaction to the immediate environment. This internalized, unconscious cognitive belief system which may distort reality and which allows the persistance of an affect regardless of external changes, predisposes the older child to depressive illness. Nevertheless, it is important to note that the form of depression found in late childhood is still not the same as in adulthood, that it is still age appropriate. The preteen's self concept is still less formed and less resilient to environmental changes than is that of the adult. The self is more responsive to success and gratification, largely due to the preteen's still limited temporal orientation. The prediction from a present state to a future experience is not seen as inexorable or beyond his control. This is because the preteen simply does not think about the future, not because he denies it.

As a result of this limited temporal orientation, children in late childhood cannot understand the meaning of the concept of infinity, and can only have a tentative emotional investment in long-range goals. Thus, as Rie (1966) notes, these children do not experience the affects of hopelessness or despair, two of the cardinal features of adult depression. Most definitions of adult depression stress a continuumlike time orientation that incorporates future representations. Children in late childhood do not view the future with dread, primarily because they do not possess the cognitively mature adult's future orientation. These conclusions seem to concur with most clinical observations of preteen children, who do not verbalize fear that depression is forever. Piaget (1954) also reports that until early adolescence, the child is wedded to the "concrete," and incapable of abstractions that would involve the projection of the self into the future.

In summary, there are now many possible factors which may participate in the preteen's potentiality for depression. As in mid childhood, the family dynamics may often include a history of depreciation and rejection by parents who were emotionally removed from the child. By late childhood, many other factors may precipitate depression, because the child now determines his cognitions through the use of active mental interpretations, rather than more passive cognitions which are fundamentally responses to immediate environmental changes. The child has developed a cognitive self-representation which he can now use to contrast with certain types of ideals. However, these children have not consolidated pictures of themselves to the extent that depression becomes characterological and pathologically unresponsive to environmental demands. Alleviation of depressive symptoms may still follow removal from a pathological family environment. We may now speak of depression in these children which is like that seen in the adult, with the advent of the cognitive equipment which allows for inappropriate prolongations of the symptoms of depression. Nevertheless, there are still crucial differences between the preteen and the adult depressive, most noticeably the undeveloped time sense and the consequent inability to experience hopelessness or despair.

ADOLESCENCE

It is not until adolescence that depressive episodes truly comparable to those seen in adults are seen clinicly. Even so, there are still some developmental features which make depression in adolescence unique. The adolescent views the logical world differently than the older child. His conceptual range is expanded to include the hypothetical, the future, the possible, and the abstract. He may behave as if he is intoxicated with his new powers of thinking. Inhelder and Piaget (1958) attribute a form of "cognitive egocentrism" to the adolescent:

"... the adolescent goes through a phase in which he attributes an unlimited power to his own thoughts so that the dream of a glorious future or of transforming the world through Ideas ... seems to be not only fantasy but also an effective action which in itself modifies the empirical world" (p. 345).

This "cognitive egocentrism" may contribute to the depressed adolescent's exaggerated cognitive distortions about himself which he derives from his experiences. His intoxication can easily become transformed into deep depression if he concludes that he is worthless or his problems are insurmountable. These conclusions are often based on very slim evidence or are severely self-condemning largely due to their lack of tempering by adult experience.

Depression in adolescents rivals adult depression in severity and often exceeds it in self destructiveness and proclivity for suicical action. Malmquist (1971), in a thorough review of pertinent literature, cites eight features which are typical of adolescent depression. They are mood swings, unresolved dependency conflicts, diverse superego activity characterized by sensitivity and proneness to overreaction, acting out or demanding externalized solutions, an insatiable seeking of affection and approval at any price, confusion in identification which is associated with an impaired self-image, acute identity diffusion (Erikson, 1959), and heightened self-condemnation. Generally speaking, the adolescent's severity of symptoms and the instability of his mood and thought are framed by a lack of adult experience, maturity, and knowledge with which to moderate his affective reactions, which leads to perplexity as he experiences the first demands to behave in an adult manner in a world dominated by adult standards.

The concept of time is now fully developed. While the preteen is not concerned with his future, the adolescent becomes concerned with little else. Adolescents often fear that actions and experiences are irrevocable and everlasting, resulting in eternal despair from which they will never recover. This preoccupation with the relationship of the present to the future is not available to the child and it is tempered by experience in the adult.

Erikson (1959) has examined the consequences of the new cognitive gains in his studies of disturbed adolescents, some of whom may be considered as experiencing severe depressive episodes. The symptoms which he cites illuminate the overwhelming quality of urgency and despair seen in adolescent depression. (Erikson (1959) notes:

"Protests of missed greatness and a premature and fatal loss of useful potential are common complaints among our patients as they are among adolescents in cultures which consider such protestations romantic: the implied malignancy, however, consists of a divided disbelief in the possibility that time may bring change, and yet also a fear that it might" (p. 126).

Another factor that influences the expression of affect in adolescence is the lack of moderation in thinking. The adolescent hangs on his experiences, inflating them so that seemingly trivial events assume monumental importance, and frequently seem to symbolize unalterable patterns. He lives in an all or nothing world. His paucity of experience leads to a lack of perspective which culminates in an attitude of finality and sometimes, as personified by depressed adolescents, desperation.

These attributes of adolescents are no doubt influenced by the social pressures which our culture imposes upon them. They are constantly reminded that they should build for the future. Everything that is important to an adolescent lies ahead, yet the avenues upon which to travel are vague and they often do not have a past which can provide them with a grounding upon which to evaluate any of their goals. Often, at this age, they leave home for the first time and find themselves living out childish, dependent strivings away from their parents, who accepted such behavior as part of the growth process. Developmentally, some adolescents are accustomed to a past of living out the dictates of others, and some form ties with new authorities, on whom they can rely for direction and meaning. Erikson (1959) states:

"Young persons often indicate in rather pathetic ways a feeling that only a merging with a leader can save them—an adult who is able and willing to offer himself as a safe object of experimental surrender, and as a guide in the relearning of the very first steps toward an intimate mutuality and a legitimate repudiation" (p. 125).

Therefore, many apparently rebellious youngsters are in reality trading new masters for old, with little alteration in basic personality structure. In the case of depressed adolescents, even this possibility has failed, and the individual finds himself in a state of emotional stagnation which he cannot alter due to fears of failure in an alien world. In such instances, suicide becomes a viable option.

In a paper on mood changes in adolescence, Jacobson (1961)

interprets the alternation between depression and grandiosity seen in adolescence as the sequential alliance of the ego with the super-ego (depression) and the id (grandiosity). In late adolescence, mood swings are modulated when there is a shift in power to the ego at the expense of the id and superego. Jacobson states:

"The ego will now play, as it were, the role of an active mediator, who employs the adolescent's worldly strivings as aids for the toning down and readjustment of the superego demands, but then in turn calls on the latter for assistance in restricting the id" (p. 177).

In this passage, the superego and id may be interpreted metaphorically, as associated age appropriate psychic strivings rather than as formal categories of mind. The superego may stand for a need to acquiesce to new external and older internalized demands, to remain married to a dependent role, one which is not separate or unique in itself. So, too, may the id stand for a tendency towards greater rebelliousness and individuation rather than solely instinctual gratification. In this way, Jacobson's formulation becomes one of conformity and dependency versus excessive freedom and assertion, with resolution lying in the primacy of the ego.

Adolescents who become clinicly depressed are often those who, because of a lack of confidence in their autonomous ability to derive pleasure from extrafamilial activities or relationships, do not venture away from their secure, if tyrannical relationship with parental figures. They find that living out parental ideals is devoid of meaning for them, yet, at the same time, they are afraid to live independently of these ideals, since this would be tantamount to betraying the parents and in their fantasies result in a terrible state of aloneness and isolation.

A striking example of adolescent depression is described by Anthony (1975) who takes his data from the autobiography of John Stuart Mill. The senior Mill privately trained his son so that he was rigorously educated by the time he reached adolescence. Anthony writes that Mill:

"one day asked himself the crucial question as to whether he would be happy if all his parental objectives in life were realized, and he was forced to answer 'No'."

Anthony then cites Mills' own words:

"At this point, my heart sank in me; the whole foundation on which my life was constructed fell down ... I seemed to have nothing left to live for."

Anthony then continues:

"He felt ill when he became aware that the realization of his father's aims in life would not satisfy him, and he regained his mental health (to the extent that this was possible) when he understood that the death of the father brought with it the growth of identity, autonomy, and responsibility for the son" (p. 448).

Unfortunately, not many adolescents are as introspective or willful as John Stuart Mill. Many continue to live out the aspirations of others, although the attainment of these aspirations leads to, at best, a fleeting, momentary security. The inhibitory impulses that are present prevent the adolescent from erecting individual goals while the guilt over disobeying the powerful other makes any self-gratification into an evil or disloyal rebellion. In addition, a heightened contact with parents who are rejecting, depreciating, and often overprotective makes the adolescent doubt his ability to stand on his own in facing the demands of life away from the security of the family.

Hendin (1975), studying depressed adolescents who have attempted suicide, found a familial environment which caused the patient to see emotional extinction as a necessary adjustment. Their lives were so devoid of gratification that depression became appropriate as a manner of warding off the impact of day to day living. Hendin coined the term "death knot" to describe the suffocating relationship between these suicidal adolescents and their parents:

"These students see their relationships with their parents as dependent on their emotional if not physical death, and become tied to their parents in a kind of death knot. Coming to college, graduating, becoming seriously involved with another person, and enjoying an independent existence have the power to free them. In fact, the meaning of suicide and depression lies in their encounter with the forces that might unleash their own possibilities for freedom" (p. 329).

Hendin characterizes these adolescents as individuals who find security in emotional numbness, in believing that living fully is a sign of disloyalty to the parents. He describes a student who, when happiest, had the impulse to either throw herself in front of a train or call her mother. Depression in these adolescents reflects the crystallization of an unconscious system of beliefs that has become a way of life. To experience satisfaction is to deny their sharing of depression with the parent, which is the only human bond they know. Suicidal adolescents, then, may conclude that depression will preserve their parental relations, and the pursuit of pleasure will deprive them of their parental relations. The obsession with death is, at bottom, an attempt to cling forever to this pathological human bond.

In summary, depressive reactions in adolescence evidence many of the factors seen in adult depression, plus some that are specific to adolescence. Many of these factors result from the cognitive development of a time perspective which cannot be tempered in a rational manner due to a lack of experience. The particular severity found in this age group may sometimes also be related to an inordinate pressure for success and conspicuous achievement which is imposed upon them. There is the usual tendency for the adolescent to see things as either/or, to inflate the importance of seemingly trivial interpersonal experiences, and to be somewhat dramatic in his view of himself. As a result, suicide may become an option, and, frequently, an obsession. At the same time, adolescence is a time of paramount importance for the recognition and treatment of depression, since at this age the individual is sufficiently malleable to escape from his former dominating authorities, and to be open to a more realistic view of himself. If identified and treated at this time, there is a possibility that the individual need not perpetuate the illness by maintaining a continually distorted estimation of his abilities, an unrealistic set of inhibitions, or a transference onto others of parental criticisms and prohibitions.

CONCLUSION

This paper has attempted to consider childhood depressive states from a developmental point of view. States of dysphoria can be observed from birth but experiences which are similar to adult forms of depression necessitate certain cognitive abilities. Some psychologically painful states precede the experience of depression, and share some characteristics with this later experiential phenomenon but are not equal to it. Rather at each stage of ontogeny, some characteristics of dysphoric states are added with the gradual maturation of the child as a total organism, culminating in the ability to experience depression in its adult form. It is hoped that the use of a developmental framework as a theoretical basis may ultimately help in clarifying and ordering the depressive-like experiences of childhood.

References

Abraham, K. (1924), A short study of the development of libido, viewed in the light of mental disorders, in *Selected Papers on Psychoanalysis,* New York, Basic Books, 1960, pp. 418-501.

Annell, A. L. (Ed.), (1971), *Depressive States in Childhood and Adolescence,* Halsted Press, New York.

Anthony, E. J. (1975), Childhood depression, in *Depression and Human Existence,* E. J. Anthony and T. Benedek (Eds.), Little, Brown, Boston.

Anthony, E. J. (1975), Two contrasting types of adolescent depression and their treatment, in *Depression and Human Existence,* E. J. Anthony and T. Benedek (Eds.) Little, Brown, Boston.

Anthony, E. J. and Scott, P. (1960), Manic-depressive psychosis in childhood, *Child Psychol. Psychiatr.,* 1, 53-72.

Arieti, S. (1962), The psychotherapeutic approach to depression, *Am. J. Psychother.,* 16, 397-406.

Arieti, S. (1967), *The Intrapsychic Self,* Basic Books, New York.

Beck, A. T. (1967), *Depression,* Harper and Row, New York.

Benedek, T. (1975), Ambivalence and the depressive constellation of the self, in *Depression and Human Existence,* E. J. Anthony and T. Benedek (Eds.), Little, Brown, Boston.

Beres, D. (1966), Superego and depression, in *Psychoanalysis—A General Psychology,* R. M. Loewenstein, L. M. Newman, M. Schur, and A. J. Solnit (Eds.), International Universities Press, New York.

Bibring, E. (1953), The mechanism of depression, in *Affective Disorders,* Phyllis Greenacre (Ed.), International Universities Press, New York.

Bierman, J. S. Silverstein, A. B., and Finesinger, J. E. (1961), A depression in a six-year-old boy with poliomyelitis, *Psychoanal. Study Child,* 13, 430-450.

Bowlby, J. (1960), Seperation anxiety, *Int. J. Psycho-Anal.,* 41, 87-113.

Buss, A. H. and Plomin, R. (1975), *A Temperament Theory of Personality Development,* John Wiley, New York.

Cohen, M. B., Blake, G., Cohen, R. A., Fromm-Reichman, F., and Weigert, E. V. (1954), An intensive study of twelve cases of manic-depressive psychosis, *Psychiatry,* 17, 103-138.

Cytryn, L. and McKnew, D. H. (1972), Proposed classification of childhood depression, *Am. J. Psychiat.*, **129**, 149-155.

Dennis, W. and Najarian, P. (1957), Infant development under environmental handicap, *Psychol. Monogr.*, **71**.

Engel, G. and Reichsman, F. (1956), Spontaneous and experimentally induced depressions in an infant with a gastric fistula, *J. Am. Psychoanal. Assn.*, **4**, 428-456.

Erikson, E. H. (1959), *Identity and the Life Cycle* (Psychological Issues, Vol. 1), International Universities Press, New York.

Erikson, E. (1963), *Childhood and Society*, Norton, New York.

Freud, A. (1953), Some remarks on infant observation, *Psychoanal. Study Child*, **8**, 9-19.

Freud, A. (1970), The symptomotology of childhood, *Psychoanal. Study Child*, **25**, 19-41.

Freud, S. (1917), *Mourning and Melancholia*, Standard Edition, Vol. 14, Hogarth Press, London, 1957, pp. 243-258.

Harlow, H. F. and Harlow, M. K. (1962), Social deprivation in monkeys, *Sci. Am.*, **207**, 136-146.

Hendin, H. (1975), Growing up dead: Student suicide, *Am. J. Psychother.*, **29**, 327-328.

Inhelder, B. and Piaget, J. (1958), *The Growth of Logical Thinking from Childhood to Adolescence*, Basic Books, New York.

Jacobson, E. (1961), Adolescent moods and the remodeling of psychic structures in adolescence, *Psychoanal. Study Child*, **16**, 164-183.

Jacobson, E. (1971), *Depression*, International Universities Press, New York.

Kohlberg, L. (1969), Stage and sequence: the cognitive-developmental approach to socialization, in *Handbook of Socialization Theory and Research*, D. A. Goslin (Ed.), Rand McNally, Chicago.

Levy, D. (1955), Oppositional syndromes and oppositional behaviors, in *Psychopathology of Childhood*, P. Hoch and J. Zubin (Eds.), Grune and Stratton, New York.

Loevinger, J. (1976), *Ego Development*, Jossey-Bass, San Francisco.

McConville, B. J., Boag, L. C., and Puromit, A. P. (1973), Three types of childhood depression, *Can Psychiatr. Ass. J.*, **18**, 133-138.

Mahler, M. G. (1966), Notes on the development of basic moods: The depressive affect, in *Psychoanalysts—A General Psychology*, R. M. Loewenstein, L. M. Newman, M. Schur, and A. J. Solnit (Eds.), International Universities Press, New York.

Mahler, M. S., Pine, F., and Bergman, A. (1975), *The Psychological Birth of the Human Infant*, Basic Books, New York.

Malmquist, C. (1971), Depression in childhood and adolescence, I and II, *New England J. Med.*, **284**, 887-893, 955-961.

Mendelson, M. (1974), *Psychoanalytic Concepts of Depression,* Spectrum, New York.

Piaget, J. (1954), *The Construction of Reality in the Child,* Basic Books, New York.

Poznanski, E. and Zrull, J. P. (1970), Childhood depression: Clinical characteristics of overtly depressed children, *Arch. Gen. Psychiatr.,* 23, 8-15.

Rie, H. E. (1966), Depression in childhood: A survey of some pertinent contributions, *J. Am. Acad. Child. Psychiatr.,* 5, 653-685.

Rochlin, G. (1959), The loss complex, *J. Am. Psychoanal. Assoc.,* 7, 299-316.

Safirstein, S. L. and Kaufman, M. R. (1966), The higher they climb, the lower they fall., *Can. Psychiatr. Assoc. J. II:* Supplement, 229-235.

Sandler, J. and Joffee, W. G. (1965), Notes on childhood depression, *Int. J. Psychoanal.,* 46, 88-96.

Shambaugh, B. (1961), A study of loss reactions in a seven-year-old, *Psychoanal. Study Child,* 16, 510-522.

Spitz, R. (1946), Anaclitic depression, *Psychoanal. Study Child,* 2, 113-117.

Thomas, A., Chess, S., and Birch, H. G. (1968), *Temperament and Behavior Disorders in Children,* University Press, New York.

Weinberg, W. A., Rutman, J., and Sullivan, L. (1973), Depression in children referred to an educational diagnostic center: Diagnosis and treatment, *J. Pediatr.,* 83, 1065-1077.

Werner, H. (1948), *The Comparative Psychology of Mental Development,* International Universities Press, New York.

PART THREE

Clinical Aspects Of Affect

EIGHT

Cognitive Aspects Of Affects And Other Feeling States With Clinical Applications

ROSE SPIEGEL

In the practice of our craft, we are aware — we are made aware, with no place to hide — of the emotions of our patients when these take over the analytic scene so that we cannot avoid the confrontation. We are learning more about the experience of countertransference. We have our great division in classification, Affective Disorders, as though all other conditions to which we give a classificatory name are not themselves affective disorders. Predominantly, we address ourselves to moods and emotions that demand attention as ailments and as what should be changed in the course of therapy — as something that should be made to go away. Thus, we deal with resentment and anger, with depression, and infrequently, to our awareness, with the moods of elation.

It is then astonishing that, in spite of the fact that affects are a universal experience for human beings and that we somehow recognize affects in each other (and, indeed, often in other kinds of living beings), we yet still lack adequate, explicit word definitions for affect, feeling and emotion. Webster is of little help, since we are given a run-around of the approximate equivalence of these terms: that affect is "feeling, emotion and desire, with an implication of their importance in determining thought and conduct." Psychoanalysts and psychologists have recognized and addressed the problem, and so far have only recognized the impasse. Beginning with Freud, the basic importance of affects in the psyche has been confronted, discussed, but not yet clearly conceptualized.

This is an expanded version of a paper presented at The American Academy of Psychoanalysis, May 1979.

This paper is the outgrowth of several converging interests: the role of affects in the Affective Disorders, as well as in the Schizophrenias; their role in relation to cognitive processes; and especially their role in communication — both internally, between the presenting personality of the patient and his or her inner self (and internally in the therapist as well), and externally, in the interpersonal interaction between patient and therapist.

In the first section, an overview of the thinking on affects and other feeling states will include attempts that have been made to define terms, Freud's concepts and their extensions by Edith Jacobson, and the challenges of Sullivan, Schachtel, Szasz, and Rado.

The second section will be concerned with the importance of distinctions between affects and other feeling states and with the basic cognitive significance beyond the usual psychoanalytic restriction, primarily as communication to the one who experiences the affect but, also, to an observer.

In the last section, some clinical applications of this point of view will be given.

CONCEPTS OF AFFECTS

Cognitive Problems in Defining Affects

In discussing affects, we are faced with the irony of our own cognitive difficulty in definition. Yet, with our limitation, somehow we function in life in general and in our professional world with a feeling (again the moot word) of understanding. How does this come about?

In the field of philosophy, the problem of language and feeling states engaged the interest of Ludwig Wittgenstein. In *Philosophical Investigations,* he grapples with the profound issue of communication of feelings. He asks:

244. How do words *refer* to sensations? . . . how does a human being learn the meaning of the names of sensations? — of the word "pain" for example. Here is one possibility: words are connected with the primitive, the natural, expressions of the sensation and used in their place. A child has hurt himself and he cries; and then adults talk to

him and teach him exclamations and, later, sentences. They teach the child new pain behavior.

"So you are saying that the word 'pain' really means crying?" — On the contrary: the verbal expression of pain replaces crying and does not describe it.

245. For how can I go so far as to try to use language to get between pain and its expression?

246. In what sense are my sensations *private?* — Well, only I can know whether I am really in pain; another person can only surmise it.

253. "Another person can't have my pains." — Which are *my* pains? What counts as a criterion of identity here?

257. When one says "He gave a name to his sensation" one forgets that a great deal of stage-setting in the language is presupposed if the mere act of naming is to make sense.

Wittgenstein is struggling with how a private experience is apprehended by means of language, or by identification with a shared experience; but he is not giving credence to empathy.

We can draw Harry Stack Sullivan into the discussion of how we "know" the experience of the other: Concerning the therapist's function as participant-observer, Sullivan stated that we can *tune into* experiences of others which we have not had independently ourselves — based upon the fact of people all being "much more simply human than otherwise" (1953). The specific term "empathy" he reserves, however, for an infant's so-called contagion of feeling from the mother.

A view the polar opposite to Wittgenstein's, in the attempt to capture what transpires in the nonverbal, or perhaps nonverbalizable, deep understanding of what another is experiencing, is given by Martin Buber in *Between Man and Man:*

> Human dialogue . . . although it has its distinctive life in the sign, that is, in the sound and gesture . . . can exist without the sign, but admittedly not in an objectively comprehensible form. On the other hand, an element of communication, however inward, seems to belong to its essence. It is completed not in some "mystical event" but in one that is in the precise sense factual, thoroughly dovetailed into the common human world and the concrete time-sequence.

A clever solution to our quandary of definition has been offered by Charles Shagass in his *Explorations in the Psychophysiology of Affect,* by the device of, in a way, giving up on it; or rather, by asking for consensus. The way we define emotion or feeling, he says, is to request the "reader"

> ... to accept what is being referred to as the quality of experience which allows him to understand "feelings," to inquire about the feelings of others and to expect them to understand when he talks of feelings. [That is,] ... the word [emotion] has meaning because of this *community experience*. ... [italics added]

I emphasize that such cognitive experience is on the basis of sharing a poorly verbalized experience with either felt understanding or with empathizing with the feeling of the other. At times, lacking these avenues, our seeming cognition is actually based on projection and identification with the other.

The enormous difficulty of precise, explicit definition is fraught with the danger of overlooking the important functioning of affects.

Since precise definition is not yet available, we can produce a working definition by collating as best we can the various concepts and facts concerning how affects function.

Freud's Concepts of Affects and Edith Jacobson's Contribution

Freud's ideas about affects stretch over the years in various statements set in the context of still other, broader discussion: in the two papers, "Repression" and "The Unconscious," in 1915; in 1917, in his lecture on "Anxiety" in *A General Introduction to Psychoanalysis;* in 1920, in *Beyond the Pleasure Principle;* in 1924, in "The Economic Problem in Masochism."

The first concepts are in terms of instincts, Conscious/Unconscious, and energy. The second cluster hypothesizes a connection to anxiety; the third, to the "pleasure principle" and a "Nirvana principle." Thus, the first focus is in biologic terms, the second in psychologic, and the third attempts a universalization with mythologic overtones. It is the last approach that has been attacked especially by the neo-Freudians.

Freud conceived instincts to be in the realm of the Unconscious and to be linked with affects in the Conscious. He designated affect and emotion as a feeling state without distinguishing between them. He equated affects with forces of energy, characteristically proceeding to a motility discharge, the motility being manifested as secretory activity and change in circulation.

It is noteworthy that Edith Jacobson points out that Freud used the model both of the reflex arc and the sexual orgasm for affect and its discharge of "tension."

To continue with Freud's hypotheses: Affects might be repressed and thereby drop out of the Conscious (in the topologic formulation), the repression resulting in anxiety — "the substitute for all 'repressed' affects" — which was itself an affect, arising in the ego, and serving as "the motor of repression." The basic paradigm for this functioning of anxiety is "physiologically established by the trauma of birth," with anxiety having the unique role, he states, of serving as a signal — a signal of threat.

Actually, the formulation *tension/affect-discharge/tension-release* is set in mechanistic terms, based on the stabilization principle of Fechner presented in 1873, namely, that every conscious "psycho-physical motion . . . is attended by pleasure . . . as it approximates to complete stability, and . . . by unpleasure . . . as it deviates from complete stability." In broader, teleologic, terms, Freud considered that the function of the affect discharge is to fulfill the pleasure principle, that is, to relieve the "unpleasure" state of (presumed) tension and, thereby, to achieve the tensionless "Nirvana," a concept he built, along with the "death instinct," on the pessimistic philosophy of Schopenhauer.

Freud linked the relief of tension and discharge of affect to both the pleasure principle and the tensionless state of Nirvana. This linkage underwent several vicissitudes. For Freud, the Nirvana principle involved a linkage with the death instinct. What he arrived at, by logic, was the troublesome conclusion that the pleasure principle was linked to the death instinct via the Nirvana principle, a conclusion he first published, in German, in 1920 (1970). It took him several years to undo this syllogism, as follows (1924):

> The life-instinct, the libido, . . . has thus wrested a place for itself alongside the death instinct in regulating the processes of life. . . . The Nirvana principle represents the claims of the libido and that modification of it, the *reality* principle, the influence of the outer world. . . . The conclusion to be derived from these considerations is that a description of the pleasure-principle as the watchman over our lives cannot altogether be put aside.

Freud gave much thought to *affect,* and asked, in his lecture "Anxiety," "Now what is an affect, in a dynamic sense?" to which he responded:

> An affect comprises first of all certain motor innervations or dis-
> charges; and, secondly, certain sensations, which moreover are of two
> kinds — namely, the perceptions of the motor actions which have been
> performed, and the directly pleasurable or painful sensations which
> give the affect what we call its dominant note.

Here the attempt at definition was in terms of what affects *do.*

Edith Jacobson also addressed the problem, pointing out the "many confusing" problems in "the search for useful classifications of affects." The essence of her suggestion is that the terms "emotions" and "affects" be synonyms for

> the whole complex set of psychological and physiological manifesta-
> tions and behavior patterns as well as the phenomena [subsumed by]
> the term "affect equivalents" and . . . all the neurological and endo-
> crinological aspects [since] . . . discovered. The term "feelings" [was
> to be] limited to the subjectively felt experiences.

She includes the "enduring feelings of love, hate, kindness." In other words, emotions or affects equal psychological and physiological manifestations and may include "feelings."

In her ultimate statement of conceptualization concerning affects, or rather, concerning moods (revised 1979; "Normal and Pathological Moods: Their Nature and Function"), she makes a sharp distinction between moods and emotion. She defines a mood as an ego state, involving generalized transference phenomena, and affecting *all feelings, thoughts and actions.* It thereby differs from emotion, which is an object-directed feeling state. But, I would differ, in that emotion does also affect all feelings -- by exclusion of many — and thoughts and actions. Moods "impart a special coloring to the whole world and hence also to the self." They may involve secondary as well as primary processes.

Jacobson's depiction of mood is rich and sensitive; her reflections on emotion are thought-provoking in exploring a basic area of human experience.

Neo-Freudian Views on Affect

Prior to Jacobson's paper on affect, which supports and explicates Freud's concepts (other than the "pleasure principle"), different trains of thought concerning affect came into being. To cite several: (1) Harry Stack Sullivan, in the 1930's and especially in 1946 (Sullivan, 1956); (2) Ernest Schachtel, in 1956 in *Metamorphosis;* (3) Thomas Szasz, in 1957 in *Pain and Pleasure;* (4) Sandor Rado, in his 1958 paper, "From the Metapsychological Ego to the Bio-Cultural Action-Self." But, though each of these approaches was engaged in modifications of or challenges to Freud's (and later even to Jacobson's) thinking, there was little or no exploration of the function of an individual's affects in relation to his cognition. In this paper, these approaches will be addressed from the relationship between affect and cognition.

Harry Stack Sullivan. In his first paper, "The Oral Complex" (1924), written when he was 31, Sullivan still bore allegiance to the "Pleasure Principle, in strict delineation of Professor Freud," in accounting for some of the symptomatology of the catatonic patient. He extended the "pleasure principle," however, to prenatal functioning, outside of awareness because of the then absence of symbolic activity.

This early flirtation with Freudian theory of primary process—though not actually so designated — was short-lived. Sullivan moved on to formulate a comprehensive theory of experience in developmental terms with associated aspects of communication, beginning with the "prototaxic" mode with its fused affect–cognition. Instead of Freud's theory of the pleasure principle, Sullivan talked of the tension of needs, manifest immediately on birth and requiring relief by the "good mother." In the progression of development and maturation, various other need-tensions occurred sequentially. Instead of an affect-discharge aimed at establishing a tensionless "Nirvana" (which seems suspiciously slack to the point of apathy), Sullivan speaks of euphoria and almost joyousness as the accompaniment of satisfaction of need-tensions. Other tensions, and painful affects, are recognizably aroused in an infant, says Sullivan, by the mothering one's disapproval, anxiety, or other disjunctive feelings or behaviors. That is, this type of infant affect and affect-behavior occurs within an interpersonal milieu; and *primary process, pleasure principle,* and *affect discharge,* are terms which do not exist in Sullivan's vocabulary.

Contrary to Freud, Sullivan does not use the sexual orgasm and reflex arc as the basic model for relief of tension. Further, beyond their immediacy, Sullivan gives to the infant's and child's painful and gratified feeling states, as evoked or manipulated by others, a central role in the development of the self-system. Sullivan's "self-system" is roughly comparable to a defense system, its development roughly comparable to character formation.

When he discusses major emotions, such as anger, rage, grief, and love, it is in terms of meaning, origin and interpersonal relatedness, and, interestingly enough, in connection with their significance for love and intimacy, *not* as tension and affect-discharge.

It is noteworthy that Sullivan's initial acceptance of the mystical qualities of Freud and Jung gave way to the operationalism of the philosophers of science and to the interdisciplinary approach.

Ernest Schachtel. Ernest Schachtel, in *Metamorphosis* (1956), challenges Freud's fundamental position of the so-called pleasure principle, pointing out that it had originally been the *unpleasure* principle and that it was "essentially a flight from or a fight against life and reality, . . . the quest to return to a state without stimulation, . . . tension and striving" − I would say, to an affect-less, that is, a vacuous, state. Schachtel does not agree with the ego psychologists that the goal is a "conflict-free sphere of the ego." Instead, Schachtel links affects with action "right from the beginning of life." For him, there are two types of affect, "one of which [is concerned with] the diffuse discharge of tension familiar in Freud's theory, the other as a positive, directed tension phenomenon which seems similar to the activity-affects of later life," i.e., calling for action, not simply as Freud's discharge of tension but, rather, purposively toward a personal goal.

These two types of affect, called "embeddedness affect" and "activity affect," respectively, are central in Schachtel's theory of feeling states. He presents an analysis of several specific emotions in terms of this theory, namely, *hope* and *joy* (which he says Freud never mentions) and *anxiety* and *pleasure.*

"Emotions," Schachtel says, "have the function not only of letting off steam (embeddedness affect) but also of creating an activity-sustaining mood (activity affect)."

Schachtel sees affect as having a role in communication – that is, we read the other's affective experience – thereby endowing affect with the ability to effect change in the outer world.

Using this approach, he develops it further in application to the Rorschach Test.

Overall, Schachtel's approach to affect is one I find sympathetic and additive to the present formulation of a conceptualization of affect, somehow adding the touch of the poet, but, as I shall point out, still incomplete. He drew upon the German literary giants, Goethe and Schiller, yet came out with quite different psychologic concepts and with an optimistic orientation toward life.

Thomas Szasz. Szasz, in *Pain and Pleasure* (1957), includes under the heading of *pain* the actual somatically based pain that is currently approached in pain clinics – and makes one wonder if he is really dealing with Freud's concept of "unpleasure" and "pleasure." In the case vignettes, which really have nothing to do with Freud's theory, the pain was in the service of attempting to establish communication.

Szasz establishes a hierarchy of pain as follows:

1. Signal to ego of threat to structural or functional integrity.
2. Call for help in terms of body.   ⎱ interpretive/
3. Call for help for nonbody; far more   ⎰ communicative
   symbolic.

His views are based in part on the English positivist school of philosophy, notably Bertrand Russell's. Pleasure he sees as reduction of physiological need – at least in neonates or in animals – such as, for example, satisfaction of hunger. But he states objections to and goes beyond a theory of simple need reduction, stressing pleasure from object-contact, such as, for example, in love and intimacy.

Szasz states,

It is clear that for both pain and pleasure, biological factors play a decisive role in the primary models of these affects and that cultural factors gain in relevance as we move toward later stages of symbolic representation.

He then plays out pleasure as communication, comparable in some ways to pain, with the difference that pleasure calls for no action.

His "Hierarchical Development of the Concept of Pleasure" is as follows:

1. The primary model: physiological need reduction.
2. Pleasure from object-contact.
3. Pleasure as an added "substance."
4. Pleasure as a signal in relation to human objects.

Szasz attacks Freud's equating physiological discharge functions with true giving; he views giving, instead, in terms of object relations.

Sandor Rado. Rado is of interest to me in connection with the affect-cognition linkage for several reasons. Although in devising the adaptational conceptual system of psychoanalysis he drops the Freudian language and concepts of affect in favor of his terms, "hedonic control" and "brute emotions," it seems to me that in some essentials there is correspondence between Freud's and Rado's referents.

In Rado's formulation, there is emphasis on a hierarchical value system, with the lowest score for "brute emotion" and the highest score for "unemotional, impartial thought," which, he states, "reflects the course of evolutionary history." Continuing this explication, he states, "Most ancient is the hedonic unit; in ascending order follow the units of brute emotion, emotional thought, and unemotional thought."

Nevertheless, there are significant similarities to Freud's thinking regarding relief of tension. Rado views emotional responses as central mechanisms "for the arousal of the peripheral organism and for the peripheral disposal of superabundant psychodynamic tensions."

He groups emotions into two categories:

1. *The welfare emotions,* such as pleasurable desire, affection, love, joy, self-respect, and pride, based on the presence or expectation of pleasure.

2. *The emergency emotions,* such as fear, rage, retroflexed rage, based on the presence or expectation of pain.

"Training transforms the innate forms of emotional expression into culturally conditioned patterns of response." The basic pattern of "hedonic self-regulation" is that "the organism moves toward the source of pleasure (reward) and away from the cause of pain (punishment)." It is this kind of formulation that, to my mind, contains the unrecognized — or at least the unexpected — implication that affect gives information to the experiencing organism; that is, that affect has a fundamental cognitive function.

What I find disturbing in Rado's formulations about "brute emotions" and an evolutionary hierarchy is a kind of snobbery. A stoical disapproval of emotion is expressed. Further, he indicates a prestige ladder in the name of "evolutionary history" of the different levels of the central nervous system that are related to "brute emotion"and its ascent to "unemotional thought."

The quality of Rado's thinking — his cognitive approach — appears to me based on the life-approach of the Stoics, though nowhere to my knowledge has he stated this, and a quasipragmatism. He has declared as his model a biologic, so-called "scientific," approach which, he states, was the fundamental early contribution of Freud that later, deplorably in Rado's view, was abandoned.

It is interesting that the first three of the above authors consider a communication aspect to affectivity, but essentially in terms of *interpersonal* communication. For Sullivan, nurturing relatedness from the mothering one to the infant results in euphoric affect; for Schachtel, we read the affects of others; for Szasz, the one experiencing an affect is involved in communicating that affect to another with a concomitant appeal as appropriate. Szasz also considers affect as a signal to the ego, i.e., a communication with oneself. The interpersonal aspect of affective communication is but one dimension of the function of affect. However, though the relation of affect to the self has been touched on, there are aspects in its functioning and significance that call for deeper exploration.

TOWARD DEFINING AFFECTS AND OTHER FEELING STATES

The Range of Meaning

I recognize that the quandary concerning terminology is not easily solved, and that we are prone to use "affect" in the large, loose sense to include the entire range of feeling. But it should be feasible, when precision is called for, to use *feeling states* to cover the range that includes affect, body feelings (in their relation to the other feeling states), mood, and emotion. "Mood" would retain its meaning of a diffuse, fixated emotional coloring (as suggested by Jacobson), "emotion" referring to the vivid, intense feeling state that has a thrust, generally but not necessarily always, for action.

Jacobson, in her discussion of affect, mood and emotion, points out important distinctions. Add to these the body feelings and states relevant to affect, mood and emotion. If the term *affect* is used both for the precise and limited meaning of pleasant/unpleasant, and also for the wide and disparate range, then confusion is compounded on a linguistic basis. This obfuscation is important both for theory and for clinical practice.

Body Feelings

The importance of the category, *body feelings,* lies in the fact that, first, by and large most of our perceptions have some modicum of affect, of pleasant/unpleasant, and, second, affect/mood/emotion generally have associated body feelings.

Often the subjective experience of the concomitant body feelings overshadows awareness of affect/mood/emotion, not only in extremes such as anxiety attacks and conversion symptoms but, also, more generally and more subtly — and not necessarily pathologically — as will be seen in the presentation of clinical material. There are situations and personalities for which addressing the body feelings opens a door to self-awareness.

Moods and Emotions

Moods and emotions, not limited to the Freudian conceptualizations, are generally presented as having some essential polar differences. The former are described as being more diffuse and passive, comparable to the receptor side of a reflex arc, while the latter are more comparable to the motor segment (of the reflex arc) both in terms of somatic expression — increased heart rate, perspiration, restlessness — and behaviorally, with proneness to take action. Furthermore, according to Jacobson, moods, in contrast to emotions, color ego states and all other experience, and are of longer duration.

This formulation of contrasts is neat and convenient, and serves us well if we have in mind the overlap, the actual continuum between mood and emotion. For example, some emotions — anger, rage — for some persons are vivid, long-lasting, and unresolved, whether acted upon or not. Some persons can control their emotions and the tendency to act on them. On the other hand, some individuals are able to alter their moods quite swiftly, such as from the "blues" to surface happy-go-luckiness, while others demonstrate a tendency toward action in terms of their moods. Somatic changes, which in the formula are compared to the motor segment of the reflex arc, may be temporary or of some duration, and do occur in moods, often falling into the purview of psychosomatic medicine.

This emphasis on the existence of a continnum between mood and emotion is far from being a quibble; it is a reminder of the fallacy of the simplistic, and of the importance of self-awareness, observation and exploration by both patient and therapist.

One important element in moods is the person's *basic mood,* which suggests but has differences from Jacobson's *general affective predisposition,* in which "we find a conspicuously frequent recurrence of special, temporarily fixated modifications of concepts of self and the world, based on generalized inferences and transferences of the past" and associated with "inherent preference for special affectomotor reactions."

Where I differ is that by the person's *basic mood* I identify elements of what has been considered innate temperament, and also aspects of character. Some basic moods involve ongoing, lasting patterns of relationship such as being alienated, being loving, or being hostile, which may be thought of as expressions of character. This is exemplified by Fromm's concept of love (in *Escape From Freedom,* 1941) as a "quality *in* a person . . . a readiness which, in principle, can turn to any person and object" and which "is not primarily *'caused'* by a specific object" [italics added].

Furthermore, aside from psychopathological manifestations, we all do have basic moods.

Affects

Affects are complex and will be considered both directly and in terms of Freud's concepts. The neurophysiological base of affects, their strict denotation and extensions of meaning, and a hypothesis as to their functioning will be presented.

In its most precise denotation, affect means pleasant–unpleasant, or even neutral. Within this strict denotation, moods and emotions are not identical with affect. The profundity of this psychologic difference is further suggested by the fact that neurophysiology has established different locations for affect, mood, and emotion. But what lends itself to confusion is that moods and emotions nevertheless have an accompanying affective tone. For instance, for some individuals the experience of anger is pleasant and gratifying, while for others it is distressing, painful, unpleasant, occurring, as may be the case, in association with a sense of guilt, shame, or a feeling of being out of control (similarly for, say, an experience of sexual erotism by an ascetic, puritanical person). Depressive moods may retain their essential affect of painful, unpleasant; or, for someone needing the self-image of victim, there may be a lurking affect of pleasant gratification.

If we maintain the meaning of affect in its strict denotation, there is clarity as to what component of experience is being referred to. Such clarity affords a stepping-stone to further, authentic exploration as to the precise nature and referents of the affective response — as for example, pleasure in the glow of sexual excitement; pleasure in fragrance; in the view of a beautiful landscape; in interpersonal communication; pleasure in achievement; in power; and so on. These examples indicate one of the limitations of the original Freudian concept of relief of tension as relieving "unpleasure," since here the tension is pleasurable, and at times deliberately prolonged (as emphasized by Schachtel, and as in Jacobson's modifications of Freud's theory).

In addition to enriching self-awareness, such distinctions, as will be seen, have heuristic value in therapy.

Affect, in the primal sense of pleasant–unpleasant, serves a reporting function, and is different from the executive function, i.e., the action component of the reflex arc. Freud's last statement about anxiety secondarily includes significant comments on affect, and appeared in 1926 as "Hemmung, Symptom und Angst," later translated into English and published in 1936 as *The Problem of Anxiety*. Anxiety, for Freud, is the first and basic affective state, and a biologic necessity. "Although we are equally ignorant of what an affect is," the attributes of anxiety are: "(1) a specific unpleasurable quality, (2) efferent or discharge phenomena [of physical sensation — as rapid breathing], and (3) the perception of these." In linking anxiety to the danger of birth as experienced by the infant, he infers that the discharge phenomena of rapid heart beat and breathing are attempts at restitution against the danger. Subsequent experiences of anxiety are signals of threat whether from within or without. Freud's concept of anxiety as having a signalling function can be taken as one instance of my general thesis, that *all* affect has a reporting function at some appropriate level. That is, affect, in terms of pleasant–unpleasant, generally has an informational function, comments on experience, and thereby has an evaluative function. Functioning within the nervous system, which itself is a network of information-gathering and sending, affect is the basis for the organism's response in primal terms of good–bad, good-for-survival–bad-for-survival, helpful–hurtful. Neurophysiologic findings are consistent with this interpretation.

We can read this in terms of a biologic level. For instance, though we cannot "know" what could be called the experience of unicellular organisms, it is observable that there is reaching-out and avoidance which we can interpret as toward the good and away from the bad in some equivalence of affect.

From sophisticated neurophysiology we learn that sensory nerves from their very periphery are involved in a reporting system of painful, unpleasant, or pleasant, with stations at every level of the central nervous system, reaching ultimate termination in the cerebral cortex with its function of clear, crisp awareness instead of the inchoate awareness of the lower centers that, however, plays a role. The exciting new discoveries of pain-relieving endorphins, not limited to humans, demonstrate the physiological profundity of affects, with psychologic concomitance and dominance. Their fundamental importance is further demonstrated by the observation that "frontal temporal lesions are associated with loss of signs of affect" (Gerard, 1960), and that split-brain patients have difficulty subjectively and in interpersonal communication with their affects and emotions.

The neurophysiologic specificity for affect indicates that there is a functional sequence of (1) a certain kind of information and (2) an interpretation of good-for-me or bad-for-me, and it is suggested that the latter is a forerunner of a psychologic value system. That is, a primal cognitive function is associated with affect, even on levels beyond our precise awareness, and consists of information as a basis for good–bad evaluation. Turning to our psychologic experiential dimension, our basic affective good–bad responses are modified by an interplay of prohibitions and permissions from the culture and from parents that are partly internalized in the superego. This in turn "affects" how we relate to ourselves and others, what our images and symbolizations are, what judgments we make, what actions we take.

The input of affect information, on whatever level, and the primitive interpretation of good–bad, serve as the basis for action, whether swift reflex, as in the blinking response to a painful dust particle on the cornea, the swift precognitive response of reaching toward or pulling away from someone on an empathic basis, or the usually conscious judgment in decision-making. These examples are all in the general domain of experience.

Empathic communication, as Sullivan emphasized for the earliest mother–child linkage, to my observation generally involves absorbing the feeling state of another, along with our affect-response, and precedes, even if only momentarily, the cognitively clear recognition. But it itself is a primitive cognition.

Traditionally the distinction is made that emotion leads to a behavioral and somatic discharge, while affect does not. This, however, is a simplistic distinction, the matter being more one of degree, for affects often have somatic manifestations and, as we have seen, may be expressed or enacted in behavior. On the other hand, emotion, which we associate with clear behavior, high visibility, and subjective intensity, nevertheless may be inhibited or altered, and not expressed directly — which has been demonstrated beginning with Freud's and Breuer's *Studies in Hysteria*. As for unpleasant, painful affects, if unresolved they make their lasting though reversible impact on body functions — which is partly what psychosomatic medicine is about — while positive affects are on the whole beneficial to us.

What about affect-drive and discharge, and the reduction of tension — Freud's concepts? My interpretation is that the discharge depends on accomplishment of the function, namely, reporting and evaluating. For example, the blinking reflex in response to the painful dust particle on the cornea was not in behalf primarily of relieving the tension of the affect, but the reverse; the tension from the affect is a continuing, forceful message that the particle is traumatic and should be removed. When this is achieved, the tension from the affect is indeed relieved, because the information-evaluating function has been consummated by action. Similar relief of affect and affect-tension occurs when a clearly psychologically experienced affect-situation is resolved. The distressing affect may then be replaced by a pleasurable one.

Another element that would help account for Freud's affect-tension-discharge observation, but would revise his theory accounting for it, has to do with metabolic factors. The suggestion is that affect and emotion require their own supportive, metabolic energy for maintenance functioning, in addition to metabolic energy for somatic expression and behavior. As we know, every tissue — nervous, heart muscle, walls of blood vessels — requires its metabolic support, both for the functioning of the whole organism and for its own maintenance. My thesis is that in Freud's affect-discharge of tension should be included the following principle: that cyclical supportive metabolic buildup/discharge characterizes all functioning process.

Besides the information-value dimension of affect and of the other feeling states, there is an intrinsic *reward-gratification* aspect in the process itself. Basically, inhibition of function is accompanied by distress and unpleasantness, while accomplishment of function is accompanied by at least a modicum of gratification and pleasure. For instance, for many depressed persons, their affect experience is preferable to affectless numbing. This is pleasure in cognition — recognizing also that anxiety and the presence of sufficiently unpleasant, painful affects, beyond an individual's level of coping, may motivate denial and lack of conscious cognition.

Summation

An approach to defining affect in terms of its functioning has been presented. I have suggested that the term "feeling states" be used to subsume affects, moods, emotions, and body feelings especially related to these, when precise distinctions are significant. The subject of emotions has not been fully addressed, partly because the focus here has been on important meanings and roles specifically of affect that so far have been overlooked. To a survey of points of view, Freudian and non-Freudian, I have added the thesis that affect is a biologically based intrapsychic process which serves as a primal *informational* resource for what I infer is ongoing *evaluation* of experience, including empathic communication, and is a building-block for a *value system*. *Teleologically,* affect is in the service of survival, whether of the individual or of the species.

The information/evaluation function involves a cognitive monitoring function. Whether there is inchoate awareness, or precise, focussed awareness is relevant and significant, but does not obliterate the cognitive functioning at some level. The closer the affect is to the reflex level of reaction, the closer to being fused are the informative/evaluative functions with swift restitutive action. On the other hand, on the whole, as the input of affect-information approaches levels of precise awareness, there is an intermediate evaluative process separate from the commentary of information, before the response of action or nonaction occurs. The relation of feeling states to cognition is one of continuous feedback.

Affect is involved in a subjective *reward* system for its functioning, even if the commentary of information is unpleasant. In the accomplishment of the function of affect in a particular situation, there is the utilization of energy and, whether sooner or much later, a discharge of the tension when the goal of the affect is accomplished. This is discussed as a perspective on Freud's discharge of energy theory. Freud's "Nirvana" theory has not been addressed here.

In terms of therapy, helping the person — whether in the role of patient or therapist, as will be seen — achieve self-awareness involves awareness of affect and emotion, at different levels of experience.

CLINICAL APPLICATIONS

Communication in the Therapeutic Situation

To be sensitive to the subjective experience of others and of ourselves requires our increased sensitivity to the range of feeling states. We tend to be simplistic and think only of the major, or what may be called the massive, states of feeling, such as depression, despair, resentment, anger, rage. Most of these the patient can tell us about, can verbalize. But at times a far wider range of feeling states is present than we psychoanalysts and psychologists are prone to consider. Our compass of emotion tends to include love, hate, resentment, ambivalence, anger/rage, depression/despair/grief, elation/mania, anxiety, shame, and guilt. This list omits many more terms, often with nuances that we are tempted to homogenize away, thus closing off our awareness of the related experience. Some closing off of exploration unfortunately lies at our door. We need the poet's range!

Case Vignettes

Vignettes of experiences with patients, which are quite ordinary and prosaic-seeming, illustrate how more deeply significant interactions may be helped to surface by the enterprise of exploring feelings — bodily feelings, moods, and emotions. The following case presentations demonstrate how this exploration of feeling states of patients (or analysts) leads to a self-awareness of psychodynamics.

How My Interest in Feeling States was Triggered

Some time ago, a woman in her 40's was referred to therapy for an *idée fixe* that she had contracted trichinosis while serving as dietician in a government post, which, she maintained, accounted for various pains — though all objective tests had been negative. After she described these aches and her concern about their persistence and the presence of an infestation, she would lapse into a tense, staring silence — tension-arousing in me. I experienced my face and jaws tensing, my heels digging into the floor. I attempted to mobilize us out of this mutual enduring of tense silence. Using my awareness of various discomforts, I asked her to describe what she was feeling. I felt that my discomfort in sitting mirrored hers. I asked about her tension in bracing herself, in sitting in a position oblique to mine. She noted she was digging into the chair posturally and with her arms, and had her feet wrapped around the chair legs. This, she said, was to control her feelings. I asked for her mood: she felt numb. "I don't like to feel a feeling because for me to feel feelings is to feel something unpleasant." I asked her to become aware of how her face was set. Her lips were in a pout that suggested to me the puckering of a baby rejecting being spoon-fed. This evoked a recollection of vomiting during car rides with her mother, and having her head held, which comforted her and gave her the feeling of having at last gotten closeness with her mother.

Re: "Resistence"

Though no one approach is an "Open Sesame" in the face of what is experienced as resistance, for the patient to be invited, encouraged, to describe any aspect of his or her feeling state, in the present or at any time in the past, often permits movement out of the entrenched resistance — given that the patient does not totally and lastingly refuse any verbal communication with the therapist.

The emphasis here is that body feelings may be tension-related or, to put it more explicitly, an expression either of an unexpressed affect or attitude, or of its inhibition. If these can be voiced — and hopefully not in a pejorative climate — we have an additional source of information. That is, awareness of the body-state, and revealing the affect or attitude that relates to it, offers a cognitive dimension and opens up information which furthers the process and goal of psychoanalytic therapy. This is distinct from affect discharge, which has generally been considered the prime element in countering the repression of affect.

What appears to us as resistance may be, from the patient's side, a mood not yet articulated and not yet with associations, recall or ideational content.

For some, it is helpful to encourage the description of the mood, which as it is articulated mobilizes recall either directly or with the intermediary of a metaphor.

A Patient with Psychosomatic Symptomatology

A young woman came for psychotherapy because of recent hypertension and asthmatic attacks, which had appeared for the first time several years before, after a serious employment crisis. An outstanding allergist had diagnosed that there were both antigenic and emotional factors. The asthma would occasionally flare into a medical emergency and for a long time she relied heavily on a variety of drugs for bouts of actual physical distress and because the anxiety that an attack was imminent. During our sessions, it became clear that at the moment she declared her anxiety and reached for the medication, her respiration became rapid and hyperventilating and preceded the actual asthma. What also captured my attention was that her verbal communication was punctuated by frequent laughs and laugh-coughs, the latter sometimes culminating in the asthmatic breathing.

Cultivating her understanding of what she was experiencing in these expulsive laughs served as handle for recognizing the linkage between repressed emotion, affect, bodily feelings, and the affect which was expressed in the laugh. Needless to say, these in turn were considered within the contextual anxiety-provoking situation and past sensitizing experiences. An example: the laugh was accompanied by amusement at what for her was the illogic or the irony of occurrences. "You find out you have hypertension and that it comes from worry and you're supposed to find out what you worry about [laugh]. So you worry about not finding out what you worry about and then your hypertension goes up." And the self-mocking in "I'm a good worrier [laugh]! You have to be good at *something*."

Particularly revealing was our exploration of an anticipated anxiety-provoking interview: "Dr. X may think what he says has content but [laugh] suppose I don't. I have to avoid an angry retort. I have to stay in the room [laugh]. I can't fight or flee. I have tremendous fear. I have to hold on." The laugh was to prevent an expression of anger as she envisioned the interview that she was afraid would boomerang disastrously.

Awareness — of what she was doing with respiration, which was within voluntary control, of feelings of rage or anger or frustration, and of her incomplete attempts to control them by being "nice" — developed concomitantly. Later on she stated that when she did assert herself without trying to be the sweet and shy little woman, if she gave the snappy retort she wanted to, there was no asthmatic attack, she could breathe freely, psychologically and physically. Incidently, her blood pressure became normal.

In contrast to the prominence of affective problems in the so-called affective disorders is the traditional picture of the low-keyed or inhibited feelings and emotions in obsessional patients. This, of course, is an oversimplification because, while the individual may be unaware of his feeling states, very often the observer — whether participant or not — notes irritation, frustration or mini-rages, or, rarely, positive emotions. One goal of therapy is for the patient to broaden and deepen self-awareness of feeling states and their meaning and genesis, with freedom from shame or sense of guilt, thereby replacing the obsessional cognitive style based on flight from feeling into intellectualization.

What has so far been described deals with another road to the unconscious, perhaps more pedestrian than royal: that of self-awareness of feeling states in the service of understanding and ameliorating maladies in living, and opening wider the door on psychosomatic ailments.

Concerning "Alienation" and "Being in Touch"

Another dimension of the deepening awareness of feeling states is for its own sake, for enriching one's experience. "Being in touch" with oneself, or with another, has become a cliché; but it is based on subtleties and profundities, for which it may serve as a marker, as a reminder. This being in touch counters the "alienation" that Fromm brought to attention in the 1950's.

> By alienation is meant the mode of experience in which the person experiences himself as an alien. . . . The alienated person is out of touch with himself as he is out of touch with any other person. He, like the others, are [sic] experienced as things are experienced; with the senses and with common sense, but at the same time without being related to the world outside productively. (Fromm, 1955)

Though set in the context of the relationship between society and the individual, the alienated mode of relating is the outcome of obliterating the authentic self and writing over it the "As If" person. The alienated mode involves distancing from one's affects and emotions out of the need to please others and to create an idealized image of oneself. Alienation brings in its wake such diffuse unhappiness as the feeling of emptiness, of boredom, of a sense of lack of direction, lack of pleasure, feelings of depression, the meaninglessness of life, a lack of caring for oneself, even amorality. What the person can still go on is the old stereotyped patterns of As If and of pleasing.

Now, for me it is axiomatic that there is no such thing as an "empty" person, though of course in ordinary, everyday parlance I experience and designate the superficiality, lack of caring, and shrunken relatedness as "emptiness." But in my responsible, professional relatedness, I seek the silent despair, the lurking, disowned depression, the need for flight into superficiality. I endeavor to have the person get in touch with *any* feeling he or she may think too ordinary to bother about.

It is to be noted that these illustrations from within the psychoanalytic situation are reminiscent of free association but not identical to it. It is true that free association does not prohibit the person's description of the experience of body feelings, mood, attitude, or emotion, but often what happens is that the person does not relate to feelings in depth, wandering instead into intellectualized tangents or organized expositions. The basic rule of reporting whatever comes to mind, without censoring, whether with a feeling of embarrassment or guilt, is easily evaded, especially by obsessive patients. Harry Stack Sullivan attempted to cope with this subtle resistance by asking the person to report "marginal" thoughts or words that flit in and out of the mind. Reminding the person to make contact with any of the range of feelings is often of added help in avoiding freezing or verbal bypassing and in bringing to light significant experiences and interactions. That is, the getting in touch with feelings mobilizes the cognitive potential.

Occasionally affect or emotion is manifested — whether by facial expression, body state of movement or tension, tone of voice, or some other nonverbal articulation — of which the patient is unaware; for instance, what I consider the private laugh and what it conveys, perhaps by hiding.

The approach presented also allows for better understanding of somatic correlates, transference and countertransference.

References

Buber, M. (1948), *Between Man and Man,* R. G. Smith, trans., Macmillan, New York.

Freud, S. (1924), The economic problem in masochism, in *Collected Papers,* Vol. II, J. Riviere, trans., Hogarth Press, London.

Freud, S. (1925), Repression, in *Collected Papers,* Vol. IV.

Freud, S. (1925), The unconscious, in *Collected Papers,* Vol. IV.

Freud, S. (1935), Anxiety, in *A General Introduction to Psycho-analysis,* J. Riviere, trans., Liveright, New York.

Freud, S. (1936), *The Problem of Anxiety,* H. A. Bunker, trans., W. W. Norton & Co., New York.

Freud, S. (1970), *Beyond the Pleasure Principle,* J. Strachey, trans., Liveright, New York.

Fromm, E. (1941), *Escape From Freedom,* Rinehart, New York.

Fromm, E. (1955), *The Sane Society,* Rinehart, New York.

Gerard, R. W. (1960), Neurophysiology: An integration, in *Handbook of Physiology,* J. Field et al., Eds., Sec. I, Vol. III, American Physiological Society, Washington, D. C.

Jacobson, E. (1971), Normal and pathological moods, in *Depression: Comparative Studies of Normal, Neurotic, and Psychotic Conditions,* International Universities Press, New York

MacLean, P. D. (1960), Psychosomatics, in *Handbook of Physiology,* J. Field et al., Eds., American Physiological Society, Washington, D.C.

Neilson, W. A. et al., Eds. (1948), *Webster's New International Dictionary of the English Language,* 2nd ed., unabridged, G. & C. Merriam, Springfield, Mass.

Rado, S. (1962), From the metapsychological ego to the bio-cultural action-self, in *Psychoanalysis of Behavior (Collected Papers, Vol. 2),* Grune and Stratton, New York.

Schachtel, E. G. (1954), *Metamorphosis,* Basic Books, New York.

Shagass, C. (1962), Explorations in the psychophysiology of affect, in *Theories of Mind,* J. Scher, Ed., The Free Press of Glencoe, New York.

Spiegel, R., Development of Sullivan's theory of participant observation, *Contemp. Psychoanal.,* 13.

Spiegel, R. (1952), Body sensing and reorientation, discussion at White Society (unpublished).

Sullivan, H. S., The oral complex, *Psychoanal. Rev.,* 12.

Sullivan, H. S. (1953), *The Interpersonal Theory of Psychiatry,* H. S. Perry and M. L. Gawel, Eds., W. W. Norton, New York.

Sullivan, H. S. (1956), *Clinical Studies in Psychiatry,* H. S. Perry, M. L. Gawel, and Gibbon, Eds., W. W. Norton, New York.

Szasz, T. (1957), *Pain and Pleasure: A Study of Bodily Feelings,* Basic Books, Inc., New York.

Wittgenstein, L. (1953), *Philosophical Investigations,* G. E. M. Anscombe, trans., Macmillan, New York.

NINE

Psychotherapy Of The Depressive Character

JULES BEMPORAD

INTRODUCTION

Since the earliest psychoanalytic investigations, disturbance in human relations has been consistently stressed in describing depressive reactions. Despite this interpersonal emphasis the majority of psychoanalytic works on the theory and therapy of depression have focused on intrapsychic dynamics. A good number of psychoanalytic authors have taken Freud's early work on melancholia (1917) as a paradigm and have encouraged an "outward" deflection of the alleged retroflected anger in their patients. This continued utilization of a pioneer work (that today appears as a transitional theoretical phase between the topographic hypothesis and the structural theory), seems unfortunate since in depression, perhaps more than in any other pathologic condition, the patient's relationships (and especially the relationship to the therapist) are of prime importance. During certain stages of treatment, for example, the actual content of sessions may be relatively irrelevent while the tenor of the therapeutic relationship is crucial. It is my opinion that the depressive requires a specific type of psychotherapeutic intervention, and I will attempt to offer some guidelines which I have found helpful. Some excellent contributions have already appeared on the psychotherapy of depression, such as publications of Arieti (1962–1975), Beck (1970), Bonime (1960–1962b), Cohen et al. (1959), Jacobson (1971), and Kolb (1956) and my debt to these authors will be evident in my frequently quoting from their works. I plan to present a fairly detailed program for the therapy of the depressive character which is relatively

185

free from technical jargon and extreme theoretical bias, sticking as close to clinical data as possible so that clinicians of different orientations can accept or reject portions of the proposed treatment plan according to their own theoretical framework. Before proceeding to a discussion of therapy, however, a brief discussion of what I consider the depressive character to encompass appears warranted, since depression may be viewed as a normal affect, a symptom, a syndrome, or a clinical entity.

THE DEPRESSIVE CHARACTER

Depression is certainly a ubiquitous experience; however, for the most of us this painful affect occurs only after a severe, realistic set-back and is fortunately short-lived. For the depressive character, on the other hand, the feeling of depression is frequent and occurs after seemingly insignificant frustrations; indeed, depression appears to be a constant mode of feeling lurking in the background during everyday life. In this respect Sandler and Joffe (1965) have been helpful in differentiating between a "depressive affective response" and a depressive illness. The depressive or psychobiological response is conceptualized as a basic ego reaction to the loss of a state of well-being. On the other hand, the depressive syndrome or illness appears to be a specific elaboration or further reaction to this loss. The individual, because of a predisposition in terms of character structure, does not remedy the loss in a healthy fashion but gives into a state of helplessness and hopelessness as described by Bibring (1953). He also calls into play a number of transpersonal defenses or maneuvers which attempt to elicit from others a return of that state of well-being. Therefore, it is the preexisting personality organization including interpersonal relationships, modes of obtaining self-esteem, and a basic view of the self, that predispose to the development of a clinical depressive illness following a narcissistic loss. The premorbid personality, in turn, is shaped by specific pathogenic experiences in childhood, which, while no longer available to conscious recall, have determined the configuration of the depressive's experience of his life space: his particular distortions, his erroneous expectations, and his characteristic defense structure. Beck (1967) has outlined a primary triad of cognitive sets which are found in depression. These include a negative view of the world, of the self, and of the future. By construing experience in a negative way, the individual succumbs to a saddened mood, a paralysis of the will, avoidance of hope, increased dependency, and even suicidal wishes. It is not clear, however, whether Beck's work on cognitive set describes the cause or the result of depression. In other words, is a negative view of the self an etiological factor or a secondary symptom (such as anorexia, early rising, etc.)? Also, while cognitive factors are certainly important in influencing affectual life, the individual's mode of relating also must be appreciated. As mentioned previously, the type of relationships which are established by the depressive are of crucial importance. It is this mode of living, even prior to a clinical episode of depression, that typifies the depressive character. Bonime's (1960) concept of depression as a practice is particularly relevant. Bonime stresses that depression is a way of living and not a disease that is occasionally manifested. Even in apparently healthy intervals the depressive character exhibits a specific mode of existence. It is, in fact, this manner of life (or ego defenses or object relations) that predisposes the individual to frequent bouts of depression.

One of the characteristics of the depressive that has been emphasized by Arieti (1962) is excessive dependency on a "dominant other" as a source of meaning and gratification. The dominant other need not always be a flesh and blood individual but may be the anthropomorphization of a system such as the army, or the church, a corporation, and so on. The depressive excessively derives his sense of self, his self-esteem, from being rewarded by the dominant other and appears incapable of securing satisfaction independent of this intermediary. In more severe cases, the esteemed other is used by the depressive to reassure him that he is not evil or malevolent. This latter type of patient had, in childhood, been made to feel the cause of others' pain and suffering in a manner similar to what Fairbairn (1952) has described as the "moral defense," so that the other is seen as the source of all good, while the self is conceived of as morally base. The lifelong task of such an individual is to seek redemption for imaginary sins (see also Klein 1948). In either case, the depressive's efforts are to maintain and insure a continued relationship with this dominant other. As Jacobson (1971) has indicated:

The personality of the manic-depressive is characterized by their narcissistic vulnerability and their tendency to react to the slightest hurt or disappointment with a profound ambivalence conflict. They suffer from an instability of their self-esteem, caused by this overdependency on the love and narcissistic supply from an overvalued, all giving love object. (p. 259).

This pathological dependency is exemplified in the depressive's fear of "autonomous gratification," (Bemporad 1971) meaning the ability to derive pleasure directly from one's activity or accomplishments. There is always an inhibition of pleasure from action; rather, pleasure is gained from a dominant other praising the individual for his behavior. To obtain satisfaction from one's own activity is frought with guilt or with fear of abandonment for such an individual, even when he is not depressed. The joy of individual accomplishment is seen as a betrayal of the dominant other.

The need for a dominant other, coupled with the fear of autonomous gratification, often produces what I have called the "bargain relationship" which is a tacit agreement that the depressive will forego independent avenues of pleasure for the promise of continued nurturance from the other. This mode of relating is pertinent to the therapy of the depressive, for whereas it is originally initiated by the parent, the depressive perpetuates it in later life and transfers this mode of relating to later significant individuals, including the therapist. Green (1946), in another context, which is, however, applicable to depression, has shown how the personality of the future neurotic is "absorbed" by the parents in childhood, so that the individual is never allowed to be free or spontaneous. According to Green, the child is conditioned to need the love of the parent and then threatened with its withdrawal if he dares to disobey the dictates of these powerful others.

Therefore, the future depressive has been trained to fear his own activities. He requires a mediator to grant him pleasure, a dominant other who breathes meaning into his life. Together with this self-inhibition, some depressives have learned to feel they are to blame for the normal misfortunes of everyday living. Punishment in childhood was predominantly through inducing guilt and an unrealistic placing of the responsibility for other's feelings onto the self. To act, thus, means to incur the loss of another's love. This type of depressive is never secure in his actions because he inflates his effects on others and his own role in the inner lives of significant persons. If he were to lose an esteemed other, it would be his fault, it would never be because the other may have freely terminated the relationship, but because the depressive obviously caused the breach in the relationship.

The depressive has a dual view of his effectiveness: he feels hopeless and powerless in terms of gratification (because he requires the dominant other to give structure to his life) while at the same time, he grossly exaggerates the effect of his behavior on others. The inflated importance given to the interpersonal transactions by the parents of the future depressive in childhood causes him to fear independent assertion forever and to seek the security of a passive, reflective role. The obsessional symptoms frequently found in depressives may partially be due to a feeling that one must always have "everything in order" in case the powerful others will demand an explanation. It is as if one were constantly expecting an "inspection" from a superior and must not be found wanting. Implicit in this mode of relating is the need to control the dominant other who matters so desperately in the life of the depressive. Much of the depressive's manipulativeness may be seen as a pathetic attempt to insure that the other will continue to supply the needed nurturance and praise.

When this mode of relating is interrupted by a loss of a source of well-being in the environment, clinical depression ensues. As Bibring (1953) has indicated, the ego of the depressive is overwhelmed by a sense of hopelessness and helplessness. There is sometimes also a sense that one is responsible for the loss and thus the recriminations that often form part of the depressive picture.

Seligman's (1975) concept of "learned helplessness" can be used to explain some types of depression — conceptualizing the core dynamic as pessimism regarding the effectiveness of one's own actions. The problem with the helplessness model is that many depressives are capable of excellent work and are convinced of their effectiveness; they derive, however, no pleasure of meaning from their efforts. It is not the realistic inability to perform but the intrapsychic inability to obtain satisfaction that seems more typical of depressives. Gratification for effort must come from without, and the loss of this external agency will often precipitate a clinical episode during which the individual will appear helpless and refuse to take any action since activity no longer insures the rewards he needs. Once again the results of a depressive condition are taken as a cause. In addition, Seligman does not take into consideration the factor of guilt which paralyzes the depressive unless he receives permission for activity from a dominant other. It is not helplessness but the inability to maintain self-worth that is basic to depression. Finally, the depressive falsely believes he is powerless (during a depressive episode) and part of the therapeutic task is to show him he is not.

Furthermore, the loss is not only external but sensed as internal as well. Since the dominant other served a powerful, if pathological, internal purpose, that aspect of the self is also lost. There is a loss of source of meaning, of the bestower of pleasure, of protector from guilt; in short, the regulator of self-esteem. As Becker (1964) stated, "To lose an object is to lose the possibility of undertaking a range of satisfying action," implying that a whole way of behaving that had brought purpose and pleasure is lost. The loss causes an extensive disintegration of one's self-image as well as the usual mode of interrelation in life.

A further, albeit often hidden, reaction to the loss is a sense of anger at having been cheated. While the depressive blames himself for the loss, he also experiences a sense of outrage in having been deprived of promised rewards from the dominant other after a life of self-negation. Often these feelings in themselves cause one to become depressed in those cases where there is no environmental loss. In this type of individual, there is a realization that his life is ungratifying and devoid of meaning. He had been promised great rewards for "good" behavior and the promise was never fulfilled. He feels an inner lack of pleasure, a dreary tiredness in life yet his self-imposed inhibitions prevent him from altering his ungratifying mode of existence. In therapy, it is found that such an individual has a similar history as well as similar attitudes toward himself and others as depressives who have endured an environmental loss. The difference is that these individuals come to realize that their bargain relationship is really not a bargain.

This extensive description of the depressive character was meant to differentiate such patients from others who might also present with depression. As stated above, depression is a ubiquitous affect that at one time or another is experienced by us all. Certainly, "normal" individuals may experience depression following a realistic set-back or loss in everyday life. However, in these individuals the loss is indeed commensurate with their reactions, and their feelings of sadness and grief are self-limited. These individuals do not exhibit the self-blame or sullen demands of the depressive character. They still have areas from which gratification may be derived. The healthier individual does not react to the depressive affect with further hopelessness and helplessness nor the manipulative attempt to induce others to rectify the loss. These individuals are able to "fight off" succumbing to depression despite losses or reversals.

There is also a group of patients who have a hopeless view of human relationships, who believe that intimacy or comradery can never be possible, and who defend against a deep sense of despair by use of drugs or alcohol. Other such individuals may fight a feeling of inner deadness by daredevil thrills or criminal excitement. Their relationships are shallow and their entire lives appear to be characterized by a sense of futility in human relatedness. Such individuals appear closer to schizophrenia or psychopathy than to depression. Guntrip (1969) beautifully described such individuals and aptly differentiated them from depressives. In contrast to these patients' experience, states Guntrip, "Depression is really a more extraverted state of mind . . . . Depression is object-relational" in that the depressive still hopes for love from others and has not "renounced objects."

Finally there is a subgroup of depressed individuals who have many features in common with the "depressive character," and yet are different in terms of their symptom picture, their mode of relating, and accessibility to treatment. These individuals exhibit symptoms similar to what had been called neurasthenia in the older literature. They are chronically tired, withdrawn people who are drawn to melancholy aspects of life, often immersing themselves in existential literature or pessimistic fiction. They are usually quite introspective while not always particularly sensitive to the feelings of others. In their everyday behavior they show a superficial distance, or even arrogance, although in close relationships they tend to be quite masochistic. Suicide and suffering hold a romantic attraction for them although their true desire for death or pain is questionable. These individuals differ from other depressives in their relentless pursuit of the "romantic agony," and their enjoyment of a depressive stance. I found the individuals of this type that I have treated to have been profoundly angry at their parents and, later, to have transferred this anger to all authority figures. Much of their behavior can be understood as an oppositional yet self-defeating vendetta against alleged (and often real) injustices inflicted upon them in childhood. On the other hand, they are similar to depressives in requiring an exalted other to rebel against as well as in their use of unhappiness to punish others. Lastly, they also show the curious mixture of an inflated sense of effect on others while feeling essentially helpless. These are interesting patients and warrant a separate work describing their treatment which is beyond the scope of the present article.

A further clarification about the type of therapy to be described herein may be needed. The depressives I am describing are "neurotic" or "characterological," they are not so profoundly depressed that the affect of melancholia overwhelms all other mental contents. As Arieti (1975) has noted, in severe cases most cognitive constructs are either repressed or excluded from consciousness and only the pain remains. These severely depressed individuals may have manifest delusions, psychomotor retardation, etc., and require a more nurturing attitude in the initial stages of therapy, as well as a heavy reliance on physical methods of treatment. When a clinical depression continues without the return of the lost sources of gratification or without clinical intervention, a self-reinforcing cycle ensues in which the patient's own behavior increases his depression. Eventually, physical symptoms such as anorexia, confusion, motor retardation, appear. During this phase of the natural course of the disorder, it is debatable whether physiological changes that have occurred due to prolonged stress make the depressive syndrome more physical than psychological. At this advanced state, psychotherapy, while still effective, should be geared to creating sufficient symptomatic improvement so that an insight-oriented approach may be instituted. The same may be applicable to severe manic-depressive psychosis.

The patients I will be describing, on the other hand, show episodes of depression but still manage to function in their everyday lives. Despite their protestations of pain and suffering, they continue to keep their grasp on reality. In these individuals, depression as a way of life is evident in the therapeutic relationship as well as in all of their interpersonal behaviors.

PSYCHOTHERAPY

The therapeutic approach to depression will center on three basic parameters: the characterological defenses; the underlying unconscious dynamic structure (in terms of evaluation of self and others); and the transference situation, which is *the* therapeutic factor.

Most depressives come for treatment only when they are in an acute state after they have reconstituted their self-appraisals and expectations from the environment subsequent to a loss of a meaningful role or relationship. Although the patient may appear agitated, confused, or retarded, underlying their behavior is a persistant demand for magical relief. It is at this initial stage that the therapist must be wary of being trapped into promising too much to the suffering human being before him who seems to be so appreciative of reassurance. At this stage the patient will praise the therapist and inflate his importance. The therapist must be careful not to become a new dominant other on whom the patient will then depend for nurturance and reflected gratification. The acceptance of this role by the therapist, narcissistically gratifying as it may be to one's professional image, is doomed to failure. Eventually the patient will demand more and more from the therapist, and when the therapist finds himself in the unrealistic situation of carrying the whole burden of the patient's life on his shoulders, his attempts to reinstate a more constructive therapeutic relationship will be met with a response of sullen anger and sense of betrayal on the part of the patient who has already formed a bargain relationship with the therapist in his own mind. Bonime (1960–1962b) vividly described the depressive's manipulations and his attempts to subtly influence others. Bonime believes that much of depression is angry behavior that results from a failure to directly modify the actions of others. As alluded to here, this anger may well be the result of a betrayal of a bond that existed only in the patient's psyche. I have seen a depressive who formerly had been in therapy, on and off, for 19 years without any real change of his underlying personality. He utilized his therapist to give him direction in life, to magically protect him from the vissicitudes of life, and to allow him to proceed with quasi-legal business deals (which he disguised in order to get the therapist's approval). This patient would try to wear a different outfit for each session to look "nice" for his therapist. The therapist was constantly with him in the manner of a mental protective amulet which would gratify his wishes and keep him from harm. Eventually (after 19 years!!), the therapist refused to take him on again for regular therapy and the patient became quite severely depressed. This patient's behavior blatantly illustrates that giving in to the depressive's demands may relieve the symptomatic superstructure but leave the underlying patterns untouched.

Jacobson (1971) also commented on the difficulties of setting a proper course of therapy with depressives who have learned to see their every move as calculated to provide a desired response from a dominant other. She writes about the therapy of one of her patients:

"There followed a long, typical period during which the patient lived only in the aura of the analyst and withdrew from other personal relationships to a dangerous extent. The transference was characterized by very dependent, masochistic attitudes toward the analyst, but also by growing demands that I display self-sacrificing devotion in return." (p. 289).

Kolb (1956) also noted that the initial relationship with the depressed individual

"bears up on the therapist heavily because of the clinging dependency of the patient. The depressed patient demands that he be gratified. He attempts to extract or force the gratification from the therapist by his pleas for help, by exposure of his misery, and by suggesting that the therapist is responsible for leaving him in his unfortunate condition."

These individuals will insist on calling the therapist repeatedly between appointments or will request extra sessions. One man called me after an initial consultation during which he appeared only midly depressed and after profusely apologizing for calling, stated that he had had some suicidal ideas then fell silent awaiting a response. When I told him I was with another patient and would return his call later, he replied in a bewildered manner that his previous therapist had always taken time, even during sessions with other patients, to talk to him when he felt "blue." The silence that followed his initial statement is an example of the depressive's expectation that another person will solve his problems. Although he had been seen only once, he immediately expected to get special preference and nurturance on demand. Such treatment may seem harsh (and is certainly not applicable to severely depressed individuals), but the initial sessions should impart a definite set of limits for therapy. The therapist's personal regime regarding phone calls, missed appointments, etc., must be spelled out in great detail and not left to an assumption of mutual common sense judgment. Even under these circumstances, some depressives will try to bend the rules with proclamations of suffering. There is no question in my mind that the suffering is real, and there is a great natural inclination to do one's all to help a fellow human being in distress. A breaking of the agreed upon rules, however, will then determine the remainder of the course of therapy. The depressive must be aware from the beginning that he will have power to help himself; that the therapist will help him achieve this goal through confrontation and interpretation, but that, ultimately, the task of therapy rests on the patient.

The patient must widen the horizons of his consciousness which were narrowed in childhood to distorted patterns of relating and a sad neglect of much that is joyful and meaningful in life. He must be made aware of his own resources for pleasure, previously unknown areas of satisfaction, and relief from the relentless feeling of guilt that accompanies each attempt at gratification. As will be discussed further, this entails a cognitive restructuring in which old experiences are brought to consciousness and given new meanings. In the therapeutic relationship, behavior is elicited, examined, and utilized for an alteration in the estimation of self and of others.

Much has been written about the beneficial role a positive attitude and reassurance play in the therapy of depression. Exaggerated reassurances, however, may be detrimental rather than beneficial, by allowing the patient to believe that the therapist shares his estimation of his own helplessness and terribly impaired state. As Bonime (1962a) has aptly written: "False reassurance at almost any time is harmful, and probably never more harmful than when a patient is depressed; he believes he is powerless, and false reassurance obscures his genuine resources instead of mobilizing them." Actually, this therapeutic stance may be relaxed in the later stages of treatment as the patient learns to share his activities and mutually participate in the therapeutic effort. From the very beginning, however, the patient must understand that amelioration is his therapeutic task and not an obligation of the therapist.

On the other hand, the therapist cannot maintain a silent analytic posture, nor is the use of the couch advisable in the early sessions. To remain silent and let the patient recount his miserable state is to further the transference distortion of an omnipotent other. Rather, the therapist should be active and forthright. Often, depressed patients, when they begin therapy, want to talk only of their depressed feelings. The therapist may initiate discussion of other topics to prevent the reiteration of symptoms. Most important, as Kolb (1956) has indicated, is for the therapist to be open and honest about his own limitations and feelings. Depressives are reared in an atmosphere of deceit and of secret obligations; they must be shown how to be direct and forthright. In addition, the therapist should treat such individuals with dignity and give them the expectation of adult behavior. Interpretations should never be phased in a pejorative manner but in a way of sharing an insight with a mature individual. Regression in therapy is definitely to be avoided, rather, the attitude of the therapist must reinforce the mature parts of the depressive's personality. Furthermore, the individual should be helped to understand that he is important as a human being in his own right, and not for what he may do for the therapist. I have found it best to interpret evidences of transference immediately, because they reveal the depressive's desire to be taken care of by a dominant other by good behavior, and to reinstate a bargain relationship.

At this beginning stage of therapy, the patient may show a rapid symptomatic improvement because he believes that he has found a new dominant other to minister to his inordinate needs. If the therapist refuses to comply with these demands for nurturance, however, patients may complain that the therapist is aloof and unsympathetic, that therapy is not helping them, that it is not worth the cost, that they wish to discontinue therapy. One young depressed man reported the following dream during this stage of therapy: he was on a cold, barren road which offered no protection and he felt painfully exposed. The dream related to the analytic situation because he felt that I was cold and indifferent, and he was having difficulty expressing himself to someone so uncaring. At the same time, he saw himself as truly exposed, unable to "cover up" his needs by his usual manipulations. As soon as I was somewhat certain of the dream's meaning, I utilized it's interpretation to demonstrate his constant need for nurturance as well as his unique opportunity to be truly honest in his therapeutic relationship. There was no need for subterfuge; what was expected and what would be returned was integrity. It is during this stage that the content of the sessions is relatively unimportant, because the patient's primary objective is to set up the therapist as a new dominant other and to reestablish a bargain relationship. These attempts should be the focus of therapy, in the effort to show the patient, by means of the transference, how all of his significant human relationships have been characterized by pathological dependency.

Eventually, a picture of an extremely inhibited and anhedonic individual will materialize, who despite considerable public achievement has never enjoyed his successes. If this image can be made apparent to the patient he may realize that he has never allowed himself to be free or spontaneous but has always had to attune his behavior to the reactions of others. This fear of self-assertion will have displayed itself not only in a lack of satisfaction but also, in some cases, in work inhibition, so that the depressive has rarely achieved his true potential. Instead he has struck to a "safe" position, afraid to venture on his own.

The therapist must be careful *not* to accept the depressive's estimation of himself as helpless, unable, or overwhelmed. These self recriminations result from a multiplicity of causes and are overdetermined. In part, they are manipulative, interpersonal techniques to insure the other's support and to evade responsibility, and they define the depressive's characterological defenses in terms of dealing with others. However, to consider only the interpersonal affects of the depressive's behavior is to appreciate only part of the total situation. The inner belief systems that form the core of the depressive's personality must also be considered. Inwardly, the depressive believes in his inferiority and truly feels incapable of facing life's demands. In childhood the depressive was made to feel weak and dependent; each attempt at independent assertion bringing a rebuke of ingratitude or disloyalty. What emerges from the retrospective accounts of depressives, which were carefully documented by Cohen and her coworkers (1954), is that they were pressed to achieve in order to insure the continuation of a needed relationship, yet at the same time too much achievement was threatening to the needed other so that real life accomplishments were treated as "repayments" for love given or as expected in order to uphold the family honor. In every case, the achievement was somehow perverted so as to rob the individual of joy in his efforts and the ability to obtain a sense of independent competence. Work and effort were utilized in the hope of pleasing the powerful parent rather than in the gradual development of self-esteem or the sense of mastery. One patient, for example, remembered how as a girl she made remarkably good grades and even came in first on two state examinations, eventually winning a university scholarship. Her mother seemed to take these impressive accomplishments for granted while criticizing her daughter for lacking social grace or being without boyfriends. On the other hand, if this woman ever made less than outstanding grades, her mother would give her long, guilt producing scoldings.

This lack of self-confidence, and the need of an external other to give meaning to life as well as to absolve guilt, may partially explain the depressive's difficulties in functioning in positions of command or leadership. They are excellent in "number two" positions, following directions without question and working hard in order to obtain the praise of their superior. Often this excellent performance promotes them into leadership positions and this sudden loss of a relationship with an esteemed superior may precipitate a severe clinical depression. In such situations, the depressive finds himself forced to make independent decisions, the correctness of which he is never sure, but which he feels must be always correct. He longs for the reflected cues from a dominant other, the constant reassurance that he is doing a good job, and relief from independent assertion.

All of these examples confirm that depressives do have an unrealistically low picture of their capabilities. Sandler and Joffe (1965), Jacobson (1971), and others have, in fact, described depression as partially resulting from the discrepancy between an unrealistic ego ideal and the real self. From a Kleinian point of view Slipp (1976) has noted that in families of depressives, the child's effort is to alter the bad parental introject into a good parental introject so that the child can feel worthwhile. Slipp describes how the parents bind a child to themselves by creating an impossible achievement situation. The point to be appreciated here is that the unrealistic ego ideal is not desired for its own sake but only in order that it can retain the nurturance of others. This self-sacrifice of a personal sense of achievement, as well as the hopelessly unrealistic expectations, are to be pointed out repeatedly to the patient. It can be shown that beneath the self-recriminations are unrealistic expectations and an erroneous feeling that one is responsible for everything that happens to him — that if he fails it is always his fault for not trying hard enough. The therapist must not reward conspicuous achievement unduly, but, rather, encourage a sense of inner satisfaction regardless of life's vicissitudes. This can be done not only through interpretations, but transferentially by showing the patient how he inflates the power of the therapist and overly regards the therapist's opinions. Here again, an open, frank attitude, in which the therapist admits his own limitations and past failures, helps the patient to see supposedly "perfect" others as merely human. Sometimes patients will become angry with the therapist for not fitting their ideal of omnipotence and this is useful material for interpretation.

The first stage of treatment consists of establishing the specific therapeutic relationship in which the patient can view the therapist as an interested, understanding individual, but one who is neither nurturing nor idealized. The depressive must gradually realize his inordinate need for other's approval, and the inappropriateness of his demands.

The next stage of therapy appears to center on the depressive's reaction (and reluctance) to relinquishing the dominant other. This is often the major struggle of therapy because it invokes cognitive and interpersonal restructuring of the individual. The patient will regress to prior modes of behavior, and even become angry with the therapist for causing him to give up the older secure, if ultimately disappointing, sources of self-esteem. One patient, for example, reported a dream in which she was being forced to do dangerous acts by an insistent man. The man was curious in that he wrote upside down. She immediately realized that from where she sat in the office, my writing was upside down. In the dream she had a sense of apprehension, confirming her fear of the possibility of altering her behavior, as had been discussed in therapy. A frequently encountered dream at this stage of therapy, is of the death of a parent. Freud (1900) described such dreams as "typical," and used them to elaborate his concept of the oedipal conflict by stating that they represented revived childhood death wishes against the parent. Further evidence for this interpretation was that the parent who was dreamt of was often, in fact, already dead for many years and therefore his or her death in dream could not represent a current wish. Another confirming point, for Freud, was the inappropriate affect experienced in these dreams. In depressives, these dreams seem to have a different meaning. They appear to represent the relinquishing by the patient of that part of themselves that the parent represented. It is an attempt to give up the original dominant other as well as the part of the self that still adheres to the original dictates. The affective component of these dreams is often a clue as to how the patient feels about this relinquishing of an ingrained mode of behavior that is characterized by a response to authority.

Contrary to the oedipal interpretation of such dreams is the clinical finding that patients may dream of the death of either the opposite or same sex parent, the choice being seemingly related to which parent was the dominant other, rather than to sexual rivalry. For example, a woman who had been chronically depressed reported the following dream prior to taking a trip by herself for the first time in her life. She dreamt that her father had died yet she could not believe it. Other people were trying to convince her of his death and her feeling was one of bewilderment. Then she was in a drug store with her brother trying to get a death certificate to prove that her father was dead, but the druggist refused to sign the certificate. This woman's father had died 20 years before the dream but remained in her memory as a despotic autocrat who favored the brother and severly intimidated the patient through fear and guilt. Although the dream cannot be fully explored here, it might be helpful to add that the patient was going to visit her brother in a distant city, and was eager to show him how she had matured in therapy. The ambivalence in the dream regarding her father's death could be interpreted as her own insecurity over relinquishing her dependent mode of life and her anxiety over renewing close contact with her brother.

Another patient reported a dream in which he was at his father's gravesite in which his dead father was lying. In the dream the patient was crying and others were trying to comfort him. He had the feeling that everyone close to him was sick. He awoke from the dream crying. In his associations, this patient remembered the actual death of his father, stating that at that time, "I felt as if my purpose in life had been extinguished." This patient had had a quasi-symbiotic relationship with the father who prefered him over his other children. He followed his father's orders to the letter in return for which his father lavished praise on him and gave him substantial sums of money. He never dared cross his father since he had the experience of witnessing what had occurred to his brothers when they had disagreed even slightly with the father. This patient had grown up in a rural area where the father, a wealthy and influential businessman, had a large estate over which he ruled like a petit monarch. Although he had slavishly followed his father's instructions, the patient had often been irresponsible in his own affairs, and had lost moderate sums of money because of his naiveté. He had the dream after losing a considerable sum of money at cards, and the dream may represent an awareness that he was now on his own, and his desperate desire to be once again taken care of by a powerful other. The dream showed his characteristic turning to others to make things right, as his father had done in the past, whenever he was in trouble.

Another patient reported a dream of his father's death after being at a family reunion during which he realized he could no longer maintain the "bargain" relationship that has existed for years. He humored his father during the day but did not feel the old need to gain his approval or nurturance. That night he dreamt that he was attending the father's funeral but he felt no emotion. It was as if the death were a neutral statement of fact.

As illustrated by these examples, the parental figure that is killed off in dreams is usually, but not exclusively, the father, for both male and female depressives. The finding may be accounted for by the peculiar childhood history that many of these patients are able to reconstruct. It appears that, generally, the mother had been quite loving and adequate when the patient was an infant, but that as the patient entered the toddler - oppositional stage, he became part of the family system in which the father was the sole authority to be placated, and the mother relinquished her care of the child to suit paternal demands. As soon as the child became an independent, willful being he or she seemed to threaten the mother who withdrew from parental responsibilities. Often such individuals were exploited as go-betweens or mediators between the weak mother and the powerful father because the mother could not directly confront her overwhelming spouse. Soon these children internalized the familial belief system that the purpose of life was to please and mollify the omnipotent father by exemplary behavior, and gradually the paternal reactions became the barometer of one's worth rather than the evolution of independent agencies by which to assess self-esteem.

The point to be emphasized regarding these "death" dreams is that the affect in the dream appears to be the key to the patient's progress. These dreams may also represent punishment for behavior that had been forbidden and thus would cause abandonment. In such instances, the patient feels a desperate feeling of aloneness and helplessness in the dream. In instances where the part of the self that still requires the nurturance or approval of the parent is weakening, the affect is one of relief or resigned determination.

At this stage in therapy, a surprising regression and resistance is sometimes encountered. Although the patient is resolved to change, and sometimes makes realistic efforts in this direction, he begins to experience a different form of depression which, for lack of a better term, may be called "deprivation" depression. The depressive, having given up the mode of doing things for the reward of a dominant other (or at least seeing the futility in such a mode of life), now sees no point in life whatsoever. He is terrified by the sense of aloneness that results from his realistic assessment that others are not watching his every move, and that he is of little consequence to most individuals. While feeling relieved of the burden of living for the reflected praise of others, he cannot conceive of living without praise. In a previous article (1973), I described a young doctor who preferred to believe that he was being evaluated by demanding authorities who scrutinized his every move, rather than feel that no one supervised (or, in his terms, cared about) his work. He was so programmed to calculate his actions as to the consequences of those action to others, that his appreciation that others are primarily concerned with their own lives and welfare, destroyed his reason for being.

This desperate need to be noticed and approved of by the dominant other was graphically portrayed in the dream of a young, depressed man who was in the grips of wanting to break from his need of his father, yet was terribly frightened to relinquish this avenue of obtaining self-worth. In the dream, he was walking past a strong, masculine male and felt saddened that this powerful man was ignoring him and, instead, was looking at two women. He felt intensely ashamed of wanting to attract the attention of the man and yet was sorry that he could no longer please him. This dream symbolized the patient's awareness that he must give up his father as a dominant other, as well as the simultaneous desire to retain the father in a needed exalted position. The dream also demonstrated the patient's competition with his mother and sister for his father's favor which to him was essential for his feeling worthwhile. Both the struggle to extricate himself from the mode of reflective gratification (having the man ignore him), and the awesome sense of emptiness that would accompany this step, are presented in the dream.

During this phase of therapy, the patient may complain of feeling empty and lifeless, often blaming the therapist for his condition. Interpretations relating this feeling to the gradual renunciation of a previous narcissistic mode can counter some of the patient's discomfort. Simultaneously, it may be pointed out that this new "aloneness" also permits freedom from imagined obligations to others, and the possibility for real involvement in life. Here again, a review of lost opportunities in the patient's past may help him view this transient period of alleged emptiness as a healthy, although painful, step. Finally, this cognitive restructuring of one's own abilities and one's relationship with others will help in preventing future depressive episodes. The relinquishing of the dominant other orientation can be seen as a liberation and not a loss. With the therapist's encouragement, feeble, and later more significant attempts, at autonomous methods of gratification will be attempted. Sometimes, an actual attempt will be preceded by a trial attempt in fantasy or in a dream. For example, a woman in this phase of therapy reported a dream in which she was intensely involved in a political argument. She recalled that in her life she had always been afraid of becoming involved in anything on her own, but followed the dictates of others and as a result found most of her activities to be devoid of joy or real pleasure. The one exception to this pattern occurred during her early college years

when she became very interested in politics and considered major-
ing in political science. She secretly joined radical political groups
and intensely enjoyed long discussions about social issues. Then
she met her future husband who forbade her to associate with
radicals and she dutifully obeyed. This brief rebellion was forgotten for 20 years until, through therapy, she again dared to feel
committed, albeit only in a dream. She remarked on how "good"
it felt to be involved in something in the dream. The fact that she
used the metaphor of an argument may have represented the resistance that not only herself, but others would mount to her
changing.

It was mentioned earlier that depressives rarely have hobbies or
interests that are not meant to win approval from others. The patient will shy away from pleasurable activities, deriding these behaviors as "childish" or "impractical." However, what he is actually avoiding is the risk of attempting anything without the sanc-
tion of a dominant other. There is an intense feeling of guilt over
enjoyment, as well as a fear that pleasure will bring abandonment.
This is to be interpreted as a remnant of the patient's childhood
experience in which he was punished (usually by threats of separation or by being made to feel selfish) if he dared to enjoy independent behavior.

This conflict over daring to experience pleasure was clearly illustrated in a dream of a depressed woman. On the day preceeding
the dream, we had discussed how she had inhibited herself in
childhood, and especially in adolescence, when she had felt uneasy
by boys becoming attracted to her. She remembered that she was
flattered by their attentions, but at the same time felt guilty about
feeling so frivolous, and worried that her interest in boys would
detract from her studies and anger her father. In the dream, there
was a beautiful room in which there were two women: one "thin
and sallow with a childish body who is downcast"; and the other
"voluptuous with shiny brown hair and beautiful intricate tattoos
on her body." The voluptuous woman was saying "Use my body
and I'm happy." Then she went into a magnificent and luxurious
bathroom exuding a great sensual aura. Suddenly, this beautiful
woman did something "disgusting" which could not be exactly
specified. The scene immediately changed to a hospital room
where the patient learned, from a teen-age boyfriend who had
been mentioned in the session, that her father was dying. The patient felt "sad and horrible" as well as guilty and abandoned, but

was helpless to prevent the death. The boyfriend tried to console her and finally said "I've always loved you" to the patient, whereupon she awakened in a state of anxiety.

This dream is complicated by reference to childhood masturbation, as well as the fact that the body had special importance to this woman because she had been anorexic in her late teens. Nevertheless the conflict between sensual pleasure and self-denial is clear in her visualization of the two contrasting women, and the sequence of the dream where pleasure gives rise to loss of the father (which is then fortunately reconciled by the love of an old boyfriend). In this dream, as in many others, the area of conflict is over sexual pleasure; this ultimately represents, however, a defying of the dominant other for one's own gratification, regardless of the mode in which the gratification is obtained. Similar dreams could be reported utilizing other modalities of pleasure with the ever present sequellae of loss and abandonment.*

It is during the psychotherapeutic attack on this pleasure anxiety that the therapist can offer himself as a model to the patient as an individual who is able to enjoy life and independent interests. If a good working alliance has been formed, the patient will understand that even esteemed doctors do not have to be deadly serious all the time, but may take time for nonproductive activity that is simply fun.

Concommitant with this shift from other-rewarded to self-rewarded activity, a transformation in human relationships hopefully will emerge. The depressive's involvement with others has been narcissistic and need-fulfilling, with the result that people were important only to the extent that they could give praise or absolve guilt. There was never an attempt to appreciate others as people in their own right. It is amazing that these individuals who are so adept at manipulating the desired response from others, are so unknowledgeable about significant aspects of the inner life of individuals. They do not seem to appreciate the core of a man but only his superficialities. As such, depressives often appear psychopathic in their subtle control of others and seeming disregard for the independent welfare of others. Yet all their efforts are directed at the effect it will produce in others. Cohen and her coworkers

---

*In terms of therapeutic progress, it is obviously important that the dream resolves itself with the patient being loved by a nonfamilial individual. It may be that the patient realized that the death of the dominant other, painful as it may be, allows her to experience closeness and love, as well as pleasure.

(1954) remarked on what they called "the stereotyped response" in depressed patients, which meant that other individuals, the therapist included, could only be viewed as stereotyped repetitions of parental figures rather than as a different, specific human being. Others are not conceived of as complex people, containing both bad and good, or as existing outside the orbit of the depressive's needs. Cohen and her colleagues believe that this stereotyping is a defensive maneuver in that the depressive is afraid to acknowledge unpleasant traits in significant others, and trace this defect to a childhood failure in integrating part-objects into a whole good and bad object. This stereotyping appears to be a manipulative estimation of others in terms of whether they can become surrogate sources of self-esteem, that is whether they will fulfill an intrapsychic need.*

In adult life, the depressive searches for a suitable individual on whom he can project the role of dominant other so that he can function in terms of obtaining esteem and escaping guilt about everyday behavior. This other is bestowed with all sorts of magical powers and directives. The depressive then distorts this other to fulfill his inner needs, and simultaneously modifies his behavior to meet what he believes the other desires. Freud (1921) was well aware of this pathological form of ego-object relationship and described it in detail in his *Group Psychology and the Analysis of the Ego*. In this work, Freud demonstrated how, in certain circumstances, the "object" is put in the place of the ego ideal so that an external other serves the purpose of a normally internal agency. As for the effects of this process on the ego, Freud commented: "it [the ego] is impoverished, it has surrendered itself to the object, it has substituted the object for its most important constituent." It is the therapist's responsibility to resist the patient's distortions, to interpret the transference, and to restore this most important constituent with an independent, intrapsychic agency.

The basic problem of the depressive is that he has remained a child in the area of obtaining self-esteem, and therefore needs others to determine his worth. As Arieti has indicated in another context, the original interpersonal relationship of parent and child

---

*However, the excellent work of Cohen et al. may not be directly applicable here in that they based their interpretations on hospitalized manic-depressives who are much more impaired than the patients I have described. Furthermore, it is again questionable how much of this stereotyping was the result of being severly depressed, and how much pertained to the individual's premorbid mode of interrelating.

has not been transformed into an intrapsychic situation of various mental agencies. Therefore, the depressive continues to parentify others, using them as an external conscience, and restricts his own behavior to obedience or rebellion. Here then, is the interface between the interpersonal and intrapsychic in depression: *Others are used in the place of internal agencies within the self, and the individual projects upon others distorted images from the past.* This dual process forms the basis of therapy with depressives, and the various manifestations of the character defenses may be traced to it. In short, the depressive has failed to develop internal regulators of self-esteem.

In order for the change to occur during this middle phase of treatment, a "cognitive restructuring" in various areas must occur; there must be an alteration of the meaning that the patient assigns to his usual experiences and anticipations. In terms of self, a decrease in expectancies and an ability to derive pleasure from one's activities is basic. New meanings are given to the usual everyday experiences with others, as well as to events in the past. Other people and their behavior are viewed differently and therefore evoke different emotions than they had previously. This "cognitive restructuring" does not apply only to interpersonal experiences. The individual is able to acknowledge thoughts and feelings which in the past he had to repress. There is an overall enlargement of consciousness as a result of the self being able to deal with intrapsychic material without fear or guilt. Fantasy life becomes richer and independent of the previously recurring themes of dependency and manipulation.

Therefore, the encouraging of independent activities, the resolution of the deprivation depression, and an alteration in the mode of interpersonal behavior, form the bulk of the second stage of treatment. As the patient actually becomes free with others, he may be surprised that he is not rejected or punished. A young woman in the initial stages of therapy reported the following dream which, in a different way, states the same theme. She dreamt she was disguised as a specific character on a daytime TV soap opera who was intensely loved by her husband and other men. In the dream the TV husband is kissing and embracing the disguised patient who enjoys the experience, but who, at the same time, realizes that she can only obtain love by being someone else. If she were discovered to be who she really is, no one would love her. This illustrates, again, the theme of having to pretend to be someone else in order to win love. The patient felt that if she were to act according to her own desires and not to please others, she would be abandoned. A crucial step is that of truly trusting others and not having to coerce their support through emotional bribery or threats. The individual may feel, for the first time, that he can be liked or loved without his usual machinations.

At the same time, behavior toward the therapist changes; he is no longer the center of the patient's world. At this stage new material may be presented — material which the patient previously feared would alienate the therapist. Therapy is no longer a game to win the therapist's love but, hopefully, a mutual endeavor in which a new mode of being is explored and solidified.

This is the time of "working through," during which current behavior is examined, related to the past or to possible transference, and either encouraged or discouraged through interpretation. Here, Beck's (1967) "cognitive" style of therapy may be useful in correcting the patient's distortions and in identifying the stimuli which elicit erroneous modes of reacting. While this type of analysis is done throughout the therapeutic process, it can, at this time be done explicitly with the patient's consent as a joint endeavor. During this stage of treatment dreams are especially crucial since they often betray old patterns of functioning despite surface improvement. The patient can begin to adequately scrutinize his own thoughts and feelings and to search out possible areas of regression, as well as areas of healthy change. He can accept more of the therapeutic task and function more as a typically neurotic individual in therapy.

The final stage of therapy deals mainly with external rather than internal obstacles to change, when the patient needs the therapist's support to continue functioning in his newly acquired mode. Realistic problems that arise during this time are the result of the patient's altering his way of relating and his way of seeing himself. This is true in most instances of psychotherapeutic change but, perhaps, more so in the case of depressives, since so much of their former pathology involved specific relationships. Parents, spouses, friends, or employers may try to prevent changes in what had been for them a comfortable relationship with the patient. Usually, their obstructions will take the form of inducing guilt or shame in the patient regarding his new independence from them. One patient's mother, for example, threatened suicide because the patient wished to move out on her own. The patient needs the therapist to fortify his resolve to break old patterns of behavior. Setbacks are to be expected, as are frequent angry denunciations of the manipulative behavior of others with which the patient had formerly complied, but of which he was unaware. Thus the final stage of treatment for depressives is similar to that for other neurotic disorders. A consistent, new pattern of being emerges and is consolidated over time despite obstacles from within and without.

The success of this stage of therapy can be ascertained by the emergence of specific characteristics which were previously absent in the patient. Almost all these characteristics revolve around the fundamental sense of freedom from the reactions of others, and the crystallization of the capability to independently assess one's self-esteem. Creativity in the arts or in applying original ideas in work is sometimes evidenced in this stage of treatment. It must be realized that every creative attempt carries with it the risk of being not only inadequate, but also rejected. Therefore, the patient's freedom to experiment and try something new bespeaks a trust in one's self and in others. Related to the outbreak of creativity is the growth of a sense of fun and humor that was lacking in previous interchanges, since to be joyful or exuberant was seen as dangerous because the old authorities insisted on serious work and diligent performance. As mentioned above, there is an expansion of interest in others, and a learning from the experience of others. This new mode of relating appears to be based on a widening sense of empathy in which the patient can identify with others and see them as separate but similar individuals. Previously, the depressive had a psychopathic type of empathy — he knew how to obtain a reaction, but could never truly place himself in the role of another and share his experiences. An ability to show anger over realistic situations will indicate that the patient feels secure enough to assert himself.

Coming to terms with the ghosts of the past is also necessary; the transition is, too often, from one of overestimation of dominant others in the past to angry recriminations against these others. Before termination of therapy, the past must be accepted without excessive rancor. Similarly, the relationship with the therapist takes on the attitude of friendship, with neither too much gratitude nor admiration. The sharing of experiences allows the patient to feel more like a copartner and less of a patient. The door should be left open however, because the patient needs the therapist as the one individual with whom he can be genuine and open until he can establish other such relationships in everyday life.

Although depressive patients can often be difficult, anger-provoking, and even boring, ultimately they may be the most rewarding in that, through therapy, they can begin to utilize their considerable talents in the service of selfless endeavors rather than in forcing others to grant them infantile devotion.

References

Arieti, S. (1962), The psychotherapeutic approach to depression, *Amer. J. Psychother.*, **16**, 397–406.
Arieti, S. (1976), Psychodynamics of severe depression: Theory and therapy, *J. Amer. Acad. Psychoanal.*, **4**, 327–345.
Beck, A. (1967), *Depression: Clinical, Experimental, and Theoretical Aspects*, Paul B. Hoeber, New York.
Becker, E. (1964), *The Revolution in Psychiatry*, Free Press, Glencoe.
Bemporad, J. R. (1971), New Views on the Psychodynamics of the Depressive Character, in *World Biennial of Psychiatry*, S. Arieti, Ed., Basic Books, New York.
Bemporad, J. R. (1973), The role of other in some forms of psychopathology, *J. Amer. Acad. Psychoanal.*, **1**, 367–379.
Bibring, E. (1953), The Mechanism of Depression, in *Affective Disorders*, P. Greenacre, Ed., International Universities Press, New York.
Bonime, W. (1960), Depression as a practice, *Comp. Psychiat.*, **1**, 194–198.
Bonime, W. (1962a), *The Clinical Use of Dreams*, Basic Books, New York.
Bonime, W. (1962b), Dynamics and Psychotherapy of Depression, in *Current Psychiatric Therapies*, Grune & Stratton, New York.
Cohen, M. B., G. Blake, R. A. Cohen, F. Fromm-Reichman, and E. V. Weigert (1954), An intensive study of twelve cases of manic-depressive psychosis, *Psychiatry*, **17**, 103–138.
Fairbairn, W. R. D. (1952), *Psychoanalytic Studies of the Personality*, Tavistock Publications, London.
Freud, S. (1900), *The Interpretation of Dreams*, Standard Edition, Vols. 4 and 5, Hogarth Press, London.
Freud, S. (1917), *Mourning and Melancholia*, Standard Edition, Vol. 14, Hogarth Press, London.
Freud, S. (1921), *Group Psychology and the Analysis of the Ego*, Standard Edition, Vol. 18, Hogarth Press, London.
Green, A. W. (1946), The middle class male child and neurosis, *Amer. Social Rev.*, **11**, 31–41.
Guntrip, H. (1969), *Schizoid Phenomena, Object Relations and the Self*, International Universities Press, New York.
Jacobson, E. (1971), *Depression*, International Universities Press, New York.
Klein, M. (1948), *Contributions to Psycho-Analysis 1921-1945*, Hogarth Press, London.

Kolb, L. C. (1956), Psychotherapeutic evolution and its implications, *Psychiat. Quart.*, 1-19.

Sandler, J. and W. G. Joffe (1965), Notes on childhood depression, *Int. J. Psychoanal.*, **46**, 88-96.

Seligman, M. E. P. (1975), *Helplessness*, W. H. Freeman, San Francisco.

Slipp, S. (1976), An Intrapsychic - interpersonal theory of depression, *J. Amer. Acad. Psychoanal.*, **4**, 389-409.

TEN

Psychoanalysis Of Severe Depression: Theory And Therapy

SILVANO ARIETI

INTRODUCTION

Since the classic works of Abraham (1911) and Freud (1917), psychoanalysis has made considerable steps forward in the interpretation of depression. For example, Rado's (1928, 1951) conception that melancholia is a despairing cry for love, an attempt of the ego to punish itself in order to prevent the parental punishment, by enacting guilt, atonement, and forgiveness; Klein's (1935, 1948) interpretation of this condition as a pathological outcome of the depressive position; Bibring's (1953) concept of depression as a conflict of the ego, a state of helplessness consequent to loss of self-esteem, are important contributions from either the Freudian or the Kleinian schools. A noteworthy contribution in the cultural school, is Bonime's (1960, 1966), who sees depression as a practice. According to Bonime, "The depressive is an extremely manipulative individual who, by helplessness, sadness, seductiveness, and other means, maneuvers people toward the fulfillment of demands for various forms of emotionally comforting response." (1966).

In spite of these significant advances, one can repeat for depression what can be said for practically every area of psychiatry: no conclusive or decisive statement has been made, and no major breakthrough leading to a definitive position has occurred. As a matter of fact, some authors have reached pessimistic conclusions about this state of affairs. Grinker and his associates (1961), considered the dynamic formulations of depression stereotyped and inadequate. Mendelson (1960), in concluding his book on psychoanalytic concepts of depression, wrote: "It would have been pleasing to be able to report that this body of literature represented, in essence, a progress through the years of a Great Investigation. It does so in part. But perhaps even more does it represent a Great Debate with the rhetorical rather than scientific implications of this word."

Mendelson adds that his book on depression represents the summary of an era. "The era was chiefly characterized by boldly speculative theoretical formulations and by insightful clinical studies . . . . This era is drawing to a close."

Is Mendelson right? Is this era drawing to a close? Must we stop groping? Why have the contributions mentioned above remained involved only with some aspects of the large human phenomenon of depression?

Depression, as a pathological variety of sadness, penetrates and involves the whole person, from his core to his highest and spiritual manifestations. We cannot limit our vision of it in order to fit it in the procrustean bed of a theory based on instincts. When Freud (1922) added to his theoretical framework the death instinct, or Thanatos theory, this concept, as far as depression was concerned, did nothing to clarify further his previous, and very useful concepts, of incorporation and introjection.

The cultural point of view that sees depression as a practice, that is as a system of manipulating techniques, is a very useful concept, especially in cases of mild depression. In the more severe cases, patients whom I have called suffering from the claiming type of depression, I (1962, 1974) have independently differentiated symptoms identical or similar to those described by Bonime. This claiming, demanding, clinging, appealing attitude, covered by the cloak of depression, is easily recognized in a special group of patients. But these maneuvers, which might explain the use of depression in some cases, do not clarify the nature of depression itself, as a specific subjective experience, nor its psychotic manifestations, nor its invasion of every aspect of human existence, to the point of endangering that existence. New ways of understanding both the feeling of sadness, which belongs to the repertory of normal emotions, and depression, an abnormal type of sadness that occurs in some psychiatric conditions, are needed. In this work I shall discuss some major points of my cognitive approach to depression, and report a successfully treated case of severe depression. Lack of space does not permit me to describe other cognitive approaches, such as the one by Beck (1967).

A COGNITIVE APPROACH TO DEPRESSION

In the emotional repertory of every human being, sadness plays an important role; usually as a reaction to something unpleasant, generally a loss – physical, psychological, or moral. Eventually the individual puts into effect special mechanisms, like a reorganization of his thinking or determinate actions in order to hasten the coming of better days (Arieti 1959, 1967, 1968). But it is not so in depression, an emotion related to sadness, which occurs in psychiatric conditions. Pathological depression, especially in its severe forms, seems excessive relative to the events that have elicited it, or inappropriate in relation to its known cause or precipitating factors, or a substitute for a more appropriate emotion when it takes the place of anxiety, anger, or hostility. In many cases depression does not seem to have been caused by any antecedent factor of which the person is conscious.

According to my studies of patients treated psychoanalytically, there is always a preceding ideology, or a way of seeing oneself in life in general, or in relation with another particular person, that prepares the ground for the depression. Although it is true that a depressive affect searches for and finds pessimistic ideas that justify the affect, initially the opposite takes place. The patient's ideology preexisted and was kept alive for a long time, in conscious or unconscious forms. Although the patient might have been aware of the importance of these systems of cognitive constructs, he was unconscious of their origin, of how much they involved, or of all the ramifications, assumptions, presuppositions, and feelings connected with them. These cognitive domains in most cases originated in childhood but continued to accrue throughout life.

At a certain time in the life of the individual, either an external event or an inner reappraisal of one's life brings about the twilight, disintegration, or loss of one or more of these fundamental constructs. Depression is the reaction to this inner loss, as well as to the inability to repair the loss. Although an external event of great importance, like the loss of a loved person, or of a position, or of a great hope, may have precipitated the episode, the significance of such loss by far exceeds the involved reality. The external event brings about the collapse of conscious or unconscious assumptions. The loss is the loss of a part of the psychological self. The sorrow at times acts as a representative of what was lost, because as long as at least the sorrow remains, the loss is not complete. The sorrow is the shadow of the absent, the echo of a voice that was heard repeatedly, perhaps with ambiguous resonance but also with love, respect, and hope. The impact of these psychological changes produces an exaggeration or distortion of reality, or may include reality and unreality in a surrealistic transformation of affects.

These cognitive constructs that suddenly or gradually undergo disintegration generally have a double entity; they consist of what seems a psychological bifurcation. One branch of this bifurcation deals with the self-image. Thus the destruction of the construct implies a new evaluation of one's self and of one's life, with all the hidden meanings, implications, and ramifications, causing a tremor to the whole psychological fabric of the individual, a profound intrapsychic process.

On the other hand, the construct has an interpersonal branch which has to do with another person, very important to the patient. I have called this person the *dominant other* (Arieti 1962, 1974). The dominant other has until now provided the patient with the evidence, real or illusory, or at least the hope that acceptance, love, respect, and recognition of his human worth were acknowledged by at least another person. Thus the interpersonal branch of the bifurcation is intimately connected with the intrapsychic, with the self-image, the way the patient experiences himself. The dominant other is represented most often by the spouse. Far less often, in order of frequency, follow the mother, a person to whom the patient is romantically attached, an adult child, a sister, the father. Also, the dominant other is represented frequently through anthropomorphization, by the firm where the patient works, or a social institution to which he belongs, like the church, the political party, the army, the club, a group or class of people, and so forth. As I have previously illustrated (1959, 1974) all these dominant others are often symbolic of the depriving mother, the mother unwilling to give the promised love. If the real mother is still living and is the dominant other, she will act in two ways — as her present role actually is, and also symbolically of her old one.

Often the precipitating factor of the psychotic depression is directly connected to the dominant other: The dominant other left or died, and the patient feels without sustenance, believes that he has finally been deprived of his love, as he was once deprived of the love of his mother. Or the dominant other has died before the relation with the patient was clarified. As Bemporad has illustrated

(1970), the patient finds that now he cannot depend any more on the dominant other for his self-esteem, approval, narcissistic supplies. It becomes obvious that he is incapable of autonomous gratification.

The second important situation which brings about this discontinuity is the realization, often only subliminally perceived or admitted, of the failure of the relationship with the dominant other. This symbolic parent, generally the marital partner, is recognized, or half-consciously recognized, as a tyrant who took advantage of the compliant, submissive attitude of the patient, rather than as a person to be loved and cherished. The patient has tolerated everything, wanting peace at any cost, but it becomes impossible for him to continue to do so. He feels that he has wasted his life in devoting himself to the spouse, in loving her or forcing himself to love her at any cost, just as he did with his mother in childhood. The realization that the spouse deserves not devotion but hate, is something the patient could not easily accept because it would have undermined the foundation of his whole life, would have proved the futility of all his efforts. In some cases the dominant other at a reality level has been active only in the past, but, by having been introjected, remains alive even if he happens to be dead. The dominant other might have been a parent who imposed an impossible goal or ideal on the patient. The patient must become a great man, win the Nobel Prize, become a great writer, a big financier, a doctor, an actress, a dancer, a devoted, self-sacrificing mother of six children, etc. When the patient senses, suddenly or gradually, that he is not going to attain this life goal, the cognitive construct is imperiled, both in the interpersonal branch of the bifurcation, with implied loss of love from the dominant other, and the intrapsychic branch, with loss of the cherished self-image. If the patient identified with the parent, the situation is even more complicated: there is a total destruction of the self-image and of the positive aspect of the relation with the dominant other. When these appraisals threaten to emerge, or actually do emerge to consciousness, a rupture to the psychological equilibrium occurs. Metaphorically, the patient bleeds profusely. Although he is alive, the hopes, ideals, and meanings for which he lived are dying or dead already. Thus he must die too, put an end to this meaningless life where only sorrow is meaningful. In these pathological cases the process of cognitive reorganization, that occurs in cases of normal sadness, is doomed to fail. The patient cannot replace the collapsing constructs with new ones, cannot renew his life or emerge again to a different mode of existence. Instead, another process occurs which brings about several degrees of pathology. The depression, rather than forcing a reorganization of ideas, slows down the thought processes. In this case, the psychological mechanism seems to have the purpose of decreasing the quantity of thoughts in order to decrease the quantity of suffering. At times the slowing down of thought processes is so pronounced (as in the state of stupor) that only a few thoughts of a general or atmospheric quality are left; these are accompanied by an overpowering feeling of melancholy.

But this is a self-defeating mechanism. When the depression becomes overwhelming, it takes possession of practically the whole psyche. Thinking is reduced to a minimum and the patient is aware only of the overpowering feeling of depression. If the patient is asked why he is depressed, he may even say that he does not know. Often the ideas or thoughts that have triggered off the depression become almost immediately submerged by the depression; they become unconscious. In these cases, the depression serves the same function that repression does in other psychiatric conditions. The cognitive components are repressed, but the painful feeling is very intensely experienced at the level of consciousness. I must add that in a considerable number of patients, although a smaller number than used to be, the depression is accompanied by a profound guilt feeling. The patient feels responsible for whatever has happened that brought about his psychological collapse. If some energy is left, it must be used for self-punishment. Vaguely it is felt that enough punishment will restore the acceptable self-image. In this group of patients the idea-feeling of guilt is often the last thought to remain conscious before it is also submerged by the oceanic feeling of depression.

In previous contributions (1962, 1974) I have described in detail the role of the psychotherapist in the treatment of severe depression. Contrary to what happens in schizophrenia, where the psychosis is a consequence of a failure of cosmic magnitude, involving as a rule the relation with the whole world, the failure of the depressed patient is experienced mainly or exclusively in relation to what I have called basic cognitive constructs and in relation to the dominant other. The task of the therapist is to study these basic constructs and the relationship with the dominant other, and the injuries that they have undergone.

When the therapist enters the life of the very depressed patient, and proves his genuine desire to help, to reach, to nourish, to offer hope, he will often be accepted, but only as a *dominant third* (Arieti 1974). Immediate relief may be obtained, because the patient sees in the analyst a new and reliable love-object. Although the establishment of this type of relatedness may be helpful to the subsequent therapy, it cannot be considered a real cure; as a matter of fact, it may be followed by another attack of depression when the patient realizes the limitation of this type of therapeutic intervention. The analyst must be not a dominant third, but a *significant third,* a third person with a straightforward, sincere, and unambiguous type of personality, who wants to help the patient without making threatening demands. He will help the patient to give up the old constructs and build new ones. He will show to him that if he had remained fixated to the old ideology or to the past ways of life, they would have fossilized his existence. Renewal and self-emergence are possible, and with them the potential for a more meaningful life.

The following case will illustrate in a paradigmatic fashion the theoretical premises that I have mentioned, as well as some therapeutic modalities. This report deals with one of the most severe cases of depression that I have ever seen; a case where the threat to previously established basic constructs and the change in relation with the dominant other were brought about by a significant event in the life of the patient: the birth of her child. Although I believe that I have clarified and brought to solution the main aspects of this case, by no means do I claim that I have understood it in its entirety. The reader will certainly discover several still untapped possibilities and issues which are in need of further discussion.

CASE REPORT

Lisette was 24-years-old when I first saw her. She was a white woman from Australia, and was in this country with her husband, who had won a scholarship to do postgraduate research in New York City. Here is a brief account of the events that brought her to me. Several months previously she had given birth to a girl. Immediately after the birth she became depressed; however, she and her family did not give too much importance to her condition, and she received no treatment. Her condition became much worse, and eventually she had to be hospitalized for a few months. She was treated with drug therapy; she improved and was discharged. A few weeks later, however, she started again to be seriously depressed. She started treatment with a psychoanalyst of classic orientation, but there was no improvement. On the contrary, the situation was deteriorating rapidly. The patient became unable to take care of the baby and was completely incapacitated. Her mother-in-law, who lived in Australia, was summoned to New York to help the patient. When she arrived, the patient resented her very much, so she returned to Australia. Then the patient's mother came and remained with her for several months. Suicidal ideas were freely expressed by the patient and suicide was an impending threat. She could not be left alone. When I first saw her entering the waiting room of my office, she was accompanied by her mother and husband, who were sustaining her on each side, almost to prevent her from falling. When I looked at her face for the first time, I saw a picture of intense sadness and abandon, so picturesque as to give me a fleeting impression that perhaps it was not genuine, but histrionic and theatrical. I had never seen such scenes before except in Italian movies. But when Lisette was alone with me in my office, her real suffering revealed itself; it was a genuine, uncontrollable, overpowering, all evolving, all absorbing, all devastating depression. The feeling of hopelessness and despair, as well as the motor retardation prevented her from talking freely. Nevertheless she managed to tell me briefly that her therapist was not doing her any good; she was sick and wanted to die. When I spoke to her mother and husband later (she was being closely watched in the waiting room by another person), they told me that I was supposed to be only a consultant. They wanted to know whether the patient should receive electric shock treatment; it was no longer possible to manage her at home. They were consulting me to find out whether I was firmly opposed to electric shock treatment in this case. In view of the failure of drug therapy, of psychoanalytic treatment, and the seriousness and urgency of the situation, I told the husband that shock treatment should be tried, and that they should consult me again afterward. The patient received 15 shocks. This is a large number for depressed patients, who generally receive an average of five. The treatment was eventually stopped, however, because there was no improvement. I remembered, from my early experiences at Pilgrim State Hospital, that depressed patients who do not improve even after such a large number of treatments have a poor prognosis. When Lisette returned to see me, she was still very depressed, very suicidal, still hopeless. In spite of 15 grand mals there was practically no memory impairment. She told me that she strongly resented going back to her analyst or for more electric shock treatment, and begged me to accept her in therapy.

I wish to describe my feelings when she made this request, partially because of narcissism on my part, but also because I believe that it is important to evaluate the feelings of the analyst at the beginning of the treatment of every seriously ill patient. I told myself, "This is another one of those hard cases that end up in my office. Will I ever get to see an easy-to-treat neurotic?" At the same time, however, I experienced a desire to face the challenge. I was very touched by that profound, seemingly infinite pain. I was also perplexed. I already understood that all this had to do with the birth of the child, but how a birth could produce such devastating depression was still a mystery to me. At the time of this consultation, which occurred about ten years ago, I was familiar with postpartum schizophrenic psychoses, but had not had much experience with postpartum depressions. What basic construct or what relation was undergoing a disintegration capable of producing such a violent and seemingly unhealing process in that young, promising, intelligent, and sensitive young woman?

When I discussed the matter with her previous therapist, he did not object to terminating his treatment, so Lisette came to me. Here is a brief history of the patient, as it was collected during the first few months of treatment.

The patient was born in a small town, contiguous to a big city in Australia. The parents belonged to the upper middle class. The father was a successful divorce lawyer, blessed with a cheerful character that made him see the world with rose-colored glasses, and helped him to make a brilliant career. His refined form of shallowness, with such effervescent optimism, made him navigate surely and fast, but without leaving a wake. The patient felt much closer to her mother, who actually was a much more demanding person. Her mother had a humanistic education, would speak about art, literature, poetry in particular, and seemed to have much more in common with the patient. She helped her with her homework while the patient was in high school and college. Her mother also made many demands and, according to Lisette, in her face there was almost a constant expression of disapproval.

Mother had been engaged to a man who died during the engagement. She often referred to this man with enthusiastic terms never used in relation to father. Although father adored mother, mother had for father only a lukewarm, amicable relation. The marriage of the parents was defined by Lisette as fairly good, but not marvelous. The patient knew that sexual life between the parents was not a thrilling one. Mother had told her that she merely obliged.

Earlier in life mother had suffered from epilepsy and also depression. Mother's epilepsy and depression had both started with the birth of the patient's brother. Mother became depressed to such a point that four-year-old Lisette had to be sent to live with her grandmother for a while. Incidentally, this grandmother, mother's mother, is the only person throughout Lisette's childhood who shines as a giver of affection, love, warmth, and care. Lisette always loved her dearly. In spite of grandmother's affection, separation from mother was experienced as a trauma by Lisette. Mother recovered quickly from her depression, but as already mentioned, she had also developed epilepsy. There was an atmosphere of secrecy in the family about mother's epilepsy. In fact, Lisette had never seen mother having an attack until she, Lisette, was 20. On that occasion, Lisette called God to help mother, but in mother's face was God's denial of her request. The truth could no longer be concealed, and she experienced a sense of horror, moral horror because of the denial by God.

Although the patient was always very good in school, during adolescence she felt inferior and unattractive. She had a negative attitude toward life. Everything that appeared good or likable, also appeared superficial, like father. Everything that was deep and worthwhile appeared inaccessible, like mother's approval. There was no doubt in her mind that mother had always preferred her brother, for whom she had strong rivalry and jealousy. She went through a period of rebellion, during which she felt people were empty, superficial, made of plastic. She did not care how she looked and was neglectful of her appearance. Because she was not well dressed and because of her bohemian ways, she felt she was disapproved of, not only by her mother but also by the upper middle class of the small town where she lived. And yet as much as Lisette was critical of these people, she seemed to need their approval and acceptance.

When Jack, a young man of the lower middle class, started to pay attention to her, she was grateful that somebody had noticed her presence. Soon she felt very much in love with him, admired his idealism, intelligence, interest in research; and when Jack graduated from school, they got married. The patient stated that her marriage was a happy one from the very beginning. The only thing that she resented in her marriage was her husband's family, and especially her husband's mother. Jack's mother was different from her son, cheap, vulgar, materialistic. Very coarse, she would eat with her fingers, and sniff tobacco. She was also narrow minded. To the degree that Jack was desirable, his mother was undesirable. Jack won a research fellowship in the United States, and everybody was very happy. In the meantime, however, Lisette had become pregnant. The pregnancy was accidental, and came at a very inopportune time. The patient was angry about it and experienced nausea. Although the pregnancy was a complication, Lisette and her husband came to the United States in May, during her fifth month of pregnancy. The baby was expected in September.

Lisette told me that during her pregnancy she had had a peculiar idea. I must make it clear that when I first heard about it, the idea did indeed appear so peculiar as to make me think of a schizophrenic disorder. Lisette told me that during her pregnancy she had the feeling that her mother-in-law had entered her. "What do you mean?" I asked, and apparently I unwittingly approached her with an obvious feeling of perplexity or even consternation. Lisette told me with a reassuring voice, "Don't worry. I did not mean it literally. My husband's sperm that had impregnated me contained genes inherited from his mother. I was displeased that inside of me a baby was growing that was partially a derivation of my mother-in-law."

In spite of this reassurance the idea seemed bizarre to me, and, in a different context, I still would have considered the possibility of schizophrenia. In fact, we know that in preschizophrenics and schizophrenics certain expressions used metaphorically are forerunners of delusions. In these cases the delusion eventually denotes literally what was previously meant in a metaphorical sense. However, in this case nothing else was schizophrenic or schizophrenic-like. I had to rely on my clinical experience with schizophrenics to evaluate the clinical picture in its totality and exclude such possibility. The future development of the case supported my clinical evaluation that there was no schizophrenia.

The patient gave birth in the month of September, and the symptomatology of a depression started to be manifested first in mild and later in very pronounced form. The childbirth represented a focal or central point from which the whole manifest symptomatology originated and irradiated in various directions. For a long time Lisette could not even talk about the birth of Clare in more than fleeting, passing remarks. The episode of the birth itself, as experienced by Lisette, was painful to such a tragic degree as to prevent discussion of it until the ground had been prepared

by the treatment. At this point it may be useful to evaluate, however, what we already know about Lisette's case and to delineate
some basic constructs.

In the life of this patient there was a dominant other, and this
person was not the husband but the mother, the mother so much
needed for approval, and from whom the approval was so uncertain; the mother with whom she would like to identify, but can
no longer. This dominant mother as a basic construct has a satellite, the mother-in-law. The patient did not have to be as careful in
her conceptions about the mother-in-law as she had to be in reference to her mother. Without guilt or compunction of any sort, and
strengthened by some realistic facts, Lisette displaced to the
mother-in-law some of the bad characteristics of her mother, and
the feeling that she had for her mother. The mother-in-law was not
only vulgar and disapproving, but she herself had made Lisette become a mother. The mother-in-law becomes, although at a quasi-
metaphorical level, the phallic mother who entered Lisette and
made her pregnant. The husband is totally dismissed; the mother-
in-law, who had made her become a mother, was a monstrous distortion of Lisette's mother. If Lisette accepted her pregnancy, she
had to accept her mother and her mother-in-law, and what they
stood for. If they stood for motherhood, that was a motherhood
she wanted to reject. Accepting their type of motherhood meant
being as they were and giving up the self-image, a cognitive construct about herself which was cherished and gratifying. The fact
remains, however, that during the pregnancy Lisette was apparently all right. It was the childbirth itself that precipitated the condition; but Lisette did not want to talk about the birth for a long
time.

From the beginning of treatment I got the impression that
Lisette could open up to me. I was immediately accepted by her as
a dominant third, and when she trusted me fully and saw me as an
undemanding, accepting, and not disapproving person, I became a
significant third. I had the feeling that although she did not consider me a source of love, she saw in me a source of strength, clarity, and hope.

For several months the sessions were devoted to studying her relations with her mother; how Lisette lived for mother's approval.
A look, a gesture of disapproval would make her sink into a deep
state of depression. To be disapproved of by mother meant utter
rejection, unworthiness. She required to be taken care of, fussed
over by mother, as grandmother did. Grandmother was really the

person to whom the patient was close. Her affection was a profuse, steady flow, and Lisette had no fear of interruption because of sudden disapproval. In contrast, mother's approval could always end abruptly whenever she decided Lisette had made an infraction, no matter how little. There is no doubt that the patient put into operation manipulations and other characteristics as Bonime has described. There was, however, in addition, the constant need for mother's approval, as Bemporad has illustrated. Not only did she want to be mothered by mother, but she wanted mother to have a good opinion of her. Mother seemed to be the only person who counted in her family constellation. And yet many of mother's actions or words were interpreted in a negative way by Lisette; not with the suspicious distortion of the paranoid, but with the adverse appraisal of the depressed. For instance, when mother said that the patient had been lucky in comparison to her, she implied that the patient was spoiled, and had an easy life. When mother said how wonderful Jack was, she meant that Lisette did not measure up to her husband. If mother was making a fuss about Clare and was calling her darling, Lisette would become very depressed, wishing mother would call her in that way. She resented mother terribly and yet could not contemplate the idea of being left alone with Clare if mother went back to Australia. Then she would be overwhelmed by her duties and she would feel completely lost.

Using the insightful formulation of Bemporad (1970), I repeatedly pointed out to Lisette that at present she was incapable of autonomous gratification. Any supply of self-esteem and feeling of personal significance had to come from mother. Mother was not just a dispenser of love, but was put in a position of being almost a dispenser of oxygen and blood. By withdrawing approval, the supply would end and Lisette would become depressed. At the least sign of forthcoming disapproval the supply would be interrupted. Disapproval would bring about in her not only depression, but guilt feelings as well, because she felt she deserved to be disapproved of. And yet a part of her wanted to be like her mother, although her mother was not like her grandmother.

I explained to Lisette that she sustained a first important trauma after the birth of her brother, when she was sent away from the depressed mother and experienced a feeling of deprivation. Moreover, she associated deprivation, loss of love, and depression with childbirth. I have found that in postpartum psychoses, of both schizophrenic and depressed types, the patient makes a double identification, with her mother and with her child. Inasmuch as Lisette identified with her mother, she was a mother incapable of giving love, a mother who would become depressed, a mother who would only love an intruder like Clare. Little Clare became the equivalent of Lisette's brother, who once deprived her of mother's love. If Lisette identified with the child, she felt deprived as a child deprived of love feels. These feelings were confusing and, of course, self-contradictory.

Lisette came to experience treatment as a liberation from mother. Mother's disapproval gradually ceased to mean loss of love and loss of meaning of life. And indeed treatment was a liberation; not so much from mother as a physical reality, but from mother as the mental construct of the dominant other. The relation with the analyst, the significant third, permitted her to stop identifying with mother without losing the sense of herself as a worthwhile human being. Moreover, anticipation of maternal disapproval did not bring about depression or guilt feeling. At the same time that mother lost importance, the satellite constructs of the mother-in-law, as well as of the upper middle class of the little town, lost power. During the early periods of the treatment, in fact, when Lisette could talk about the people in her home town, she was still worried about what they would think of her, in spite of the distance of more than ten thousand miles. At the same time that mother, as an inner object, and the related constructs, were losing value, the husband was acquiring importance. The patient had always admired and respected the husband, but the husband had never been put in a position where his withdrawal of approval would be of vital importance. Now the husband could be enjoyed as a source of love. Lisette's desire for sexual relations returned. The patient became also more capable of sharing interest in Jack's professional and scientific activity. Before she was interested only in humanistic subjects, as mother was.

Up to this point, treatment had consisted of changing the value of some basic constructs so that their loss would not be experienced as a psychological catastrophe, and so that new, more healthy constructs could replace the disrupted and displaced ones. In other words, the patient was searching for and finding a meaning of life which was not dependent on the old constructs, not connected with pathological ideas.

After several months of treatment it was felt that the patient could manage her life alone and mother returned to Australia. The patient had a mild fit of depression, caused by their separation, but no catastrophe occurred. After a while Lisette was asking herself how she could have tolerated her mother in her home for so long.

It took some time after mother left for the patient to bring herself to talk about a most important issue: the experience of childbirth. Lisette explained that when she discovered that she was pregnant, she decided to take a course for expectant mothers on natural childbirth. According to the basic principle of natural birth, the woman in labor does not succumb to the pain, she maintains her grip on herself. The woman in labor should not scream; the scream is ineffectual despair, is being no longer in control of oneself. In spite of the preparation, however, Lisette, while in labor, could not bear the pain and screamed. It was a prolonged, repeated, animal-like scream. While she was screaming, she wanted to kill herself because to scream meant to give up as a human being, to disintegrate. But she screamed; she screamed, she screamed! What a horror to hear herself screaming, what a loss of one's human dignity.

During many sessions the patient discussed her cognitive constructs about childbirth. She resented being a biological entity, more an animal than a woman. Biology was cruel. Women were victims of nature. They became slaves of the reproductive system. You started with the sublimity of romantic love and you ended with the ridiculous and degrading position of giving birth. While giving birth, you were in a passive, immobile position, which was dehumanizing. Nurses and doctors who meant nothing to you, saw you in an animal-like, degrading position. You revolted and screamed and lost your dignity. Lisette wanted her husband to be present in her moment of greatness, during her childbirth, but instead he was witness to her descending to her utmost degradation. Childbirth was the death of love, the death of womanhood. You were no longer you, but a female of an animal species. You became what these dominant adults made you, and, what is even worse, you needed them. You wanted to be liked and loved by them when actually you despised them. You were no longer yourself; already dead because the ideal of yourself, of what you were or what you wanted to become was no longer tenable. You gave up the promise of life. You went through a dissolution of thoughts and beliefs. The pain increased, became insurmountable.

Eventually Lisette felt only pain, physical pain, but also moral pain. She could not think any more. She felt depressed, and the waves of depression submerged her more and more. But at the periphery of her consciousness, some confused thoughts faintly emerged: She did not want to be a mother; she did not want to take care of the child; she would not be able to take care of the child; she could not take care of her home; she should die. It was impossible for her to accept what she had become — a mother — and the concept of motherhood did not hold for her the sublimity which culture attributes to it: rather it held negative, animal-like characteristics. She felt she had probably become an animal-like mother, like her mother-in-law.

At an advanced stage of the treatment Lisette was able to recapture all these thoughts that had occurred to her after the birth of Clare, thoughts which had become more indistinct, almost unconscious, as the depression occupied more and more her consciousness. Treatment permitted the ideas that precipitated the depression, and that the depression had made unconscious, to emerge.

Although they were revealed to me in an intricate confused network, it was not difficult for me to help Lisette disentangle and get rid of them because we had already done the preliminary work. Once we dismantled mother as the inner object of the dominant other and as an object of identification, it was easier to bring the associated ideas back to consciousness. When Lisette gave birth, she rejected motherhood, together with her own mother; and yet she was identified with her mother, who had become depressed after giving birth to Lisette's brother. Thus, by rejecting her mother, she was rejecting herself. In the beginning of treatment she became aware gradually that her suffering was partially due to her not receiving approval and gratification from her mother, but later on she became aware of her greater suffering due to the loss of her basic constructs, which were not replaced by others. Lisette realized that the depression had been so strong as to prevent her from searching for other visions of life. She understood that the physical pain that she sustained during childbirth was symbolic of the greater and more overpowering pain caused by the incoming twilight of the basic constructs. Eventually, the therapy permitted her to accept the loss of these constructs without experiencing depression. Even her attitude about being a member of an animal species changed greatly. She came to accept that we are animals and procreate like animals but we can transcend our animal status. And there is beauty in our animal status, too, provided we are able to fuse it with our spiritual part. The patient was able to reassess old meanings in a nonpathological frame of reference and came to accept new meanings. Treatment made rapid progress. My fear that it would be difficult to change the husband's role in Lisette's life proved unfounded. Contrary to the other males, the father and brother, who were not significant figures, the husband rapidly acquired importance and was fully experienced as a source of love, communion, and intimacy.

Treatment lasted a little over two years. The family has returned to the native country. In a span of seven years there have been no relapses.

Some general thoughts about psychotic depression occur to me when I compare this condition to schizophrenia. Both the schizophrenic and the psychotic depressed lament what they have come to know and feel about life. However, whereas the schizophrenic rejects and symbolically destroys the cruel world, and attempts through projection and special cognition to rebuild his own private universe, the person who is depressed to a psychotic degree does not reject the world, as a mother does not reject a bad child. The psychotic depressed does not even reject his suffering, but accepts it, all of it, and the suffering expands more and more, relentlessly and endlessly into a psyche that seems endless in its capacity to experience sorrow. This sorrow is not completely unfounded. There is always a resonance in our heart for the sorrow of the depressed, which is similar to ours, and a partial truth which is connected with the human predicament. When we successfully treat a patient who is depressed, we do not ask him, of course, to give up his identity, but, rather, whatever lie or impossible value had become connected with that identity. We do not help a human being to lose a sense of commitment, but only the commitment that seduces and saps the self. When we successfully treat a patient who was depressed to a psychotic degree we experience a burst of joy because we have helped a suffering person who is happy to have known us. But we also feel a secret joy, because we have come to know him, and in knowing him we know more of ourselves. Lisette reminded us that we are barely out of the jungle and we can easily resume a purely animal status, not because we are animals — which we are — but because we are humans with ideas. Lisette showed us that no matter how unusual, drastic, or unpleasant the external circumstances happen to be, we ourselves are the great contributors to our own sorrow because of the strange ways in which we mix and give meaning to our ideas and feelings. The study of the circumstances of life is important; but even more important is the study of our ideas about these circumstances, of our ideals and what we do with them, and of how we use them to create feelings. This study may enlighten not just our pathology, but our so-called normality, not just our despair but our hope, not just our loneliness, but our ways of helping each other and reinforcing the human bond.

References

Abraham, K. (1911), Notes on the psycho-analytical investigation and treatment of manic-depressive insanity and allied conditions, in *Selected Papers on Psychoanalysis,* Basic Books, New York, (1953).

Arieti, S. (1959), Manic-depressive psychosis, in *American Handbook of Psychiatry,* 1st ed., Vol. 1, S. Arieti, Ed., Basic Books, New York.

Arieti, S. (1962), The psychotherapeutic approach to depression, *Amer. J. Psychother.,* **16**, 397–406.

Arieti, S. (1967), *The Intrapsychic Self: Feeling, Cognition and Creativity in Health and Mental Illness,* Basic Books, New York.

Arieti, S. (1968), Depressive disorders, in *International Encyclopedia of the Social Sciences,* Macmillan Co. and The Free Press, New York.

Arieti, S. (1973), The intrapsychic and the interpersonal in severe psychopathology, in *Interpersonal Explorations in Psychoanalysis,* E. Witenberg, Ed., Basic Books, New York.

Arieti, S. (1974), Affective disorders: Manic-depressive psychosis and psychotic depression: Manifest symptomatology, psychodynamics, sociological factors, and psychotherapy, in *American Handbook of Psychiatry,* Vol. III, S. Arieti, Ed., Basic Books, New York.

Beck, A. T. (1967), *Depression. Clinical, Experimental, and Theoretical Aspects,* Hoeber, New York.

Bemporad, J. R. (1970), New Views on the psychodynamics of the depressive character, in *The World Biennial of Psychiatry and Psychotherapy,* Vol. 1, S. Arieti, Ed., Basic Books, New York.

Bibring, E. (1953), The mechanism of depression, in *Affective Disorders,* P. Greenacre, Ed., International Universities Press, New York.

Bonime, W. (1960), Depression as a practice: Dynamic and therapeutic considerations, *Comprehen. Psychiat.,* **1**, 194–198.

Bonime, W. (1966), The psychodynamics of neurotic depression, in *American Handbook of Psychiatry,* Vol. 3, S. Arieti, Ed., Basic Books, New York (Republished in this issue, p. 301.)

Freud, S. (1917), Mourning and melancholia, in *Collected Papers,* Vol. 4, Basic Books, New York, (1959).

Freud, S. (1922), *Beyond the Pleasure Principle,* International Psychoanalytic Press, London.

Grinker, R. R., R. J. Mille, M. Sabshin, R. Nunn, and J. C. Nunnally (1961), *The Phenomenon of Depressions,* Hoeber, New York.

Klein, M. (1935), A Contribution to the psychogenesis of manic-depressive states, in Melanie Klein (1948), 282–310.

Klein, M. (1948), *Contributions to Psychoanalysis,* Hogarth Press, London.

Mendelson, M. (1960), *Psychoanalytic Concepts of Depression,* Thomas, Springfield, Illinois.

Rado, S. (1928), The problem of melancholia, *Int. J. Psychoanal.,* **9**, 420–438.

Rado, S. (1951), Psychodynamics of depression from the etiological point of view, *Psychosomatic Med.,* **13**, 51–55.

ELEVEN

Interpretation Of Affect And Affective Interpretation

ILDIKO MOHACSY

BENNETT SILVER

We will begin with a question: Should therapists use their own affects in interpreting the affects of their patients?

Over the years, as our technology has advanced, social critics have time and again voiced the worry that the machine age will eventually catapult us into an emotionally sterile world, a world without affect. That this fear is unfounded should be obvious, above all to the psychoanalyst. Affect is the substrate of our conscious and unconscious life. In Spitz's (1965) words, affect is the trailbreaker of all development. Perception, cognition, language, motor behavior — all of these unfold only in an affect-charged atmosphere, the atmosphere of the parent–child relationship. We do not simply learn to talk, but to talk to mother. We do not just crawl; we crawl to and away from mother. Thus all our capacities, as they develop, are ineradicably stamped with affect. And though, as adults, we may try to ban affect from certain areas of functioning, it invariably resurfaces. In Stanley Kubrick's film fantasy *2001: A Space Odyssey,* there is a telling moment when the spaceship computer, Hal, refuses to obey the commands of one of the scientist-astronauts. Hitherto cold and businesslike, the scientist begins to plead desperately with the machine, begging it to respond. This is a supremely ironic situation. Even in a hypothetical future presumably cleansed of affect, even in the face of a machine devoid of affect, the human creature, under stress, reverts to affect.

Presented at the Mid-Winter Meeting of The American Academy of Psychoanalysis, New York City, December 1979. We would like to thank Joan Ross Acocella for her editorial help in the preparation of this paper.

231

The psychological point is quite valid. Hard as they may try, human beings can have no relationship, take no action, speak no word, that is not ultimately founded upon and enacted with emotion. Even the projections of our greatest ego ideals have affective manifestations. In the Old Testament Moses has outbursts of frustration. In the New Testament Jesus angrily curses the fig tree because it has no fruit for him. God declares himself to be jealous and is repeatedly moved to anger against his "chosen people." He also makes a prideful wager with Satan concerning Job. Even the divine, it seems, is not immune to the explosive influences of affect.

To come to our subject, psychopathology, its origins in affect have long been recognized. As Freud (1914) points out, it is the feelings that cause the sickness. And, for the most part, it is feelings that provide the way out of the sickness. To the extent that psychotherapy is a "cure," it is a cure via interpretation of repressed affect.

As many have observed, a correct interpretation of affect often precipitates regressive behavior on the part of the patient. While such regressions may be threatening to the less experienced therapist, they can be extremely beneficial, and as Winnicott (1954) pointed out, they should be encouraged. For the regression is a sign that the patient's defenses against the denied affect have momentarily collapsed, making it available for exploration. As Peto (1960) has conceptualized the process, a part of the ego, under the pressure of the interpretation, disintegrates, and its constituent parts, remembered images of self and object, enter into a fluid state. In this state, split-off parts of the ego emerge into the center of consciousness, unleashing a flood of infantile affect. This is a frightening moment for the patient, as the regression indicates. However, it is also a valuable moment, for it offers the patient the chance to reintegrate banished images into the self. This in turn allows him to form a more realistic picture of the self and the world, to graduate from primitive defenses to more mature ones, such as sublimation, and thereby to improve his interpersonal relationships and his adaptation to life in general.

The unfolding of this process can be demonstrated in the therapy of a twelve-year-old boy named Joey who was treated by Dr. Silver at Mount Sinai Hospital under the supervision of Dr. Mohacsy. When Joey was two years old, his father disappeared with a young woman whom he had gotten pregnant, leaving Joey and his sister in the hands of their depressed and disorganized mother. When the boy was five, the mother, unable to cope, finally put him up for foster care. In two years he went through three foster homes, finally ending up with a stable and affectionate family with whom he remained from the age of seven to the time of his hospitalization, at age twelve.

Despite the support of his foster parents, Joey never adjusted well. Though he was quite intelligent and excelled academically, he did not relate well to his peers, who teased and ostracized him. In Joey's behavior there was much to impede social adjustment — he was moody, stubborn, and immature — but what truly doomed him with his agemates was his effeminacy: he talked, moved, and gestured like a woman. He later admitted to his therapist that he cross-dressed in secrecy and had done so since the age of four or five. He claimed that he was a woman in every respect except anatomy and that all he needed in order to solve his problems was a sex-change operation.

Joey's gender-identity confusion was merely the symptom of a far broader developmental failure, namely, that he had never separated his own identity from that of his mother. At age 2½ — that is, at a crucial period in separation–individuation — the experience of being abandoned by his father presumably terminated any movement toward psychic independence from the mother. In consequence, the child failed to establish not only a masculine identity but any coherent identity whatsoever separate from his mother's. Long after his removal to foster care he nourished an obsessive fantasy of going off with his mother on a cruise to a tropical island, where the two would live together forever in blissful symbiotic fusion. This yearning to be reunited with the mother further reinforced his feminine leanings. After the father's departure, the mother had told Joey repeatedly that his father was evil and worthless. "Thank God you're like me and not like him," she said. When at last the child was sent away from her, a logical defense against anger at her was to assume that the cause of his exile was some fault in himself — namely, his masculinity.

In the year preceding his admission to the hospital, his sexual-identity confusion was compounded by two episodes of sexual abuse. First he was molested by a 15-year-old boy living as a foster child in the same family. Then he was subjected to anal intercourse by his natural mother's boyfriend. Not surprisingly, Joey showed increasing signs of psychological distress during this year. According to his foster parents, he was hostile and argumentative, his thoughts seemed to wander, he talked to himself and to inanimate objects, and seemed possibly to be hallucinating. Finally the foster parents brought him to the hospital.

The psychotherapy of this very disturbed boy was far too complex to discuss here in detail. We will concentrate on what seems to us the central component of the treatment, the interpretation of affect, as it emerged in three representative sessions.

The first important affect to be handled in the treatment was Joey's anger toward his mother. This anger was very great. What the boy wanted most in the world was to be with the mother. Yet she had not only abandoned him to foster care; now she was allowing him to be shut up with his miseries in a hospital. Yet it was extremely difficult for him to tolerate awareness of his rage against her. The reasons are easy to imagine. For one thing, because of his psychic fusion with her, anger against her would be challenging to his very self. Furthermore, to take a more practical view, he probably felt at some level that if she knew of his anger toward her, she might abandon him altogether. We may assume that the splitting in which Joey engaged was, in part, a solution to this problem. His mother, as he explained it, was good and innocent and put upon. It was not she who was responsible for his predicament. The culprit was the social worker at the adoption agency. When Joey spoke of this man, he clenched his fists and pounded the table. Once the treatment began, the split-off rage was redirected, in the transference, to the therapist. When Joey and Dr. Silver spoke of the mother — of her inability to take Joey back home, of her failure even to arrive for scheduled visits with the boy — Joey indirectly showed much anger toward the therapist. He would twirl furiously in the therapist's swivel chair. Or, seemingly as an accident, he would break the toys in the office. Occasionally he splashed the therapist with water.

In the early sessions, so as not to introduce too much threatening material, the therapist confined his interpretations of this anger to the patient-therapist relationship. He said that he realized that Joey was angry at him for making him talk about his problems. He assured the boy, however, that he, the therapist, was not angry at *him;* on the contrary, he understood and sympathized with his angry feelings. In giving Joey this reassurance, Dr. Silver was creating what Winnicott (1954) called a "holding" environment — an environment in which the boy could trust the therapist to "contain" his angry feelings and not to retaliate or be destroyed by them. That the hours devoted to establishing this "holding environment" were well spent became obvious when the therapist at last touched upon Joey's rage toward his mother.

This happened in the eighth session. At the beginning of the session, the therapist informed Joey that his mother had cancelled his first weekend pass with her. The boy began twirling in the swivel chair, an action that they had already established was a sign of anger. The therapist commented that Joey was angry at him for bringing him this bad news — and also *that he was angry at his mother for letting him down.* The response to this direct interpretation of affect was an immediate regression. The boy began crawling on the floor and saying, "I want Mommy." The therapist remarked that Joey was experiencing strong feelings that he had great trouble talking about and that these feelings made him feel as small and helpless as a baby. He then suggested that Joey might like to *draw* his emotions, since this was what young children did when they could not explain what they were feeling.

Joey eagerly grabbed the crayons and paper. His first drawing was a violent scribble. The therapist commented that it looked like anger. Then Joey drew what he called a "cuckoo" person, with eyes crossed, tongue hanging out, and limbs every which way. The therapist said that this must be how Joey felt inside: disorganized and out of control.

Joey then proceeded to draw a very complicated and revealing picture. Saying "Doggie, Skippy," he first drew a dog. In answer to the therapist's question, he said (still in baby talk) that Skippy had been his pet when he was two years old. At that time, he added, they lived in Massachusetts, and he drew the shape of Massachusetts on the same sheet. In Massachusetts, he explained, the whole family had been together. He then drew his mother, his sister Cathy, and himself in a corner of the page, adding another picture of himself with a toy named "fishie" in the center of the page. Now he began to list the members of the family in another corner of the page. The father, conspicuously missing from the family portrait just mentioned, finally surfaced in this list. Not for long, though. As soon as he had completed the list, Joey went back and crossed out "daddy," saying "No daddy. Daddy bad. Daddy creep." Immediately after eliminating his father, Peter hastened to ennoble his mother. Going back to her stick figure in the family portrait, he covered it with the crown and mantle of a queen. Finally, in another corner, he drew a house with three figures — his mother, his sister, and himself — going inside. This drawing, in its totality, offered a graphic representation of Joey's problem: his rejection of the male image in the person of the father, his identification with the female image in the person of the mother, and his need (obvious in the queen outfit) to protect his mother from his anger at her, lest she be destroyed and he with her, since his self was still symbiotically joined to hers.

Of these meanings Dr. Silver interpreted only a small part. He reiterated that it was probably very hard for Joey to feel anger toward his mother, since this made him afraid that she might *never* come to see him again. He added that it must feel good for Joey to pretend he was two years old and remember how happy it was then, with the whole family together. As for the specific issue of the father, the therapist sidestepped it for the moment.

In response to the interpretation, Joey abandoned his regressive behavior. He now produced a fourth drawing, this time of an ocean liner carrying himself, his sister, and his mother. Attached to the ocean liner was a smaller boat.

The image of the ocean liner recurred again and again, with obsessional frequency, in Joey's artwork, and it is worthwhile digressing for a moment to summarize the many meanings it had for him. In the first place it stood for the idealized mother — solid, sturdy, and punctual. (Revealingly, Joey's ships were generally labeled "Princess line" — a name that should recall the royal outfit given to the mother in the drawing described above.) In this positive aspect, the ship also came to represent the therapist, who was in fact solid, reliable, and punctual. Again in its positive aspect, the ship revealed the boy's symbiotic yearnings — the little boat umbilically attached to the large, sturdy ship, as seen in this particular drawing. However, a ship can also sail far away. In this sense, the ship symbolized the mother's maddening unavailability. It also represented Joey's own journeying in pursuit of his mother and — at a more deeply repressed level — in pursuit of his father. In addition, it symbolized Joey's desire to turn the tables and be the one who sailed away rather than the one who was always abandoned. Finally, on a more superficial level, the ship was an image of Joey's desire to escape his problems — his anger, his fears, his feelings of abandonment — and cruise away to some more tranquil world.

Again, in the case of this particular drawing, Dr. Silver gave only a limited interpretation of affect, concentrating still on the boy's ambivalent feelings toward his mother. He remarked on how solid-looking and well-anchored the big ship looked — perhaps the way he wanted his mother to be, and perhaps also the way he viewed the therapist. He added that the little ship made him think of Joey and of how good it would make Joey feel to be securely tied up to a "big ship." In response, the boy sighed and asked the therapist to keep the drawings.

The effect of this intense session was to enable Joey to confront his anger toward his mother and thus to begin reintegrating the split-off images of the "bad mother." This process in turn made it possible for Joey to begin exploring another affect that was even more heavily defended against. This was the longing for the lost father. In the next few sessions Joey began, of his own volition, to talk about his father. His feelings were highly ambivalent. On the one hand, he claimed that he would "get" his father for abandoning the family. On the other hand, he fantasized that the father had become rich and famous, and he imagined himself becoming friends with him. It was both interesting and disturbing to Joey that his father, whom he claimed he had nearly forgotten about altogether, was now occupying his thoughts. "Why am I thinking so much about that bastard now?" he asked. The answer was twofold. First, as mentioned earlier, the integration of the "bad mother" made way for the resurfacing of the "good father." The second cause was of course the transference. In the treatment Joey was learning that men, as well as women, could be nurturing and kind. As he began to internalize these positive male images, memories of the loved father inevitably began pressing toward the surface of consciousness.

In another session, a few days after the one just described, Joey was very angry at his mother, who had once again failed to show up for a scheduled visit. He sat in the swivel chair hitting his thighs and biting his fist. Dr. Silver pointed out to him that he was redirecting onto himself the anger that he felt toward his mother. As before, the correct interpretation of affect triggered an immediate regression. He scribbled with the crayons, crawled on the floor, used baby talk, and began sucking on a toy baby bottle. He then placed the bottle in the therapist's hand and resumed sucking on it, saying "Mamma." The therapist accepted the maternal role. Immediately afterward, when Joey started to scribble on the wall, the therapist stopped him, saying, "If your mother can't be here, you want to make sure that I will take care of you and also that I will protect you from being hurt by your angry feelings or from hurting others with them."

With these words, the regression ended as abruptly as it had begun. The boy sat down in a chair and began speaking in an age-appropriate manner, complaining that his mother was unfair to him and that she didn't realize how much she let him down. Joey then drew an extremely detailed and sophisticated map of the Caribbean. On a separate piece of paper, he wrote "Princess Ships, Berth 93A, Port of Los Angeles, 3000 miles away." The therapist remarked that Joey's mother, like the Princess ships, must seem to him at times thousands of miles away, not only in the sense of physical absence but also in her failure to understand his feelings. Joey then asked the therapist to speak to his mother about this and to act as his advocate with her.

Two sessions later, Joey returned to the subject of his father, and the minute he did, the regression once again took over. Interestingly, however, this time it was more a mock regression than a real one, for what the boy articulated, in his pseudo-baby talk, was a clear statement of his essential problem, the problem underlying his gender-identity confusion and his separation difficulties. He said, "Want Daddy – Daddy stupid – love Daddy – hate Daddy – Mommy no want Daddy – if Joey say hello Daddy, Mommy say bye-bye Joey." Dr. Silver restated Joey's ambivalent feelings toward his father and his fear that to accept his father would mean losing his mother. In response to this interpretation of affect, Joey went to the desk and drew a picture of the family's happy home before the father left. Anchored to the rather phallic chimney of the house was a small sled, reminiscent of the little boat attached to the big ship in the earlier drawing. In that drawing, however, the big boat represented the mother. Here the chimney clearly suggested the father. Above the house Joey drew a happy sun and an incipient tornado – in other words, the father's impending departure.

Expanding on this theme, Joey drew another picture, a poignant representation of the family before and after the tornado. In the "before" picture, he once again depicted the happy sun and the family portrait, this time with the father included. In the "after" picture, the tornado descends, the father disappears, and the rest of the family are blown away on the winds of the storm.

These self-revealing pictures demonstrated Joey's growing acceptance of his love for the father. The reintegration of the male image was evident in other areas of his behavior as well. For one thing, the transference, both positive and negative, was becoming extremely intense. Joey took to calling the therapist "Daddy" on the unit. At times he would cling to the therapist like a baby; at other times he would scream at him violently and run away.

There were other signs of the increasing male identification. Joey reported to Dr. Silver that he had had his first heterosexual dream, involving a ten-year-old girl on the unit. At the same time he said he had been having homosexual dreams about a younger boy on the unit. He claimed that he was "somewhere between feeling like a man and feeling like a woman" — a far cry from his sentiments upon admission, when he claimed that he was in fact a girl imprisoned in a boy's body.

Finally, Joey's ocean liners began to undergo a sex change. Hitherto they had always been "Princess" ships. Now he drew a "Royal Viking Sun." He gave this picture to the therapist with the offhand remark that he was "getting tired of always drawing the Princess line." A few days later he drew an oil tanker. His reponse to this latter drawing neatly exemplified his ambivalent feelings about his burgeoning male identification. First he looked at the oil tanker and crossed it out, writing "censored" over it. Then, after a pause, he turned the paper over and drew the tanker again, this time more carefully and in brighter colors. He inscribed it to Dr. Silver and presented it to to him, asking him if he would hang it in his office.

The treatment of this boy continued beyond the sessions that we have described and included many other elements that we have not had time to elucidate. Our purpose has been to show just how effective — and immediately effective — the judicious interpretation of affect can be. In this case, the interpretation of the boy's anger against his mother and of his longing for his father initiated his emergence from the defensive guise of femininity. Prior to treatment, femininity was Joey's way of coping with the loss of his father and the ever-threatened loss of his mother. If he were a woman, this would make him loveable to his mother. At the same time, by making him like the abandoning mother, it would lessen his dependence on her. At a deeper level of unconscious logic, a feminine identification allowed Joey the fantasy of having a child, thus giving him control over a relationship and mitigating his anguish over separation from his mother. We might even speculate that femininity also represented to Joey the possibility of giving his father a child, as did the woman with whom the father ran away, and thus winning the father back. In sum, feminine behavior for this boy was an overdetermined defense against abandonment. By confronting Joey with his feelings of abandonment, Dr. Silver lessened the need for the defense. At the same time, by fostering the transference and by unearthing the buried love for the father, he revived the boy's dormant masculinity. In this way, the boy's ego, or a part thereof, was "disintegrated and reintegrated," to return to Peto's metaphor. The images of "bad mother" and "good father," formerly split off, were restored to his picture of himself and the world. And once freed from the necessity of concealing these images, the boy could go on to develop more mature defenses against his admittedly difficult circumstances.

This technique, the interpretation of affect, is by no means a controversial one. On the contrary, it has been recognized as a central component of psychotherapy since the turn of the century. We would like now to raise an issue that *is* controversial, and that is what we have called "affective interpretation" in the title of this paper. By affective interpretation we mean interpretation in which the warded-off affect is not only identified verbally but also *expressed* by the therapist. Let us, for the sake of argument, conceptualize two styles of interpretation. First, the therapist may call the patient's attention to his underlying emotions through strictly intellectual means — that is, by poker-facedly stating the content of the emotion. Alternatively, the therapist may combine the verbal identification of the emotion with a subtle portrayal of it, using tone of voice, facial expression, and other modes of so-called "body language" to express the emotion at the same time that he names it. It is our belief that the former style is simply impossible — or, if possible, then inhuman — whereas the latter style is not only natural but, when used in a controlled clinical setting, immeasurably increases the effectiveness of the interpretation.

As we noted, this is a controversial topic at the moment. Indeed, recently an entire issue of the *Bulletin of the Association for Psychoanalytic Medicine* (March 1979) was devoted to this matter. It seems, however, that the controversy is based to some extent on a misunderstanding. As Kernberg pointed out in the *Bulletin,* the human potential movement of the fifties and sixties, with its concomitant upsurge of rapid and cathartic therapies, pushed psychoanalysis toward one pole of false dichotomy, at least in the public mind. To quote Kernberg, "the psychoanalytic principle of technical neutrality has been misinterpreted as implying a cold, scientific, objective stance to the patient, in contrast to an affective, warm, 'encounter-like' sharing and active intervention which various of these [newer] psychotherapies promote" (1979, p. 77).

For those who wished to characterize psychoanalysis as cold, there was no scarcity of texts to cite. Perhaps the most notorious of these was Freud's discussion of the analyst as a mirror in "Recommendations to Physicians Practicing Psychoanalysis." "The doctor," Freud writes, "should be opaque to his patients and, like a mirror, should show them nothing but what is shown to him" (1912, p. 118). Many have read these words as meaning that the ideal therapist leaves his emotional life behind when he enters the consulting room; to the patient he presents a flat, cold, impersonal surface, undistorted by any feelings of his own. But as Sandler, Dare, and Holder (1973) have protested, this is a serious misreading of Freud. A human being, no matter how carefully trained, cannot act as a mirror in the literal sense of reflecting only what comes from the outside. In order to act as a mirror, the therapist must to some extent identify with the patient, tapping emotions that originate ultimately in his own personal hostory. For what else can he use to reflect back to the patient what the patient has revealed to him?

That Freud was unaware of this fact seems most unlikely. The impact of the therapist's personality on the course of analysis was not a central focus of Freud's writings. It was Rank and Ferenczi in Europe and especially Sullivan, working independently but simultaneously in the United States (Thompson, 1952), who first gave this matter the great attention that it still enjoys today. Yet Freud unquestionably recognized the importance of the therapist's personality, and there is ample evidence in his writings (e.g., "Notes Upon a Case of Obsessional Neurosis," 1909) that he expressed feelings to his patients. It is our belief that all good therapists do so, often without being aware of it, like Molière's *bourgeois gentilhomme* speaking prose without realizing it. In particular, they will use their own emotions in interpreting the patient's emotions. In volume and tone of voice, in sitting forward or leaning back, in knitting the brow or raising the eyebrows, in lowering or raising the eyes, they will to some extent express the affect as they identify it verbally in the interpretation.

This measured use of affective interpretation has many benefits. For one thing, the implied sympathy cements the therapeutic alliance. Indeed, it is difficult to imagine how a therapist might establish a decent working relationship with a patient — what Witenberg aptly calls "a mutually respectful eye-level relatedness" (1973, p. 10) — without expressing affect. However, the primary function of affective interpretation is that it furthers the patient's recognition and acceptance of the affect that is being interpreted to him. It should be kept in mind that what we are generally interpreting to our patients are warded-off affects, affects that the patients have powerful reasons *not* to confront. In order to overcome this resistance, a deadpan interpretation is, I think, insufficient. The intellectual communication must be combined with an emotional communication — cognition must be joined to affect — in order for the interpretation to penetrate the defenses and actually touch the unconscious.

Bertha Bornstein makes this point quite strongly in her description of the case of "little Frankie." Underlying the child's aggressiveness and anxiety was a profoundly repressed sadness, originating in the crushing experience of being barred from his mother's hospital sickroom while his father was admitted. As Bornstein points out, the child's longing for his mother had to be re-experienced before his conflict could be successfully interpreted, "lest the ego be pushed into a course beyond its integrative power" (1949, p. 187). To reintroduce the affect into his consciousness, Bornstein, in her games with Frankie, relied heavily on expressions of sympathy, pointing out how lonely the little boy must have felt, excluded from his mother's presence and too young to understand why. Frankie responded to these compassionate words with increasing sadness, which betrayed itself in his facial expression and which he was able to tolerate because of the support of the analyst's sympathy.

A recent case of Dr. Mohacsy's presented a similar problem. The patient was a suicidal 15-year-old boy who was constantly relating to the therapist stories and fantasies of a grotesque and disgusting nature — animals defecating on one another, vomiting on one another, sprouting gruesome deformities, and so forth. While telling these tales, he would laugh or produce a characteristically crooked smile. The pain lurking beneath this show of mischievous pleasure was manifestly clear. As Anna Freud (1936) has written, it is a peculiarity of child treatment that the analyst, in tracking down the affect, is largely independent of the child's willingness or truthfulness; because of the ego's inexperience, the affect generally reveals itself either in its true form or poorly disguised as its opposite. Behind this child's bizarre stories and mask of gaiety was a deep self-hatred. He saw himself as stupid and loathsome in comparison to his father, whom he considered brilliant — an evaluation that the father had done much to foster. Recognizing the pain underlying his grisly stories, Dr. Mohacsy began to respond to them with expressions of sympathy. During one session, for example, the boy's perverse imagination hit rather close to home: he said, as a "joke," that his parents used cockroach spray on him every morning. Upon relating this, he laughed. The therapist did not laugh, so he repeated the statement and laughed again. The therapist then told him that far from being funny, it was extremely sad that he thought so little of himself as to imagine his parents spraying him with insecticide. She said this with a look of great compassion. The boy's smile then faded, and he began to describe how inferior he felt at home with his father. Here in the office, he said, he seemed to himself much more intelligent, and he indulged in the fantasy that his father would watch him through a one-way mirror during one of his therapy sessions and recognize that he was not so stupid after all. This was the first time that the boy acknowledged the connection between his gruesome stories and his feelings about himself.

So far we have cited only child and adolescent cases; however, everything we have said regarding affective interpretation applies equally to the treatment of adults. We will illustrate with two vignettes, again from Dr. Mohacsy's practice.

The first involves a 35-year-old psychotic woman who has been in psychotherapy with Dr. Mohacsy for three years. One day this patient came into the office and immediately began talking about her mother's success as an actress and her father's devotion to her brother. These were not new topics; the patient's jealousy of her mother and her brother had preoccupied her for years and were intrinsic unresolved conflicts in her psychopathology. On this particular day, however, she reported these feelings in a monotonous voice, with an empty gaze and an expressionless face. She added that somehow the office seemed different to her today. The chair in which the therapist was sitting seemed different; even the therapist seemed different. Her foot was shaking, and she pointed to it, claiming that she could not stop "it" from shaking. She said that she felt she was falling apart — the same feeling she had had prior to her last hospitalization. It seemed to Dr. Mohacsy that these manifestations of depersonalization and derealization were defenses against intense rage and frustration, and she began to worry that the patient's resulting state of confusion might lead to self-destructive behavior, either deliberate or simply through inattention. To break through her defenses, the therapist used affective interpretation, saying, "I feel that you are *so* angry; you are in *such* a rage. I feel your anger in my fists, in my throat." While saying this, she clenched her fists and showed the anger in her facial expression. Suddenly the patient's confusion was dispelled. Instead of looking through the therapist, she focused on her, and her foot stopped shaking. She left the session in an organized state, saying she felt better now.

A second example involves a 26-year-old woman with a severe narcissistic character disorder. This woman, an actress, had been in treatment with Dr. Mohacsy for two years and had repeatedly expressed her dissatisfaction with the therapist. Dr. Mohacsy had no imagination, did not understand her (the patient's) creativity, could not stimulate her, and so forth. Above all, she claimed that the therapist did not care about her — this despite the fact that Dr. Mohacsy was endlessly juggling her schedule for the sake of the patient's acting jobs, fitting her in at 8 A.M. one week, 8 P.M. the next week, even midnight on one occasion. Eventually the therapist began to worry that the woman's depressive complaints might lead to a serious withdrawal, such that she would simply stop coming for her appointments. So one day when the patient protested again that the therapist did not care, Dr. Mohacsy said to her, with properly modulated affect in her voice: "How is it that I cannot convey to you that I *truly* care — that I feel that everything you do, everything you say, everything you feel is very important to both of us?" Then, with a certain sadness in her voice, she added, "You make me feel so helpless." This aroused some important associations in the patient. She said, "I guess I act sulky and sullen with you the same way I used to with my mother. I never answered any of my mother's questions. I always pushed her away from me. Once when she tried to touch me, I bit her hand. I was full of anger. I asked my parents to buy me a punching bag so that I could get out my anger, but they never did." To this the therapist replied, "And now you have your punching bag. *I* am your punching bag *and* your mother in these sessions." The hour ended, and for the first time in a long time, she smiled as she left, instead of slamming the door as usual. This improved mood lasted into the next session, when she told the therapist that she was feeling better than she had in months.

Affective interpretation should operate not only in therapy but also in supervision. The supervisor has a multifaceted task. He must empathize not only with the patient but also with the supervisee, entering emotionally into their relationship. The affective cross-currents passing between them can be discerned in the supervisee's presentation of the material. In his words and gestures, though he may not be aware of it, he will convey the emotional impact that he and the patient are having on one another. The supervisor's task is to call the supervisee's attention to the affects underlying his presentation and to do so, again, via affective interpretation, using tone of voice, gestures, and facial expression. It should be added that the affects in question involve not only the dyadic relationship of patient and supervisee but also triadic transference and countertransference manifestations among patient, supervisee, and supervisor. The latter should also be interpreted affectively to the supervisee. In supervising the case of Joey, described earlier, Dr. Mohacsy made full use of affective interpretation in her meetings with Dr. Silver and encouraged him to use it in his sessions with the boy. We believe that this technique accounts, at least in part, for the speed with which the therapeutic process moved. As noted earlier, very painful material emerged as early as the eighth session.

Having said these many words in support of affective interpretation, we must add a cautionary note, namely, that the affect must not be allowed to displace the interpretation. Empathy alone will not carry psychotherapy. What is required is a subtle mix of empathy and informed judgment. Ferenczi made this clear as early as 1919, in a statement that has been paraphrased many times since. He writes: ". . . on the one hand analytic therapy requires of [the doctor] the free play of association and fantasy, the full indulgence of *his own unconscious;* we know from Freud that only in this way is it possible to grasp intuitively the expressions of the *patient's unconscious* that are concealed in the manifest material of the manner of speech and behavior. On the other hand, the doctor must subject the material submitted by himself and the patient to a logical scrutiny, and his dealings and communications must let themselves be guided exclusively by the result of this mental effort" (1919, p. 189). In a similar formulation Arlow (1979) recently drew a distinction between what he calls the two stages of empathy. In the first stage the therapist identifies with the patient; subject and object for a moment become one, as the therapist's unconscious reverberates in response to the patient's unconscious. This process, however, quickly gives way to the second stage, in which the transient identification is replaced with cognitive processing of the material that triggered the identification. Thus the therapist goes from thinking *with* the patient to thinking *about* the patient. The second stage leads, in turn, to the interpretation itself, a product of both affect and cognition.

Keeping this two-stage process in mind, we would propose that the therapist should express in the interpretation only those emotions that can pass inspection in the more rigorous cognitive-processing stage, what Arlow calls the stage of thinking *about* the patient and what Ferenczi calls logical scrutiny. In other words, the therapist must carefully screen the affective coloring that he gives to the interpretation. The countertransference must be used, but only in the service of the analytic task, to guide interpretation and lend it power (Greenson, 1967). We most certainly are not suggesting that therapists should ventilate their own feelings during the therapeutic hour or in any way use affect to satisfy their own needs. What we do advocate is that therapists deliberately and judiciously use their own capacity for affective responsiveness to satisfy the *patient's* need — that is, through interpretation, to make the unconscious conscious. That it can do so with great effectiveness has been shown in the four cases we have described here.

So, to return to the question that we posed at the beginning: Should therapists use their own affects in interpreting the affects of their patients? The answer, in our opinion, is yes. Indeed, it is difficult to see how interpretation can do its job without affective coloring.

References

Arlow, J. A. (1979), The role of empathy in the psychoanalytic process, *Bull. Assoc. Psychoanal. Med.,* **18,** 64–69.

Bornstein, B. (1949), The analysis of a phobic child: Some problems of theory and technique in child analysis, *Psychoanal. Study Child,* **3/4,** 181–226.

Ferenczi, S. (1919), On the technique of psychoanalysis, in *Further Contributions to the Theory and Technique of Psychoanalysis,* Hogarth Press, London.

Freud, A. (1946), *The Ego and the Mechanisms of Defense,* International Universities Press, New York.

Freud, S. (1955), *Notes Upon a Case of Obsessional Neurosis,* in *The Standard Edition,* Vol. X, Hogarth Press.

Freud, S. (1958), Recommendations to physicians practicing psycho-analysis, in *The Standard Edition,* Vol. XII, Hogarth Press, London.

Freud, S. (1958), Remembering, repeating, and working through, in *The Standard Edition,* Vol. XII, Hogarth Press, London.

Greenson, R. R. (1967), *The Technique and Practice of Psychoanalysis,* Vol. 1, International Universities Press, New York.

Kernberg, O. F. (1979), Notes on empathy, *Bull. Assoc. Psychoanal. Med.,* 18, 75-80.

Peto, A. (1960), On the transient disintegrative effect of interpretations, *Int. J. Psycho-Anal.,* 41, 413-417.

Sandler, J., C. Dare, and A. Holder (1973), *The Patient and the Analyst: The Basis of the Psychoanalytic Process,* International Universities Press, New York.

Spitz, R. (1965), *The First Year of Life,* International Universities Press, New York.

Thompson, C. (1978), Sullivan and psychoanalysis, *Contemp. Psychoanal.,* 14, 488-501.

Winnicott, D. W. (1958), Withdrawal and regression, in *Collected Papers: Through Pediatrics to Psycho-Analysis,* Basic Books, New York.

Witenberg, E. G. (1973), Psychoanalysis today, in *Interpersonal Explorations in Psychoanalysis: New Directions in Theory and Practice,* Basic Books, New York, pp. 3-11.

TWELVE

Anger As A Basis For
A Sense Of
Self

WALTER BONIME

Ours is an angry culture. This has a direct effect on the development of personality. Many who come into our offices have been
particularly warped. A patient of mine says: "The only efficacy I
feel, the only worth I feel, is when I'm angry – and that's why I'm
angry all the time."

There are many forces at work to account for the pathology:
the daily difficulties of getting about, getting ahead, getting fed,
getting enough time to rest or to think; deprivations, both material
and emotional; frustrations of the normal struggle for autonomy;
and the consequent desperate struggle for the pseudo-safety of
dominating.

What we live in, and live with, is a pushy, angry culture at its
best, and at its worst it is savage. Personalities evolving in such circumstances, shaped by them, show serious derivative distortions
of the sense of self.

The sense of self is a subjective experience, the feeling of one's
own self functioning. People develop a sense of individuality,
of a familiar unique being, in terms of the feelings they experience while performing, perceiving, sensing, responding, cogniz-
ing, in isolation or in interaction. The sense of "me" develops
slowly, with intellectual, affective, sensory, and physical growth.
The forces active in the society at large are also active in the family, though modified by the individual personalities in each family.
In a family milieu which has predominantly nurtured the individual's potential for this growth, a healthy and vigorous sense of
"me" evolves. Such an individual, by and large, can "cope." Where

Presented as the William V. Silverberg Award Lecture, New York, New York, December 6, 1975.

this nurture is denied, or where the growth potential is cultivated in the service of another person, or where it is blocked by social inequities, then those who are stunted, exploited, or confined become hostile, not only toward the depriving, enslaving and restricting forces, but hostile altogether, as a way of life. Their sense of self develops in an internal milieu of anger.

The anger may be open and violent, or it may be manifested in less obvious forms. There may be subtle rebellion, stubbornness, delinquency, depression, and psychosomatic disturbances. The significant point is that in the type of personality I am discussing, whatever form the anger takes, the individual will struggle to maintain it, for it is only in these angry modes of functioning and the simultaneous subjective sensations that the individual feels his identity.

This kind of struggle to maintain an identity, however pathological and painful, contributes to the intense resistance we encounter in treating various clinical conditions such as depression and its psychosomatic masks, addiction, criminality, competitiveness, controllingness, and aspects of catatonic and paranoid schizophrenia. The patient whose foundation in identity is his anger, whether or not he so categorizes himself, battles to stay angry.

Naturally, this is not a new concept. But in our angry society perhaps we must now pay more attention to anger as a basis for a sense of self. Others have referred to the same dynamics. To quote Guntrip (1966) on Fairbairn:

> . . . aggression is not the ultimate factor it has been classically assumed to be . . . . it arises out of the desperate struggle of a radically weakened ego to maintain itself in being. As one patient said, "When I'm very frightened I can only keep going at all by hating."

Adler (Ansbacher 1956) says,

> The tendency to anger is related to a competitive striving to escape from a sense of being overcome . . . . children make use of such explosions to conquer by terrifying . . . .

And Rado (1956) (as condensed by Fromm-Reichmann 1959) thinks that "coercive rage increases self-esteem . . . ." Lesse (1974) speaks of a "child's compensatory rage . . . a compensatory mechanism that finally dominated the patient's personality." Not one of the people quoted above refers to an "aggressive instinct" (Freud 1939). There is enough functional constriction in our own culture to generate anger without any need to postulate an aggressive instinct. There is the denigration of women, blacks, the young, the old, all of whom are scorned in various ways, and who have some healthy reasons to be angry. But among these there are some who experience themselves as authentic people *only* in their hostility.

Pathological anger is often so covert and difficult to recognize that discerning and dealing with it clinically are enormous tasks. Growing up in an angry milieu, most people to some degree experience their individuality as participants -- either attackers or defenders — within angry forces. The culture as a whole supports the attractiveness of violence — automotive Jaguars on the road; tigers in the gas tank; shark jaws in the sea; towering infernos in the cinema, often the towering inferno of a man as well as a building; everywhere power to control, outdo, destroy. For the pathologically angry person, reenforcement is everywhere, and if there is no other way in which he can experience his own being, he will absorb the cultural reenforcements and increase his anger in order to maintain his identity. It is sad and clinically significant when a young patient says, "The real me is the angry me." It sounds like a pun on Descartes: I rage, therefore I am.

Many clinical inferences at once present themselves. It is important for the psychotherapist to discern the anger; to avoid becoming entangled, frustrated, defeated through its influence on the therapeutic process; and to try to see its relationship to resistance and anxiety. To the extent of one's ability, it is essential to respond compassionately and firmly to the hostility directed against us as therapists.

It is sometimes quite explicitly expressed. For example, a physician patient declared at the beginning of a session:

> As I came in I had a feeling of "fuck Walter"; I said to myself, "You're going in there to find your associations — bluster makes it easier for you to say things you're embarrassed about. When it's put in a blustery, angry, fuck-you framework, it's easier to have it come out."

Much of it is expressed as noncommunication, negative therapeutic reaction, anxiety. The crucial stake these people have in holding on to their anger accounts for much of the avoidance of the psychotherapeutic alliance. This avoidance can frustrate and exhaust the therapist. It may generate hostility in him, may lead to inattention, to hopeless diagnosis, reliance on physiological approaches, to transfer of the patient to a colleague, or even to the total bankruptcy of the therapist engaging with the patient sexually, for reassurance as to his own effectiveness. All the while, the patient is angrily struggling to keep his pathological sense of identity. We have to seek constantly to recognize, endure, evaluate the modes and purposes of this anger, to keep attempting to engage and reengage the patient so that he will make his own efforts to recognize and change his hostile, self-defeating ways.

The patient is, as already indicated, also *frightened* by the prospect of disintegration should he give up anger. The therapist needs to illuminate this fear for the patient, illuminate it as an obstacle in psychotherapy.

Some patients can be quite forthright in conveying their fear of becoming vulnerable. They may maneuver provocatively to avoid a collaborative, trusting relationship both within and outside of the therapeutic setting. A married woman in her early twenties said to me directly: "When I feel angry, I feel stronger. I can fight you better." This patient even sat on the windowsill above and behind me. Later she said, ". . . embarrassment, love, even friendship — that would put me at a disadvantage."

Another woman realized that she "always wanted to feel like an oppressed person. That makes me feel alive. I have to keep facing the fact that [when] nothing is going wrong, then I become dead." This patient had pleaded for my help so that she could be brave enough to make a decision, and then for a long time she blamed me for forcing her to make that decision.

But patients can and do develop perspective when therapists do not get entangled in the hostility. For example, a teacher of social psychology said: "Last week when I sat up at the end of the hour, and you summarized, I was surprised at your not being angry at me for insulting you in the dream." In a friendly and serious way I interpolated that he did not insult me only in the dream, but that the dream relfected his generally insulting attitude toward me when he was awake. He went on: "When I left here I started thinking about my rage at you. I thought I was strong because of rage. Then I thought of a cornered rat's 'titanic' rage. I realized that there was nothing titanic about my rage. I was a spoiled brat."

This man's efforts in the analytic experience had begun to be accompanied by a quite different subjective feeling of self, something that gave him awareness of an alternative to anger as a basis for strength and being. Experience of alternatives, in these cases, becomes motivation for further therapeutic risk.

Our work is beset by additional cultural contradictions; by attitudes which camouflage and deny anger, and also flaunt anger. Concealed anger in the form of cool, sophisticated self-control, and overt anger in the form of table pounding, patriarchal or executive wrath, are both admired. We have one social norm that professes to support personal autonomy, and another that demands many types of arbitrary conformity. Corporate employees are expected to show initiative, and at the same time to be "ideal company men." Through such contradictions, the cultural milieu provokes more anger and, dynamically, tends to imprison the patient who is already dependent on anger as a subjective substitute for identity.

Hence, also, widespread and frequently exacerbated depression (Bonime 1966), almost the most common emotional disturbance of our western culture.

I will say a word about despair, a component of depression which in the past I have only alluded to. The angry individual whose identity depends on anger lives in pain. He is trapped in patterns that produce, simultaneously, both his agony and his feeling of identity. To sever the critical linkage without losing his sense of "me" feels to him utterly impossible. This hopelessness produces despair. And the despair is further deepened by a subliminal awareness of the future, of the continuing pain and emptiness, from which there is no exit, because the anger which is his basis for survival must be maintained. The agony of such a trap can motivate suicide, alcoholism, drug addiction, and other despairing forms of so-called escape from pain.

In a relatively normal, relatively nonneurotic life, despair, discouragement, sadness, remorse, and grief all exist as reactions to unhappy life circumstances. These emotions occur in intensities varying with the emotional involvement of the individual and the severity of the events. Catastrophic or unbearable situations can bring about a despair that has nothing to do with depression. All these normal unhappy affects can, however, occur along with depression, from which they must be distinguished in order to understand the individual's total emotional experience. A depression-prone person is distinguished by his *anger* over the painful disturbances of his life. Normal grief and temporary despair can exist alone, and may dissolve with the advent of new sources of meaningful life. But the despair evolving from a sensed entrapment in a depressive way of life will not yield to opportunities for bettering life. It can be dispelled only with the overcoming of the core of anger.

In psychotherapy we seek to help our patients toward appropriate expression of hostility. We try also to help them to detect irrational hostility. All analysis, all psychotherapy, can be defined as helping a person to develop a healthy sense of self. We strive for a patient's access to nonpathological gratifications, to help him to identify and to develop his resources for growth and enjoyment.

Consistently, this kind of insight is what we reach for where anger is the foundation for an individual's sense of being. The patient who may know objectively what constant anger does to a life, can, by a long struggle, eventually grasp the feelings and forms of his own anger . . . can know, subjectively and cognitively, how it affects his own life. He can thereby contemplate alternatives, and risk other modes of functioning. Then, based on different kinds of functioning, he slowly acquires a different and comfortable sense of self. He finds he can be a person without being angry.

References

Ansbacher, H. L. and R. R. Ansbacher (1956), *The Individual Psychology of Alfred Adler,* Basic Books, New York, 310.

Bonime, W. (1966), Psychodynamics of neurotic depression, in *American Handbook of Psychiatry,* 1st ed., S. Arieti, Ed., Basic Books, New York, 239-255.

Freud, S. (1939), *Civilization and its Discontents,* Hogarth, London, 85, 94.

Fromm-Reichman, F. (1959), *Psychoanalysis and Psychotherapy,* Collected Papers, D. Bullard, Ed., Univ. of Chicago, Press, Chicago, 240.

Guntrip, H. (1966), The object-relations theory of W. R. D. Fairbairn, in *American Handbook of Psychiatry,* S. Arieti, Ed., Basic Books, New York, 237.

Lesse, S. (1974), *Masked Depression,* S. Lesse, Ed., Jason Aronson, New York, 73.

Rado, S. (1956), *Psychoanalysis of Behavior,* Grune & Stratton, New York, 235-242.

THIRTEEN

Anticipation, Hope, And Despair

MAURICE R. GREEN

INTRODUCTION

Expectations, anticipations, and hopes quicken the imagination, enliven the curiosity, increase the appetite and desires and energize the action of all of us. However, unrealistic and exaggerated expectations and anticipations lead to false hopes that pave the way for bitter disappointment, desperate frustrations and tragic despair. We see this today in the anti-scientific, anti-intellectual attitudes of many bright talented people who reject the scientific enterprise for superstitious dogmas of various cults and for magical counter-culture rituals. Psychiatry, and especially psychoanalysis, is dismissed because it did not deliver on its exaggerated promise of better lives, more efficient learning, and a saner society. Parents are bitterly disappointed that their children are of a different sex than they had hoped for, different intelligence than they expected, and have different friends and values than they anticipated. Children are disappointed in their parents for being less than they expected themselves to be, for being frightened, less courageous, less assertive, more confused than they hoped they would be in taking action in this troubled world. Schools disappoint parents and children and are in turn disappointed themselves by diminishing moral and financial support, less than they anticipated when they had planned for the future. All the institutions of our society — schools, hospitals, courts, prisons and even the

Presented at Joint Meeting of American Academy of Psychoanalysis and AAAS Section N & J in Boston, Massachusetts, February 23, 1976.

most sacred of them all — the family — are questioning their basic premises, are disappointed in their anticipations, confused in their hopes and fending off the shadow of despair.

Let us now examine the emotional states of anticipation, hope and despair — what they are in human living psychologically and even biochemically; for we are one — an integrity who requires wisdom and freedom; but, also oxygen and carbon dioxide.

The human being is unique among living creatures for its time-binding power, through its immensely complex symbol processing apparatus for storage and communication of information. All living things participate in this process to some extent. The genetic code itself is certainly a storage and communication of information. This not only facilitates the survival of the individual life form within an average expected environment but by means of evolutionary selection-processes encodes new information in enabling the species to survive changing environments. Our inner environment must remain remarkably constant in temperature, acid–base balance, hydration, and innumerable other indices for our individual organisms to survive the extreme changes in our life habitat and circumstances that characterise our various situations on this small globe. Social, psychological, physiological, and biochemical levels of transaction operate simultaneously with the most subtle and abstract symbolic processes to encompass past, present, and foreseeable future into some kind of steady state.

The human brain itself is specialized in devoting one half of its cortical substance to logical discursive linguistic symbolic processes and the other half to metaphorical imagic patterned holistic and aesthetic symbolic processes. We are shaped by the expectations built into our structure in our genetic inheritance interacting with our human experience.

VARIETIES OF AROUSING AND ANTICIPATING EXPERIENCES

Surprise, novelty, startle, and the orientation reaction have often been lumped together under the rubric of anticipation. However, William R. Charlesworth (1969) has taken pains to distinguish the subtle differences.

Surprise, novelty, and the orientation response are basic not only in the beginning of life but throughout life to sustain curiosity, discovery and the genuine learning that is part of human growth. The startle response is an innate response occurring in all new-born healthy infants, characterized by an involuntary, expressive display of fear or distress associated with extension of legs, back and arms (the Moro reflex), pronounced visceral changes, changes in skin conductance, heart rate, respiration, and blood pressure. The startle response is triggered off by any very sudden intense stimulus such as a sudden loud noise, sudden bright flash of light, and so on. They are events that occur too rapidly for anticipations to be formed.

Surprise, on the other hand, is characterized by a discrepancy from strong anticipations or expectations — a misexpectation. Surprise can occur only in the context of relevant expectations wherein something other than what is expected or anticipated takes place. Surprise is always produced by the magician or the sleight-of-hand expert — now you see it, now you don't. Look at the audience of the magic show. They all show the expression of surprise carefully described by Charles Darwin:

> He said, (p. 278, 1955) "The degree to which the eyes and mouth are opened corresponds to the degree of surprise felt; but these movements must be coordinated; . . .
> . . . The explanation lies, I believe, in the impossibility of opening the eyes with great rapidity by merely raising the upper lids. To effect this the eyebrows must be lifted energetically . . . Moreover, the elevation of the eyebrows is an advantage in looking upwards; for as long as they are lowered, they inpede our vision in this direction."

Darwin explains the open mouth of surprise to be part of increased attention to sound as well as sight, for breathing through the open mouth makes less noise interference with hearing than breathing through the nose. Also, in terms of the increased readiness for muscular action that follows surprise, the open mouth will allow a more rapid full and deep inspiration.

The orienting reflex described by Pavlov and later elaborated in the Russian literature, especially by Sokolov, and in this country by Berlyne, is characterized by a number of responses that follow a novel experience including:

1) An increased sensitivity of the sense organs
2) A directing of the sense receptors towards the novel stimuli by skeletal muscle action
3) A rapid inhibition of all on-going behavior

4) A change in the E.E.G. showing a heightened arousal
5) Vasoconstriction in the limbs
6) Vasodilation in the head region
7) Increased galvanic skin response
8) Change in respiratory rate
9) Change in heart rate
10) Active curiosity and set for exploratory behavior.

However, there is now considerable controversy and confusion as to what the term, O.R. response, should cover, which we need not elaborate here.

Since the 1950's the Russians, and others in this country, have been demonstrating the dynamogenic properties of the anticipatory orientation reflex for classical conditioning. Berlyne and others in America particularly stress the emotional invigoration given to attentional and learning processes by the disparity between incoming information and stored information leading to behaviors that structure the old information. This arouses curiosity and learning behavior with the development of sets of new anticipations.

The physiological state of coping with unpredictable and novel situations is especially powerful in stimulating an increased production of 17-hydroxy-corticosteroids from the adrenal cortex (Henry, Ely, and Stephens 1972). The organization of psychophysiologic defenses, as described in psychoanalyitc literature, is critical in determining the precise level of these stressor substances in the circulating blood. Information from the human and nonhuman environment in the direction of greater novelty, strangeness, alienation, and unpredictability is transmitted via the limbic system and amygdala to the hympothalamus increasing the pituitary-adrenal cortical response of alarming and arousing the entire organism and facilitating very rapid discrimination processes. If this highly aroused organism is informed of danger, the forward extension of the brain-stem reticular formation in the anterior hypothalamus is stimulated to activate the adrenal medulla for producing more adrenalin, dopamine and norepenephrine, and preparing the organism for attack or flight by the effect this has in providing skeletal muscles with maximum nutrition, by increasing the heart rate, output and volume of blood passing through the muscle. If on the other hand, the organism prepares to attack or run but has information that it can not cope in any direction blood levels both of the alarm reaction, the 17-HCT and of the "defense reaction," the catecholamines, adrenaline and noradrenaline, reach very great heights, as Sachar et al. (1970) demonstrated in their study of acute schizophrenic crises.

In addition to growing up in a closed organized, lawful world, secure in predicting anticipation and control, the child at the same time is also growing up in a highly probabilistic, unpredictable world wherein causes are not known and events are obscure in their antecedents and anticipated consequences. The capacity of the infant and young child to assimilate the new information, re-organize his activity and develop effective anticipatory defenses and anticipatory coping strategies, but above all, foresight, closely hinges on the security he experiences with the presence and absence of parents or surrogates with whom he has had mutual fulfilling pleasureable and playful interaction.

ANTICIPATION AND AROUSAL

The anticipation of ordered sequences of events is the cornerstone of our growth. We must assimilate new experience in growth, not merely new, but genuinely novel experience, which raises the hackles; that feels unfamiliar, alien, possibly alarming at first — that stirs the organism and arouses its vigilance; this characterizes the primitive basic affect state of undifferentiated anticipation or arousal.

Anticipation, the immediate response to novel experience, is a complex psychological state that is very brief and almost instantly becomes a state of heightened arousal, inhibited acoustic sensitivity, rapid scanning movements by the eyes so that any danger in the environment may be seen, heard, or smelled, as described above.

However, once the information is assimilated, the novel experience recognized, the unfamiliar becomes familiar, anticipation then becomes part of desire if it is a pleasant kind of event that is forthcoming — hunger, thirst, lust, curiosity, dependency, and other appetitive cravings. However, if there is no hope of fulfillment, the appetitive desire subsides. Even thirst, it has been shown, requires signs and indications of the presence of water in order to persist. The complete absence of water is not enough, there must be information present to arouse the anticipation of water. This is probably true of all the appetites and desires including lust. Young soldiers sequested away from the stimulation of the opposite sex for long periods began to feel castrated at the loss of their sexual appetite and often accused the kitchen of putting saltpeter in their food.

Anticipation, in the directional sense of all action tendencies of the human organism, is to be found at every level of conscious and unconscious experience beginning before birth and continuing to the point of death. It is almost synonomous with life itself. Foresight is the constructive use of anticipated patterns of experience.

Short-term memory, long-term memory, affective memory, inherited patterns of activity, together with imagination and quick scanning and repeated appraisals make up the action of foresight. "Foresight, the functional activity which makes the neighboring future so important in human life, depends upon the adequacy and appropriateness of one's acquaintance with the past, as well as upon observation of the present" (Sullivan 1954, p. 303).

Such foresight enters into our subjective feelings of immediate anticipation, surprise, curiosity, fear, and other emotional states that are both cognitive and affective at the same time. "Cognitive" applies to the structured information accumulated to anticipate ordered sequences of events in the world; "affective" applies to the felt experience of the person, in time, of competing and collating motives at work in his life.

Hope is an ambiguous or uncertain anticipation of something desired. The term is used in a very narrow sense to hope something trivial, such as better weather tomorrow, or no burned toast this time; or it can be more weighty and general to hope for a better world; or a cessation of inflation – at least some change in that direction. Hope based on constructive appraisal of on-going trends and actions is another term for foresight. Hope is also used in a popular sense and spelled with capital letters to mean an essential virtue – a virtue essential to the good Christian life, faith, hope, and charity. Psychiatry, whose normative expectancies follow the Protestant ethic, secularizes Hope as essential to its own Good Life termed Health and Growth. The Existenialists, mistrusting religion and hope as impractical illusions dismiss Hope as dangerous to man's well-being and truth. However, Camus (1955) adds there are many kinds of hopes and despairs.

Psychoanalysts, more akin to the existentialists, pay little attention to Hopes, concerned rather with the hermeneutics of ego, self and desire. Harold Boris (1976) postulates a dialectic between hope as what ought to happen in the assumed order of events, and desire as what one wants to happen within that order. William

Alanson White (1916) believed hope and fear made a dynamic dialectic underlying all human development. Winnicott saw hope for a false self as a cardinal resistance to growth. Fromm regarded hope as an essential life force. However, we shall leave Hope in general, as for immortality, salvation, progress or other rhetorical abstract generalities – and look to specific hopes for specific ends in particular contexts.

Here it is important to distinguish between hopes that one can actively implement, and a helpless hope that passively yearns to be implemented by others: the invalid hoping that the nurse will come in time to bring the bed pan.

Hope is the felt anticipation of anything desired. Wiliam Alanson White (1916) said that hope was a general tendency to expect fulfillment; and that fear was a sense of a painful failure of fulfillment. Hope and fear together directed attention and shaped consciousness in a kind of dialectic of personal growth, like the hope – disappointment dimension of Mowrer (1960). George L. Engel (1963) states that the affect, hope, is a derivative of confidence with an ambiguous quality. It implies a shift away from complete self-reliance towards expecting something of support or gratification from others in the environment either on empirical, rational or even magical grounds.

Schachtel insists (p. 38, 1959) that the affect of active hoping helps in the mobilization of energies. However, Schachtel agrees with Camus that magical hope is destructive and wasteful by distracting the individual from the necessity to take full responsibility through his own effort and concern. In magical hope, the time of the present is emptied and the emphasis shifts to the future. "The present may be experienced as an unwelcome obstacle, as an empty span to be waited out, as time to be killed, time without meaning, fullness, weight. It may stretch endlessly in boredom, restlessness or futility . . . ."

D. W. Winnicott (1971) distinguishes between the hope of the true self and the false self. The hope of the true self in psychosis may be represented by the individual's regression as an attempt to relive certain experiences of his environment. Hopefully, these experiences will succeed this time, instead of failing, in facilitating the development and maturation of the personality. In character disorders, the hope of the true self is represented by the anti-social acting out, and the hope of the false self by compliance. Winnicott describes how the therapist by announcing his hopelessness for the false self gives his patient the first experience of genuine hope for his true self. The acting out of the anti-social adolescent sometimes expresses his hope for correcting a certain failure in his relationship to his parents.

Thus we see the true self, realistic anticipation, confident hope and protesting despair as experiences of fluid, free-flowing energies in the growth of human relationships.

The affect of hope, itself, does have an activating effect in mobilizing energies for facilitating the expected and desired outcome. Many theorists including Thomas French in psychoanalysis, Kurt Lewin, Tolman, Rotter, Atkinson, and Cofer and Appley stress the salutary effect of anticipating success or gratification in their motivational theories. More recently, Stotland (1969) generated six hypotheses to establish his thesis for the overriding importance of any kind of hope to the well-being of man. He does not limit hope only to that which requires the individual's own activity; he includes hope from the behavior of other people, from acts of nature or from God. William James refers to the practical value of optimism as against pessimism. And we are perennially reminded of the power of positive thinking by one preacher or another. But to be complete, let us list Stotland's six hypotheses:

1) The greater the expectation of attaining a goal is, the more likely the individual will act to attain it.

2) The more *important* a goal is, the more likely is the individual to *attend selectively* to aspects of the environment relevant to attaining it.

3) Increased *importance* of the goal, also leads to more overt action to attain it.

4) Increased importance of the goal leads to more *thought* about how to attain it.

5) Increased expectation of goal attainment leads to more *thought* about how to attain the goal.

6) Increased *expectation* of goal attainment also leads to more selective *attention* to aspects of the environment relevant to attaining the goal.

In other words, the greater the anticipation of actually having what is merely hoped for, the greater will be the attention to getting it, the more thought there will be about getting it and the more action will be taken to get it. In Boris' terms, as "what ought to be" approaches what is, hope gives way to desire and action.

For the practical purposes of earning a living, crossing the street, training your dog, preparing meals, performing adequately as a sexual athletic partner, such optimistic hope facilitates these matters. However, the serious art, literature and philosophy of our time is preoccupied *not* with celebrating Hope with all its practical value for attaining useful ends; but it is preoccupied with grief at the loss of the value and meaning of ends, and with despair at the quality of our being — not despair of particular goals or anticipations but despair over living authentic loving lives instead of an empty, sterile busy existence. From T. S. Eliot's *Wasteland* to Samuel Beckett's *Waiting for Godot,* we hear a consistent lyric despairing cry of protest against the enfeebling anesthetizing empty wasteful urban blight of the past 200 years. Over a hundred years ago, early in our modern technological bureaucracy, Soren Kierkegeard exhorted us to confront the abyss of our shallow empty self-centered hypocritical lives — to experience fully the hopeless dread of the Sickness Unto Death.

Despair, however, is also an expectation and not an end-state. Despair is the anticipation of almost certain loss, defeat, failure, irrevocable guilt or injury to oneself or one's loved one. This can be expressed in a very angry, agitated, desperately dangerous person — anticipating but not yet resigned, a desperation of protest. Or it may be expressed as a tearful, sobbing helpless supplicant. In our culture, even today, we regard this as childish, unmanly or womanish, effeminate, sissy. Or despair can become inspissated into a chronic long-lasting condition — what Leslie Farber called a life of despair wherein false pride and vanity inhibit the *corrective* and reconciling action of genuine guilt and remorse preventing efforts to live wholeheartedly in the fullness of one's integrity.

Hopelessness, in itself, is a key variable for predicting suicidal behavior among depressive patients (Beck, Kovacs, Weissman 1975).

Developmentally, such despairing experience does not begin until the integrity of early attachments are consolidated between the infant and parental caretakers. This vulnerability begins in about the 5th – 7th month of life when the infant or toddler will reject the stranger while the *familiar* mothering figure is gone. If the absence persists, the infant or *toddler* will search for her, cry for her, lose interest in his toys or food, and be frightened of the strangers. Sometimes this can be gradually reconciled if the infant receives a good deal of affectionate cuddling and reassurance.

This type of experience of separation and attachment seems to be the precursor for later experiences of anticipation, hope and despair in human relationships throughout life. It is interesting to note here, that the biochemical substratum of acute loss can be detected within a few weeks after birth, and persists throughout life until old age and death. There is a marked increase in the 17-hydroxycorticosteriods and an inhibition of growth hormone manifested in the blood of infants deprived of essential mothering.

This is seen again in mothers of children dying from Leukemia − not while they are hysterically protesting and still hoping for their child's life − but at the very end when they suddenly grow calm and quiet and more attentive to the dying child a day or two before the actual death occurs. It is at that point that the 17-HCT and inhibition of growth hormone reach their extreme level (Anders et. al. 1970).

Knapp (1963) describes hopelessness or despair as the feeling reflecting the greatest degree of disorganization in response to stress, experienced as feeling left out, overwhelmed, drained, empty with no desire to do anything and no expectation that anything can be done, with no capacity to relate or to accept help when proffered. Physiologically, the organism is in a state of conservation-withdrawal with an intense metabolic activity. Bowlby (1973) describes this as a protest of detachment in response to sustained unpredictable behavior or to prolonged and repeated separations. Biochemically, it is associated with a sustained rise of hypothalomic–pituitary adrenal stimulation showing an increased secretion of Adreno-cortisone stimulating hormone from the pituitary and increased plasma cortico-steriods, and a depletion of noradrenaline (Levine, Goldman, and Cooser 1972).

DEVELOPMENTAL ISSUES

Developmentally, anticipatory responses become more elaborated beginning about a week after birth with the manipulation of the food-recognition reaction. This is one of the more dramatic examples of the wide range of discrete and complex experiences that very early become more organized, in which the infant selectively attends and responds. By the third week an infant shows rythmic limb movements, smiles and vocalizes after fixation. After 8 weeks, the infant will turn from a familiar, repeatedly exposed pattern to look at a novel one. Neonates also respond selectively to different tones, from different locations and of different duration. Both smell and taste sensitivities are well developed at birth. There are a variety of autonomic responses, activity levels, preferences, and perceptual sensitivities appearing within a week or so of birth and remaining stable beyond the first months and years of life.

In the light of research using direct observation, often with the help of video-tapes of infant behavior in the earliest months of life, we have a substantial documentation of the rich variety of discriminating relationships between the infant and its multifaceted inanimate and peopled environment. Hence, the uniqueness with which each individual comes into life makes for unique anticipations, hopes and desires, of and for those near and dear to him throughout life.

Smiling and babbling must have feedback of similar responses to develop fully and prepare the way for more elaborate social behavior. These develop in preferential and heirarchical ways with the mothering ones who provide feedback of social imitation and information being held, greeting, following, climbing, exploring, and clinging. Preferring particular inanimate objects does not take place until after 9 months of age when they seem to function more or less as substitutes for attachment figures, usually very familiar objects.

Attachment of the child to particular mothering ones is based on the innate orienting response to turn towards, look at and listen to the faces and sounds of the caring ones. The ones who become preferred were the caring ones who responded more quickly — who imitated social interactions regardless of sex. Familiarity of both persons and objects are increasingly preferred; and strangeness, in itself, of other persons and surroundings is disturbing; the child then requires the proximity of the preferred caring person as a base for exploring.

Children who have had lengthy and/or repeated experiences of being alone without their mothering one in the first years of life tend to be more passive, more detached, more unloveable and more vulnerable to alarm and danger responses. Bowlby states, ". . . during childhood, an individual s attachment behavior was responded to in an inadequate or inappropriate way, with the result that throughout later life he bases his forecasts about attachment figures on the premise that they are unlikely to be available." Such experience results in anticipations qualified by chronic distrust and persistent anxiety.

The child comes into the world genetically programmed for attaching himself to others *anticipating* a face with two eyes and a nose — a face that will move enough so that he can separate the figure of this face from its ground. Any person, or even a puppet, that meets these criteria captures attention. The attachment to a single special unique person occurs much later — within 4 to 6 months. However, as soon as the child has a relationship of *confident-anticipation* with such a mothering one, he will initiate separation to an increasing degree and be able to enjoy contact with many others, as well.

Schecter (1973) and his co-worders at Albert Einstein have concluded that playfulness is more important than tension reduction or drive-connected behavior such as sucking, clinging, following, crying, or smiling activities in the hopeful fulfillment of the mother–infant attachment. He states, (p. 24, 1973) "We have seen how, through reciprocal playful experience the infant comes to *anticipate* and learn that he can evoke a social response even when he is not hungry, cold, hot or in pain." Correspondingly, as the child develops a sense of social potency — that is, a confidence in or hope of making an impact on others — he learns that he can effectuate not only relief of tension, but positively stimulating and even playful patterns of response in relation to a human partner as well as intimate objects of various kinds.

ATTACHMENT AND SEPARATION

Bowlby and others have been so impressed by the profound importance of attachment experiences in infancy, for later life that they almost describe it as kind of model for the most problematic aspect of human living at all ages. There is no question that attachment, companionship, loss, and isolation are important in very different ways at different times of one's life. One can even consider the religious recluse, the retiring hermit or wandering tramp as a kind of structured attachment behavior within the structure of our society. Of course, there are many problematic issues basic to human living other than attachment and separations.

In later life persons can maintain deep fulfilling attachments over long distances of separation for long periods of time. In infancy, separation from affectionate cuddling can be disastrous. As described above, it has been shown that there is an inhibition of growth hormone in infants who have been neglected and deprived, but the growth hormone comes back to normal after the infant has had a few weeks of affectionate attention and cuddling from surrogate figures. By the way, this same inhibition of growth hormone occurs temporarily throughout life in association with severe depressive states associated with sudden loss. Such experiences can lead to a feeling of "badness," or unworthiness that may undermine remaining relationships.

John Bowlby states (p. 123, II, 1973), ". . . children and adults are frequently apprehensive about events that they believe may be going to occur and of objects and creatures that they suspect may be going to appear. Such fear is associated with future contingencies." These anticipated fears loom very large in clinical work. Much behavioristic and psychoanalytic assumptions about these fears are wrong; in other words, there are innate, genetically programmed anticipatory fears in humans, just as there is a genetically determined fear in the mouse of a large shadow coming up suddenly on him. Such genetically evoked "natural" fears are:

1) Strangeness
2) Sudden change of stimulation
3) Darkness
4) Extreme Height
5) Sudden rapid approach of a person or object and strange animals

Those fears that are conscious in childhood nevertheless occur throughout life, however modified or inhibited they may be by particular kinds of experiences. However, three kinds of experiences especially are effective in diminishing such fearful anticipations:

1) Observing others in the same fearful situation such as parents, older brothers and sisters, and neighbors and schoolmates.
2) Exploratory behavior that habituates ones to becoming familiar with what was strange to begin with.
3) Actively participating in the fearful situation with the encouragement and support of a trusted friendly companion.

In other words, the security of attachment relationships is the major antidote to innate fears.

Bowlby's major theme is that the fear of separation or loss, of someone to whom one is attached, is innate and persists throughout life, and is camouflaged or not noticed more than any other fear. He says, (p. 201 Hoccit), ". . . of the many fear arousing situations that a child, or older person foresees or anticipates, none is likely to be more frightening than the possibility that an attachment figure will be absent or, in more general terms, unavailable when wanted."

Bowlby's position in summary is that confident-anticipation (hopes) occur, with much less proclivity to any kind of fear, when an individual has security and trust in an atachment figure available to him whenever he desires it; that such confident anticipation, or the converse, fearful anticipation, are gradually developed throughout infancy, childhood and adolescence and tend to persist unchanged for the rest of one's life; and finally that the actual anticipations of accessibility or response from those one is attached to now accurately reflect the experiences one has had in the past.

SEPARATION, DISTRESS AND DESPAIR

Engel (1963), more than anyone else, has called attention to the adaptive and survival functions of distress following separation. For example, a young nursing rat separated from its lactating mother will show a lower and lower heart rate, proportional to the length of separation. The provision of milk effects little change, but a foster mother with no milk restores the heart rate to normal and interrupts the aroused, restless exploratory activity of the young rat. He calls this response the conservation–withdrawal response which seems to be part of depressive illnesses.

Engel postulates species and genetic proclivities for the conservation–withdrawal response which we might call the psychophysiologic corollary of despair. Engel states (Knapp 1963, p. 63), "immobility type reactions are most likely to develop when one has limited freedom of movement or can develop no effective responses to deal with the threat . . . transient and prolonged immobility patterns also may occur when they are separated from a companion or groups (traumatic neuroses of war). Such reactions also occur in defeat when fighting or running is not effective to ward off an enemy; submission may prevent injury or death by suddenly becoming motionless (helpless) averting the gaze and lowering the head or trunk (bowing and crawling to authority) and even lying supine and limp. This anticipation of defeat or loss is manifested by:

1) Sudden or sustained decrease in muscle tone especially the anti-gravity muscles exemplified by sagging face and jaw, rounded shoulders, flexing knees, and general slump.
2) Subjective feelings or behavior expressing; fatigue, weakness, loss of energy, constriction of attention to and interest in environment.
3) Later on – sleepiness, apathy, and detachment occur.
4) Such a "defeat" response also occurs in response to a serious physical injury or severe infection."

Depression has much in common with submission in the kinesics of body movement, gesture and expression. Joseph Becker (1974, p. 195) compares the features of depressive illness with the characteristics of one who has lost dominance and must submit to a stronger person. He quotes Price's speculation that depressive behavior serves adaptive functions within dominance heirarchies wherein the defeated, formerly dominant, must affirm his new subordinate, nonthreatening, defeated position by giving up access to food and sex, avoiding formerly equal companions, showing signs of unworthiness and inferiority by submissive self-defeating behavior, forgetting or avoiding privileges and habits of previous dominant status, and avoid associating with previous allies in dominance. Much of depressive behavior, therefore, anticipates the other's response of forgiveness, pity, charity, and kindness. However, as there are many kinds of hopes and despair, there are also a variety of depressive syndromes from a variety of causes. A severe loss of a loved one, however stressful to the heart, soul, and biochemistry of the grieved one, does not necessarily lead to despair or depression. The normal state of grieving, however painful, also has in it the incorporation of pleasant happy memories and a gradual acceptance of the loss with the development of other interests and relationships.

Since loss does not necessarily result in a depressive illness, explanations and theories of such illness have been elaborated (since ancient times) that propose genetic predisposition, tempermental indulgences, explorations, strategies or biochemical failure in adaptation. All of these explanations seem to be valid now to varying degrees in the variety of depressive syndromes we see clinically. Animal experiments and longitudinal studies of human development have confirmed the observed relationship between inadequate or absent parenting behavior and the development of depressive tendencies in their offspring. However, it is only recently that our biochemical research has helped us to distinguish between the learned helplessness that is acquired from certain kinds of parenting behavior (Gero 1936), and the physiological helplessness that occurs with the depletion of noradrenaline in humans and animals that can be experimentally produced by chemicals such as reserpine or by experiences such as sustained unpredictable shocks or prolonged unaviodable stress (Weiss et al. 1975). The use of monoamine oxidase inhibitors and tricyclic anti-depressants is very effective in blocking noradrenaline depletion, and moderately effective in restoring noradrenaline subsequent to depleting experiences. Clinically, when properly used, it provides relief from physiological debility enabling the therapeutic alliance to function more powerfully in helping the patient so engaged to improve his way of living with himself and others.

Anticipations of acceptance, respect, admiration, friendship or on the contrary of rejection, disinterest, withdrawal, irritation, ridicule, or anger, continually rise and fall in the waves of experience in new relationships with new people as one proceeds through life. Daydreaming, as Dr. Singer has pointed out, and the creative use of fantasy and imagination are invaluable in helping us prepare for the variety of potential futures, which then can be subjectively discriminated and conceived through applying foresight and experience or unfolded into works of art. The loss of foresight, the loss of a sense of future, is seen especially keenly in alcoholics, who, without a sense of the importance of the consequences of their behavior, act in a way that becomes destructive or self-destructive without intending to do so. Marijuana affects the sense of future by prolonging the subjective experiences of intervals of time, like the music of John Cage, so that one seems to have much time, dulling the keen edge of life's brevity. One can approach important transitions in terms of the characteristic ways we cope at each time with the polarity of hope and despair, of confident anticipations and of dreadful anticipations.

Time does not permit us to describe life transitions from this point of view. Nevertheless, we can list them briefly:

The entrance into school life and group activity — the hope for belonging, the dread of ostracism; the hope for success and the dread of failure. Then preadolescence with its unique capacity for affectionate sharing, introduces the hope for intimate companionship and the dread of loneliness. Adolescence with its flowering of sexuality, brings in the hope for a willing partner and the dread of being rejected. In adult life, one hopes for fulfilling work with dignity and dreads becoming a slave or automaton to the wage check. And in old age, all the hopes of yesteryear come together in wanting continuity with all that has gone before. The consolidations of happy memories, the letting go of what is gone, the enjoyment of present involvements and finally the preparation for the final letting go, with an affirmation of what was and might well continue to be the value of one's life in the life of others.

Unrealistic and magical hopes we have been warned by Kierkegaard, Camus, and many others, sow the seeds of bitterness, emptiness and waste.

Today, in relation to our joint hopes for a better way of life, the movement of self-help in all kinds of treatment modalities and social programs offers some realistic hope. Miles Shores (1974) has written cogently of the importance of making hopes and expectations realistic to the point of aggressively and painfully, if necessary, correcting false hopes and unreasonable expectations.

In summary, we have described the experiences of anticipation, hope, and despair phenomenologically and also biologically with an attempt to precisely delimit the adaptive function of these emotional states. Biochemical concomitants of these states can now be described. It is useful to distinguish between the learned helplessness of depressive psychology and the biological impairment due to noradrenaline depletion. Misleading expectations, false hopes, and the life of despair are noxious influences for life and work in human communities.

References

Anders, A. (1970), Behavioral state and plasma cortisol response in the human newborn, *Pediatrics*, **46** (4), 532–537.

Beck, A. T., M. Kovacs, and A. Weissman (1975), Hopelessness and suicidal behavior, *J. Amer. Med. Assoc.*, **234** (11), 1146–1149.

Becker, J. (1974), *Depression: Theory and Research*, Winston: Washington, D.C.

Boris, H. N. (1976), On hope: Its nature and psychotherapy, *Int. Rev. Psychoanal.*, **3** (2), 139–150.

Bowlby, J. (1973), Seperation, anxiety and anger, in *Attachment and Loss,* Vol. II, Basic Books, New York.

Charlesworth, W. R. (1969), The role of surprise in cognitive development, in *Studies in Cognitive Development,* A. Elkind and A. Flavell, Eds., Oxford Univ. Press, London.

Darwin, C. (1955), *Expressions of the Emotions in Man and Animals,* Philosophical Library, New York.

Engel, G. L. (1963), Toward a classification of affects in, *Expression of Emotions in Man,* P. H. Knapp, Ed., International Universities Press, New York.

Henry, A., A. Ely, and A. Stephens (1972), Changes in catecholamine-controlling enzymes in response to psychosocial activation of the defense and alarm reactions, in *Physiology, Emotion and Psychosomatic Illness,* Elsevier, Amsterdam.

Knapp, P. (Ed.) (1963), *Expression of the Emotions in Man,* International Universities Press, New York.

Levine, A., A. Goldman, and A. Cooser (1972), Expectancy and pituitary-adrenal system, in *Physiology, Emotion and Psychosomatic Illness,* Elsevier, Amsterdam.

Sachar, E. J. (1970), Psychological factors relating to activation and inhibition of the adrenocortical stress response in man: A review, in *Progress in Brain Research,* A. deWied and A. Wejinen, Eds., Elsevier, Amsterdam.

Sachar, E. J. (1975), A neuroendocrine strategy in the psychobiological study of depressive illness, in *The Psychobiology of Depression,* J. Mendels, Ed., Spectrum, New York.

Schactel, E. (1959), *Metamorphosis,* Basic Books, New York.

Schector, D. (1973), On the emergence of human relatedness, in *Interpersonal Explorations in Psychoanalysis,* E. G. Witenberg, Ed., Basic Books, New York.

Shores, M. F. (1974), Psychotherapy and the real world, *Mass. J. Mental Health,* 4 (4).

Sullivan, H. S. (1953), *The Interpersonal Theory of Psychiatry,* Norton, New York.

White, W. A. (1916), *Mechanisms of Character Formation,* Macmillan, New York.

Winnicott, D. W. (1971), *Therapeutic Consultations in Child Psychiatry,* Basic Books, New York.

FOURTEEN

Notes On Loneliness

GEORGE SATRAN

SUMMARY

Loneliness in this article is discussed in order to make it more discernable. Psychoanalytic literature has been surveyed relevant to loneliness and related issues. Noted is the importance of individualism in America, citing Thoreau as a model for individualism. Edgar Allan Poe's story "The Man of the Crowd" is discussed to illustrate desperate loneliness. The topic of loneliness connects to issues of empathy, loneliness in treatment, the countertransference response to loneliness, the study of self experience, and the problems created by the use of the term identity. The historical perspective indicates how we are time bound to the vocabulary, theories, ideas and myths of our era, to which, in our loneliness, we cling.

Loneliness is one of the most common types of human distress and can lead to behavior geared to lessening its intensity. Yet the feeling state of loneliness remains a neglected one in psychiatry and psychoanalysis. Fromm-Reichmann (1959) noted that loneliness is "not even mentioned in most psychiatric text books" (p. 325). Grinstein's Index (1966) had but 12 entries under loneliness. Weiss (1973) comments on our ignorance of the various expressions of loneliness.

In this paper I will survey the psychoanalytic literature related to loneliness, discuss Thoreau's *Walden* which has become part of the myth of the individual in America and use Edgar Allan Poe's story "The Man of the Crowd" to illustrate one of the most desperate of lonely states. Included are comments about empathy with the lonely, the therapist's loneliness, why the topic of loneliness has

This article is a revised version of the paper given at Grand Rounds, Roosevelt Hospital's Department of Psychiatry, in November 1975.

been avoided until recently, and a clinical sample of some problems of loneliness in therapy. The purpose of this paper is to spotlight the feeling state of loneliness and, hopefully, make it more readily discernable in the reader's work.

My interest in this topic stems from consultation work with medical and surgical patients in the hospital who are most often lonely. A person who is ill becomes more dependent and usually craves company. The critically ill and those near death may experience intense loneliness. Death, however, has become a popular topic. We have learned that people think much more about death than we previously realized. Books and countless articles have been written about death. Loneliness on the other hand remains relatively unexplored. A second source of my interest in this topic, in addition to working with the physically ill, is an ongoing sense of the disparity between what is written about patients and their treatment, and what actually goes on in the private often lonely worlds of patients.

One reason suggested for the little written about loneliness is that there is no theory for studying loneliness. But Fromm-Reichmann (1959) saw this as more of an emotional challenge than a theoretical problem. She wrote that loneliness "is such a painful, frightening experience that people do practically everything to avoid it" (p. 325). Weiss suggests that many of us severely underestimate the role of loneliness in our own experience and as a result underestimate it in others. A therapist who was once lonely may no longer have access to the part of himself that was lonely and may be impatient with this problem.

Weiss (1973) describes two types of loneliness. The first type is the loneliness of emotional isolation secondary to the loss of a close emotional attachment and is seen in the widow or the abandoned lover. This loneliness can only be helped by a new attachment or getting back the lost one. Weiss' second category is the loneliness of social isolation secondary to the loss or absence of a social network as the divorced, some people who move to new neighborhoods, those who are socially stigmatized, the aged who have lost their networks of social contact, and the isolated housewife. The loneliness of social isolation is based on loss of engagement with peers whereas the loneliness of emotional isolation is based on loss of one key person.

Emphasis on the self in psychoanalysis may help bring loneliness into sharper clinical focus. Study of the self leads to a closer study of self-experience including loneliness. Although Sullivan, Fromm, and Horney used the term self, it is only recently that all of psychoanalysis has emphasized the self. For Freud the ego first equalled the self, but with the coming of the structural theory in 1923, id, ego, superego, the ego became an abstraction, a cohesive organization of mental processes, a precipitate of identifications. Self-experience along with phenomenology, the observable, was less important. More recently Kohut, Mahler, Jacobson, along with Guntrip and Winnicott have emphasized the self and its evolution. There may now exist a greater readiness to look more carefully at self-experience and such states of the self as loneliness. The study of the self is a background issue for psychoanalytic consideration of loneliness — how self-experience has been a neglected area of study and how loneliness as a special type of self-experience was relatively ignored. Simplistically, the ego could not be lonely; a self can.

Of major significance in the history of psychoanalysis is that Hartmann's monograph *Ego psychology and the Problem of Adaptation* was published in German in 1939 and not translated into English until 1958. Hartmann writes "that pure phenomenological description . . . which we could disregard previously is essential for and maintains special importance in ego psychology" (pp. 6–7). What was observable had been unimportant and loneliness as a superficial phenomena had also been unimportant. There was a lag in the study of the obvious (Leites 1971).*

Ideas about attachment and separation have come into prominence in psychoanalysis along with ideas of the self, and as a result loneliness is more noticeable. Bowlby (1973) theorizes that "proximity promoting mechanisms" were important for survival in early man. Vulnerability to loneliness when separated from those who matter may be seen as a residue of man's primitive heritage. Attachment behavior and loneliness are part of life "from cradle to grave." Parkes (1973) describes "restless lonely searching behavior" in patients who are bereaved which parallels primate searching behavior following loss.

The words we use in psychoanalysis may at first expand our knowledge of human experience but after a while may blur our view. Identity is such a word. Identity initially was useful in looking at self experience. It later became an impediment. There are other words with great appeal, such as "splitting," "symbiosis," and the "anniversary" which are initially clarifying but eventually become substitutes and slogans for clinical observation.

Another reason for the lack of interest in loneliness is the

*R. Stoller in his introduction to Leites' *The New Ego* (1971, p. 33) elaborates this point.

unpredictable way ideas are spread in psychiatry and psychoanalysis, i.e., the politics of the spread of information, ideas and theories.

Freud rarely writes of loneliness. There are no specific entries to loneliness in the index to 23 volumes of his work. In his Introductory Lectures (1917) while discussing phobias he writes, "Solitude, too, has its dangers and in certain circumstances we avoid it; but there is no question of our not being able to tolerate it under any condition even for a moment" (p. 399). Freud was certain of his own capacity to be alone. In the same work he writes that for children the first phobias are "those of darkness and solitude" (p. 407). Longing in the dark is transformed into fear of the dark. A child who is afraid of the dark says that "if someone speaks it gets lighter" (p. 407).

In *Inhibitions, Symptoms, and Anxiety,* (1926) Freud expresses a different point of view about being alone for adults. In discussing agoraphobia he writes,

"The phobia of being alone is unambiguous in its meaning, irrespective of any infantile regression: it is, ultimately, an endeavor to avoid the temptation to indulge in solitary masturbation" (p. 127).

In the same work he writes.

"Only a few of the manifestations of anxiety in children are comprehensible to us . . . when a child is alone, or in the dark, or when it finds itself with an unknown person instead of one to whom it is used — such as its mother. These three instances can be reduced to a single condition — namely that of missing someone who is loved and longed for" (p. 136).

A child may be lonely and yearn for the mother while an adult fears masturbation. Longing is not readily acknowledged in the adult.

In *The Uncanny,* (1919) Freud wonders "what is the origin of the uncanny effect of silence, darkness, and solitude" (p. 246) and observes that "they are actually elements in the production of the infantile anxiety from which the majority of human beings have never become quite free" (p. 252). But what is this infantile anxiety? Weigert (1970) notes that "In German the uncanny — das Unheimliche — refers literally to loss of home. The uncanny sense of having lost one's home goes with feelings of emptiness, alienation, depersonalization" (p. 67). Freud interprets the yearning for home as distorted incestuous desire and minimizes the range of emotion surrounding the missing mother. When Freud (1926) developed the sequence of crucial danger situations in a child's life there was little or no awareness among analysts as to what typical real situations they would apply. The anxiety situations of loss of love and the object were not readily related to the actual separations in the patient's childhood. Thus, the child's loneliness, as a sequel to separation, also went unnoticed. This is crucial because the theory of anxiety over object loss existed for many years without precise connection to the separation experience which could bring it about and the loneliness occurring after the loss.

Guntrip (1973) compares the careers of Freud and Bertrand Russell and points out that Freud ignored loneliness whereas "Russell's early life left him profoundly bogged down in the problem of what to do with an ineradicable loneliness and emptiness at the heart of him" (p. 271). Guntrip feels that Freud never penetrated in his own analysis to the inner core of hopeless loneliness — the core of all serious mental disorder. In Freud's self-analysis, begun after his father's death, when Freud was 40, Freud discovered the oedipus complex. Freud had never experienced catastrophic loss, deprivation, or the failure of parental relationship. Even in Freud's adult life he worked comfortably at home and ate lunch with his family. Russell, however, lost his mother and sister when he was two. His father died before he was four. Guntrip emphasizes a vital moment in Russell's life. Russell was living with Alfred North Whitehead, the philosopher. Mrs. Whitehead was in great pain from a chronic illness. During a meeting with Mrs. Whitehead, Russell noted her distress and had the sudden revelation of "The loneliness of the human soul" (p. 278) and reflected "nothing can penetrate it except the highest intensity of the sort of love that religious teachers have preached — in human relations one should penetrate the core of loneliness in each person and speak to that" (p. 278). Guntrip feels this is the fundamental truth in human nature and that Russell at age 29 had noted the "central fact of human personality." He had discovered what 50 years later is being examined under various headings: self-experience, the real relationship in analysis, alliances, and the effects of separation individuation on the entire life cycle.

Guntrip regrets that in 1901 Russell had no chance to study himself and understand his loneliness. Russell had four marriages. Every 10 years he would fall out of love. Guntrip relates this to a

restaging of Russell's core of unmothered loneliness. Guntrip
(1975) describes his own two analyses. The first, with Fairbairn,
taught him about the oedipus complex. Later in life he worked
with Winnicott and discovered his early experience with loneliness
which arose after his brother's death when he was three. Winnicott's technique reflects appreciation of the alone state. After
Guntrip's first session, Winnicott said, "I've nothing particular to
say yet, but if I don't say something you may begin to feel I'm
not here" (p. 152).

Slochower (1975) considers Freud's unstated philosophy of life
and notes that Freud wrote so little about the mother but that she
may have been the key secret in his life. Jones wondered whether
Freud might have wanted to hide his deep attachment to his mother. Freud felt he was "his mother's undisputed darling" and knew
for life "the feeling of a conqueror" (p. 13). Freud's mother died
when he was 75. Freud then felt that he would be able to die but
didn't attend her funeral. Again emphasis on the oedipus complex
seems to have obscured appreciation of earlier conflicts, attachments, longing, and loneliness.

Sullivan, by citing needs for intimacy and tenderness, emphasizes loneliness. In the *Psychiatric Interview* (1954) he considers
the patient's attitude toward solitude, whether he seeks solitude or
runs from it. He asks, "Are you ever so lonely you become restless" (p. 163). Loneliness for Sullivan has "driving power." With
other gregarious animals he felt we share a recurrent need for contact with other people often felt as loneliness. He noted that a
child needs his parents as an audience for his play or loneliness will
occur. The more lonely a child has been, the more difficulty the
child will have separating reality from fantasy. A lonely child will
have a tendency towards social isolation.

Sullivan felt there were developmental components leading to
the adult experience of loneliness, a developmental line so to
speak. In infancy the need for contact is followed by the childhood need for the adult audience, the preadolescent need for a
chum, and the adolescent need for acceptance. The need for group
affiliations in the adult follows naturally. He stresses the need for
a chum in preadolescence and how beginning in preadolescence
loneliness can be a force strong enough to overcome anxiety in
order to achieve companionship. Sullivan (1953) felt that "tone-
less things" were said about loneliness and, "Anyone who has
experienced loneliness is glad to discuss some vague abstract of

this previous experience . . . . But it is a very difficult therapeutic performance to get anyone to remember clearly how he felt and what he did when he was horribly lonely" (p. 262).

Fromm (1941) in *Escape From Freedom* observes that the experience of separateness arouses anxiety. After primary bonds with parents are severed, after "individuation," the individual faces the world as completely separate entity. An "aspect of the process of individuation is growing aloneness" (p. 29). Fromm feels that two courses are open to overcome the unbearable state of powerlessness and aloneness. The first course is to become one again with the world via love, work, and positive freedom. The other course is to give up freedom, "escape from freedom," and try to overcome aloneness by latching on to an authoritarian movement — such as, in his time, Nazism, becoming a conformist, or getting involved in destructive relationships. Emergence of the self leads to both strength and the awareness of being alone. In broad macroscopic fashion Fromm outlined what Mahler has microscopically delineated by direct observation of children and their mothers.

The existential position separates secondary loneliness following loss from the primary loneliness of being human and having knowledge of one's potential death (von Witzleben 1958). Such primary loneliness may increase with age. Weigert (1960) notes how modern ego psychology has brought psychoanalysis closer to the existentialists. She also observes how the existential psychiatrist enters into the world of the patient. Havens (1973) underlines the existential position as one of the "Approaches to the Mind." Havens notes that the existential method is one where the therapist "is to feel what the patient feels" (p. 156). While "focusing on the inner experience of the patient" (p. 157), the existential position allows, via its empathic stance, a window into the loneliness of patients.

Fromm-Reichmann at the time of her death left her unfinished paper, "On Loneliness" (1959). She had pondered the problems of loneliness for many years but never got around to writing about it. This is the fate of many considerations of loneliness. She notes that loneliness is poorly conceptualized, is uncanny, and how such varied states

"aloneness, isolation, loneliness in cultural groups, self-imposed loneliness, compulsory solitude, and real loneliness are thrown into one terminological basket" (p. 325).

She contrasts the fear of being alone that some people may experience even thinking about an afternoon alone, with the need to be alone before any creative work can be done. She learned from schizophrenic patients that severe loneliness in its "quintessential form" is of a nature that is inconceivable to others and cannot be shared via empathy. This point is critical, how hard it is to empathize with the lonely, how helpless we may feel when this is the patient's complaint. Most people have difficulty talking about their loneliness. They may be too ashamed to mention it and again the listener may not like to hear it.

Fromm-Reichmann also observes how loneliness and anxiety get mixed up. She feels that if loneliness and anxiety were more sharply differentiated from one another we would appreciate that loneliness plays a more significant role in the dynamics of mental disturbance than we are ready to acknowledge. Since psychiatrists share a fear of loneliness with nonprofessionals, she wondered whether there might not be a "tacit conspiracy among psychiatrists to accept unchallenged the conceptual merger between anxiety and loneliness" (p. 334). Emphasis on anxiety has limited our grasp of other feeling states, including loneliness. Bibring (1951) defined depression as a basic ego state, equal in importance to anxiety. This came from a spokesman of orthodox psychoanalysis. Yet his point of view has only gradually gained acceptance. Anxiety was still the ignition system which sparked defense. Engel and Schmale (1967) have noted how helplessness and hopelessness may precede physical illness. Brenner (1975) now notes that depressive affect as well as anxiety can lead to defense. A range of defenses against loneliness can be postulated.

Klein (1963) writes of "The Sense of Loneliness" experienced by everyone. As with Fromm-Reichmann's paper, it was published after her death. Klein notes "that early emotional life is characterized by the recurrent experiences of losing and regaining" (p. 104). Longing for the preverbal mother contributes to the sense of loneliness. Paranoid and depressive anxieties enhance loneliness and are never overcome. Klein also relates loneliness to her idea that certain components of the self are split off and cannot be regained. The good breast mitigates loneliness. In schizophrenia, loneliness is coordinated by fragmentation and confusion. Klein lists dependency, the urge toward independence, and denial as defenses against loneliness. She notes how internal and external influences combine to cause loneliness. Her conclusion is that loneliness though diminished can never be eliminated.

Kaiser (1955) saw man's problem as isolation and felt the basic behavior of all patients in treatment as an effort to get emotionally close to the therapist and have an "illusion of fusion." He termed this tendency the "universal psychopathology." Kaiser's focus was that patients are propelled by two tendencies, a need for contact, and an aversion to any awareness of separateness. In this connection Masserman (1956) indicates that if man becomes too aware of his separateness he becomes psychotic. This is individualism gone awry. Masserman felt one of man's illusions is that he is deeply connected to others. In every treatment, at minimum, a patient is with another person.

The conception of the genital character may have implied achieving maturity without loneliness. Novey (1955) recognized that genitality had been glamourized as an overly differentiated and separate state. He also noted that the notion of analyzing transference completely was untenable, and that benign delusions about relationships to others were not analyzable. Follow-up studies of analytic patients always show that they maintain strong feelings toward their analysts based on both transference and the real relationship. Novey had the interesting idea that feelings toward parents as a parental unit, rather than as separate mother and separate father, were over-looked by patients and therapists. This he felt insured a sense of separateness. If parents are seen jointly the sense of self is threatened. Separateness is a necessity.

Novey's book *The Second Look* (1968) deals with the actual histories of patients and how people in analysis often, as he did, go back to where they had lived in childhood to try to recapture the experience of their childhood. As actual experience in childhood has become more and more important, i.e., what really happened – loneliness is clearer. For example the father (Abelin, 1975) has now been noticed in child development as a factor in the child's world of separation-individuation. He can also be missed. Another area of actual experience is the impact of the loss of parents on children at different ages. Only in the past decade has the "parent loss" case (Fleming, 1972) come into prominence. If lifelong abortive and incomplete mourning reactions were unnoticed, so were the varied manifestations of loneliness paralleling these reactions.

Winnicott (1958) considers "The Capacity to be Alone" to be based on the experience of having been alone as a child in the presence of the mother. Without the experience, the capacity to be alone does not develop. The supportive environment is built into the personality and leads to the vital ability to be alone. Intra-psychically someone is thus always present, and the residue of experience with the mother who "temporarily identified with her infant and for the time being was interested in nothing else but the care of her infant" (p. 420) enables someone to be alone. The paradox is that to be alone comfortably, one must carry along the experience of having been alone in the mother's presence in child-hood.

Recent emphasis on the self makes loneliness more noticeable. Kohut's *The Analysis of The Self* (1971) has eight references to loneliness. Kohut describes patients with mirror transferences who have "memories of frightening childhood loneliness" (p. 124). He notes how "a person's seeming isolation and loneliness may be a setting for a wealth of object investment," (p. 228) just as many observable relationships may conceal narcissistic experience of the world and loneliness. In another example he describes a patient who after a relationship with his father failed, retreated to fanta-sies of relationships with playmates alternating with "depressively tinged brooding loneliness" (p. 249).

Kohut also describes the protective quality of isolation. A patient who lost his mother in childhood dreams of living alone under a lake, yearns to go fishing, but if he opens the window to fish the lake would flood the house and drown him. Kohut also touches on the loneliness of the artist or writer who may need a listener during a period of creative work, particularly when new areas are being explored. The Freud-Fleiss relationship where Freud overvalued Fleiss was such a relationship. In similar fashion Melville needed Hawthorne while Melville was writing Moby Dick. Melville was enthralled by Hawthorne and wrote him embar-rassingly adoring letters. As one might expect Hawthorne became uneasy about this adulation and discouraged Melville, but not be-fore the book was written. Thus Kohut, by studying the self, sees the loneliness in his patients.

There is a myth of self-sufficiency in our country epitomized by Thoreau's *Walden*. Thoreau writes,

"Why would we be in such a desperate haste to succeed and in such desperate enterprises. If a man does not keep pace with his compan-ions, perhaps it is because he hears a different drummer. Let him step to the music which he hears, however measured or far away."

Thoreau lived for two years in a cottage he had built. He wrote Walden in 1854 and inadvertently created a myth of solitude, a myth of getting away from it all, a myth of self-sufficiency, and individualism. The myth is that of a man, perhaps nowadays a woman, who goes off alone to a simple life. Leon Edel (1975) incisively notes how Thoreau's myth has "exercised magic" for many generations and continues to do so, although we're running out of places in which to be alone. The myth exists in all of us and is part of America: to get away from it all, to live by oneself. But there is also a "mystery." What led Thoreau to do this? Thoreau writes that he wanted "to front only the essential facts of life and see if I could not learn what it had to teach, and not, when I came to die, discover I had not lived." Thoreau fished, didn't eat meat, drank no coffee, and kept a journal of what he observed. An initial reaction is that he seems like Robinson Crusoe. But Edel observes that Thoreau wasn't on a desert island. Walden was two miles from Concord, Massachusetts and Thoreau's home was only a mile away. Edel quotes a woman who knew Thoreau who wrote that Thoreau was a good son; who loved his mother, and "even when living in his retirement at Walden Pond, he would come home everyday" (p. 274). Fact and myth vary. The myth is one of Thoreau being alone. Yet his mother and sisters visited every Saturday bringing special foods. The Emersons and Alcotts invited him to dinner. Children would visit and the anti-slavery women of Concord met at his house. Rumor had it that when Mrs. Emerson rang the dinner bell, Thoreau came bounding through the woods and over the fences to be first in line.

In the chapter in *Walden* called "Solitude" Thoreau writes "I find it wholesome to be alone — to be in company wearisome." In the next chapter called "Visitors" he adds "I think I love society as much as most and am ready to fasten myself like a blood sucker to any man that comes my way." Thoreau lived two lives, the experiment at Walden and the life of Concord where he yearned to be able to live. In the 1840's a man really could go to the frontier, but Thoreau never left home. He had gone to Harvard 14 miles away. He admired and imitated Emerson and worked for him. He clung to Concord and to his mother. After living with Emerson for awhile, Emerson helped him get a job in Staten Island but Thoreau didn't like New York and came back to Concord. Edel describes how around this time Thoreau and a friend while trying to cook some fish, accidentally started a fire, and burned 300 acres. All of Concord was disgusted with him. He was a "rascal," an "idler," and a "woodsburner." It was this event that preceded his experiment at Walden.

An adolescent patient I treated was shocked to learn that a writer she admired actually lived with a wife who worked as a sales-lady. Her Thoreau needed others. This adolescent patient and Thoreau were struggling to individuate, to delineate themselves. Loneliness and defenses against loneliness in adolescence may account, in part, for why adolescence is often forgotten and why as Anna Freud noted, it is often by-passed in the treatment of adults. Thoreau thus created a legend which taps our urge to march to a different drummer. Edel observes that this legend shows how "a legend can be more powerful than the truth – indeed in the end it can become the truth" (p. 281).

deTocqueville, the French critic, visited America in 1831 and wrote "Democracy in America." To describe what he observed he used the French word "individualisme." Surprisingly, there was no word in English for individualism at that time (Matthiessen 1941). The first English translator of this book decided to use the work individualism "however strange it may seem to the English ear because it illustrates the introduction of general terms into democratic language and partly because I know of no English word exactly equivalent" (Matthiessen 1941, p. 6). So in 1835 individualism entered the English language and is now defined as "self-centered feeling or conduct, as a principle." This is part of our American background. One is an individual and individuals may find it difficult admitting loneliness.

Edgar Allan Poe's short story "The Man of the Crowd" portrays a man's craving for others and taps the loneliness and potential desperation in everyone. Poe prefaces the story with an epigram from La Bruyère, "Ce grand malheur de ne pas pouvoir être seul" – this great unhappiness, the inability to be alone. The story begins as the narrator, convalescing from a nearly fatal illness, looks at crowds of people passing as he sits alone in a coffee house in London. The narrator catalogues the range of human society – the decent, pick-pockets, gamblers, peddlers, prostitutes, soldiers. He notices two classes of people, those who are comfortable, satisfied, and show no impatience, and a restless group with "flushed faces" who talk and gesticulate as if feeling in solitude because of the very denseness of the crowd. He sees beggars whom "despair had driven out looking for charity" and "feeble invalids upon whom death had placed a sure hand." He sees lonely women making a last grasp at youth, a leper, and innumerable drunkards. Finally he sees a "decrepit old man" who shows malice, avarice, a wild history, vast mental power, and extreme despair. The narrator is impelled to follow the old man, and as night falls he follows him into a crowd of people. The old man relaxes until the crowd thins out, when he rushes with urgency to another crowded street. At one point someone accidentally touches the old man and he shudders. He craves the crowd but must not be touched. The narrator is at a loss to understand the old man. Empathy is blocked in this story as is so often the case when we encounter the desperately lonely.

The old man becomes agitated when the streets are empty and then goes to the slums of London where people are still up and about in the filthiest and most desolate areas. Daybreak is finally near and with a shriek of joy the old man finds a crowded bar that is still open and he walks back and forth among the throng. Finally the bar closes and with the most intense look of despair he doesn't hesitate but goes back to the heart of London to continue his rounds with the daytime crowd. After 24 hours of following this man the narrator "grew wearied unto death" and stops in front of the old man and gazes at him. The old man doesn't notice him and keeps walking. The narrator stops following, remains deep in thought, and speaks for the first time in the story saying "this old man is the type and genius of deep crime; he refuses to be alone. It will be in vain to follow him."

Poe was an orphan and lived in London from ages six to ten, and the story is, no doubt, derived from this time of his life. Literary critics have essentially missed the loneliness in the story. In fact, Poe's biographer (Quinn 1941) places the narrator in a private club, a much less lonely place than a hotel coffee house. Bonaparte (1949) in her psychoanalytic biography of Poe stresses that the old man is wandering because of oedipal guilt and misses the urgency — the "preoedipal," addictive desparation of his loneliness — as did psychoanalysis in her time. Poe suggests that crime arises from the inability to be alone. The theme of the double resonates in this story where a man fails to recognize his lonely twin. Overall the story is a dreamlike expression of the most urgent desire to regain contact with other people.

A 25 year old woman who falls into the popular category of borderline patient had great difficulty being alone. She would appear after a weekend, where she chose to be by herself, and complain of extreme loneliness. At times she would go to the shopping centers just to be with people. She often called to hear my voice or to check whether I would return her call. She regularly contemplated getting away from treatment in order to be by herself. She was both a Thoreau and a "woman of the crowd." I noticed great difficulty empathizing with her loneliness, particularly when she would rapidly shift to minimizing her need and denigrating me. Another problem for the analyst with the lonely patient is our actual importance as a real person for the patient. The very intensity of the patient's yearning may lead the analyst to disavow its importance. Actually for periods of time with certain patients we are their main link to the human environment and this role may become a burden. Winnicott (1949) deals with the issue of "Hate in the Countertransference" with psychotic patients. Another facet of work with the lonely occurs when they emerge and value others, and we may mourn the old days when we were all important. Loneliness however, is not just a problem for the borderline and psychotic patient. It is part of the fabric of day-to-day human experience and the everyday practice of psychoanalysis and psychotherapy.

More people probably live alone in New York and other large cities than ever before in history. More people deal with day-to-day aloneness if not loneliness. It's the rare person who lives alone and chooses to stay by themselves many evenings or even one evening. The telephone is not only a means of delivering messages; it is a connection to other people. One gets the impression that people must refuel with the population or at least with the streets of the city. Poe's story in a bizarre fashion captures this yearning for being in a group. Living alone is a relatively new phenomenon in human history. One wonders whether a thousand years ago anyone lived alone.

The popularity of the word identity masks consideration of self-experience, including loneliness. The word identity intellectualizes a blend of different feelings about the self, including feelings of separateness and difference from others. The word identity approaches self-experience, while at the same time it obscures it. Significantly, the word has caught on in an era where statements about the self abound such as openness, authenticity, and encounter. Just as pseudo-intimacy and pretensions impede contact between people so does the word identity block scrutinizing individual experience. By using the word identity so readily to describe a patient's sense of self, we may miss his or her loneliness.

Leites in *The New Ego* (1971) deplores the use of words which confuse and attempts to elucidate the qualities of the self implied in the term identity. His outline (p. 144) includes: (1) "The sense of existing," which can have different intensities and can range to include the psychotic state of feeling non-existent. (2) "The sense of separateness," which he feels for some authors is the whole referent of identity – how separate a person feels. (3) A "sense of permeability," the degree to which a person feels he absorbs or gives off emotions, both good and evil. (4) A "sense of the ineffable quality of one's being" – the I am I phenomena and how one feels different from others. (5) "The sense of permanence" of the self – a sense of continuity or discontinuity of the self with the past. (6) The "sense of the self's inaccessability" – the degree to which a person feels their private world is knowable or not knowable. (7) A "sense of unity" and cohesion as against "being fragmented." (8) The impact of beliefs about the self upon all the other senses of the self – for example, how beliefs about gender will influence all other senses of the self. Leites' work is an important attempt to categorize self-experience. Just as ego functions have been listed in the past, we need greater precision in looking at self-experience.

Empathy with the lonely is difficult. A patient's complaint of loneliness is heard in different ways by the therapist depending upon where the therapist is in his training and in his life. A prominent analyst once remarked that his patients never complained of loneliness. This may be accurate because many patients throughout long treatments may not talk about their most private concerns. In a therapeutic setting patients are different than when they are alone. Many private worries including loneliness, though ruminated about in the solitary state, may remain unstated in treatment in the therapist's presence. Or again, loneliness, is so private an experience that it is rarely defined with another person. And moreover, the other person, whether a friend or therapist, may not want to hear about it. Implied is a responsibility for the analyst to try to get at the patient's private experiences which fade in the interpersonal psychoanalytic situation.

Empathy is mysterious and the literature on empathy does not do justice to the difficulty approximating another person's feeling state. We grope around and try to grasp how another person feels while in mercurial fashion the field is shifting. Limitations in our capacity to empathize are rarely acknowledged. A recent exception is Shapiro (1975) who cautions the therapist against thinking he fully understands his patient. The structural theory for some analysts may have blocked empathy as they looked for ego functions and actually thought about patients in metapsychological terms. As the structural theory loses power loneliness is more readily noticed.

We assess a person's relationships with others as to significance, intensity, and durability. Patients know other people. They meet new people. As a relationship with another person begins, for example of a romantic sort, various possibilities exist ranging from great anxiety, "will he or she like me" to near delusional confidence. What may be called an ability to tolerate suspense in a new relationship may be a prerequisite for having one. The ability to tolerate suspense is related to the capacity to be alone. In a not unusual case a young woman patient painfully related her inability to tolerate the uncertainty of waiting to learn if a man was interested in her, and almost decided to break off the friendship, rather than wait to see if he was interested. In Winnicott's formulation, a background of being alone comfortably at one time with the mother might enable a person to tolerate suspense as a relationship develops. But things are more complicated, and this patient's entire history of relationships with others as well as the actual man she was getting to know were additional factors in her situation.

A notion that might be useful is one of trajectory of involvement with others. A person will have a characteristic velocity of engagement in relationships. It follows that a person will have a characteristic trajectory at a given time with a particular person and hopefully will have a repertoire of trajectories with different people. Different people are known for different periods of time at different levels of intensity with varying potentials for being missed.

Mahler's work (1975) depicts the life-long counter point, the ebb and flow of awareness of separation and attempts to resist separation. Object constancy is unfortunately a concept too often viewed statically, as if it is achieved once and for all in childhood. Pine (1974) expands the concept and notes that the mental representation of the object once formed "does not remain static" but is "reshaped and extended" (p. 312) throughout life. "Flexible adult functioning" includes the ability to "evoke one or another aspect of the object representation" (p. 313). Also implied is that the self in different modes can also be reactivated. Schecter (1974) writes of "relationship constancy," a concept which includes self and object components. The entire range of past relationships becomes a governor of longing and may allow freedom within a setting of closeness. Stierlin (1970) uses the term "gyroscopic function" of internal objects which can modulate longing. A basic mood of longing exists in normal childhood as a model for adult loneliness.

People who decide to become therapists, among other motivations, have chosen to work where intimacy and separation coexist. Therapists at different stages in their lives have different feelings of loneliness and will carry these feelings into their work. Therapists for example with satisfactory personal lives are more likely to be clear about separateness from patients. Personal analysis has not prevented many lonely therapists from becoming sexually and otherwise involved with patients as a reaction to isolation and sadness in their personal lives. The ability to work with lonely patients will vary in the course of the therapist's career. A related issue is the limited social life of many therapists. Some people in the mental-health world only speak to colleagues in their field and some analysts will only have friendships with members of their own analytic society.

The phenomenon of transference neurosis is related to loneliness. Some elements of transference neurosis in an analysis are not always transferences from the past. More specifically, some of the difficulties patients may experience in treatment may be a current reaction to loneliness in the therapeutic relationship. Of course patients who react in such a way have roots in their past reactivated in the analytic situation. But the denial of the real relationship between patient and analysis existed for many years and this problem was ignored. Stone (1961) underscores the legitimate gratifications a patient is entitled to in analysis and how certain stilted maneuvers in analysis may impede rather than enhance the crystallization of transference. The benefit a patient achieves is always determined, to some degree, by the personal equation or therapeutic fit. Green (1975) notes that his decision about a patient's analyzability is based on whether he feels he is or isn't the analyst for the patient. If the loneliness a patient experiences in treatment stems from a defective or absent therapeutic alliance, we have an iatrogenic neurosis rather than transference neurosis. Questions surrounding optimum anxiety levels in treatment have always come up. A new question may be how much loneliness need a patient experience if treatment is to proceed? And what is the optimum distance and optimum loneliness for a given patient with a given therapist at a given time in their lives?

References

Abelin, E. (1975), Some further observations and comments on the earliest role of the father. *Int. J. Psycho-Anal.*, **56**, 292-302.

Bibring, E. (1951), The mechanism of depression, in *Affective Disorders,* P. Greenacre (Ed.), New York, 1953.

Bonaparte, M. (1949), The Life and Works of Edgar Allan Poe, Imago, London.

Bowlby, J. (1973), Affectional bonds. Their nature and origin. In *Loneliness,* R. Weiss (Ed.), MIT Press, Cambridge, Massachusetts.

Brenner, C. (1975), Affects and psychic conflicts, *Psychoanal. Q.,* **44**, 5-28.

Davidson, E. H. (1956), *Selected Writings of Edgar Allan Poe,* Riverside, Cambridge, Massachusetts.

Edel, L. (1975), Walden: The myth and the mustery, *Am. Scholar,* **44** (2), 272-281.

Engel, G. and Schmale, A. (1967), Psychoanalytic theory of somatic disorder, conversion, specificity, and the disease onset situation. *J. Am. Psycho-Anal. Ass.,* **15**, 344-365.

Fleming, J. (1972), Early object deprivation and transference phenomenon: The working alliance. *Psychoanal. Q.,* **41**, 23-35.

Freud, S. (1917), *Introductory Lectures on Psychoanalyses,* Standard Edition, Vol. 16, Hogarth Press, London, 1963.

Freud, S. (1919), *The Uncanny,* Standard Edition, Vol. 17, Hogarth Press, London, 1955, pp. 217-256.

Freud, S. (1926), *Inhibitions, Symptoms, and Anxiety,* Standard Edition, Vol. 20, Hogarth Press, London, 1959, pp. 77-175.

Fromm, E. (1941), *Escape from Freedom,* Farrar and Rinehart, New York.

Fromm-Reichmann, F. (1959), On loneliness, in *Psychoanalysis and Psychotherapy,* Selected Papers of Frieda Fromm Reichman, D. Bullard (Ed.), University of Chicago, 1959, pp. 325-336.

Green, A (1975), The analyst, symbolization and absence in the analytic setting. On changes in analytic practice and analytic experience. *Int. J. Psycho-Anal.,* **56**, 1-22.

Grinstein, A. (1966), *Index of Psychoanalytic Writings,* International Universities Press, New York.

Guntrip, H. (1973), Sigmund Freud and Bertrand Russell, *Contemp. Psychoanal.,* **9**, (3), pp. 263-281.

Guntrip, H. (1975), My experience of analysis with Fairbairn and Winnicott, *Int. Rev. Psycho-Anal.,* **2**, 145-156.

Hartmann, H. (1939), *Ego Psychology and the Problem of Adaptation,* International Universities Press, New York.

Havens, L. (1973). *Approaches to the Mind,* Little and Brown, Boston.

Kaiser, Hellmuth (1955), The problem of responsibility in psychotherapy, *Psychiatry,* **18**, 205-211.

Klein, M. (1963), On the sense of loneliness, in *Our Adult World,* Basic Books, New York, 1963.

Kohut, H. (1971), *The Analysis of the Self,* International Universities Press, New York.

Leites, N. (1971), *The New Ego,* Science House, New York.

Mahler, M. (1975), *The Psychological Birth of the Human Infant,* Basic Books, New York.

Masserman, J. (1956), Faith and delusion in psychotherapy: The UR — Delusions of man. *Am. J. Psychiatry,* **110**: 324-333.

Matthiessen, F. O. (1941), *American Renaissance,* Oxford University Press, New York.

Novey, S. (1955), Some philosophical speculation about the concept of the genital character. *Int. J. Psycho-Anal.,* **36**, 1-7.

Novey, S. (1968), *The Second Look,* Hopkins Press, Baltimore.

Parkes, C. M. (1973), Separation anxiety: An aspect of the search for lost object, in *Loneliness,* R. Weiss (Ed.), MIT Press, Cambridge, pp. 53-67.

Pine, F. (1974), Libidinal and object constancy, a theoretical note, in *Psychoanalysis and Contemporary Science,* Vol. 3, L. Goldberger and V. Rosen (Eds.), International Universities Press, New York, pp. 307-313.

Poe, E. A. (1840), The man of the crowd, in *Selected Writings of Edgar Allan Poe,* E. H. Davidson (Ed.), Cambridge, Massachusetts, 1956, pp. 131-139.

Quinn, A. H. (1941), *Edgar Allan Poe: A Critical Biography,* D. Appleton-Century, New York.

Schecter, D. (1975), Notes on some basic human tasks, *J. Am. Acad. Psycho-Anal,* **3**(3), 267-276.

Shapiro, T. (1974), The development and distortions of empathy. *Psychoanal. Q.,* **1**, 4-25.

Slochower, H. (1975), Philosophical principles in Freudian psychoanalytic theory: Ontology and the quest for matrem, *Am. Imago,* **32** (1), 1-39.

Stierlin, H. (1970), The functions of inner objects, *Int. J. Psycho-Anal.,* **51**, 321-329.

Stone, L. (1961), *The Psychoanalytic Situation,* International Universities Press, New York.

Sullivan, H. S. (1953), *The Interpersonal Theory of Psychiatry,* Norton, New York.

Sullivan, H. S. (1954), *The Psychiatric Interview,* Norton, New York.

Thoreau, H. D. (1854), *Walden and Civil Disobedience,* S. Paul (Ed.), Boston, 1957.

de Tocqueville, A. (1840), *Democracy in America,* R. D. Heffner (Ed.), New American Library, New York, 1956.

Weigert, E. (1960), Loneliness and trust, in *The Courage to Love,* Yale University, New Haven, 1970, pp. 53–72.

Weiss, R. (1973), *Loneliness: The Experience of Emotional and Social Isolation,* MIT Press, Cambridge, Massachusetts.

Winnicott, D. W. (1949), Hate in the counter-transference, *Int. J. Psycho-Anal.,* **30,** 69–74.

Winnicott, D. W. (1958), The capacity to be alone, *Int. J. Psycho-Anal.,* **39,** 416–420.

von Witzleben, H. (1958), On loneliness, *Psychiatry,* **21,** 37–43.

FIFTEEN

Symbiosis, Narcissism, Necrophilia: Disordered Affect In The Obsessional Character

EDWARD S. TAUBER

What is the aim of psychoanalysis? It is, broadly speaking, the same as the aim of life when that aim encourages and facilitates a commitment to life. This means to grasp the human condition, to be able to give and receive love, to develop the powers of reason, to acknowledge what is alive as against its illusory representations, and to tolerate uncertainty and insecurity. The goal of the therapeutic task is to meet these challenges. It is imperative also that the therapist note, explore and define those psychobiological trends which oppose and defeat the processes fostering the engagement of life productively.

In this paper I address myself to what in my clinical experience I regard as a specific triad of underlying affectively charged, interpersonal themes representative of disordered affect. Disordered affect is observed in varying intensity or degree in all individuals who struggle unsuccessfully to enter life productively, but it appears to stand out with special clarity in the obsessional character.

Before formulating my hypothesis concerning the roles of symbiosis, narcissism and necrophilia in respect to the nature of disordered affect, I will first define what I mean by "disordered affect."

Disordered affect, as I use the term in this presentation, is a *holistic* concept; i.e., all affective expressions of relatedness to the self and to others are inclined away from aliveness and adventure, coupled with an exaggerated inability to tolerate uncertainty or healthy independence. The affective investment in life experience is *miserly*. The sense of joy lacks conviction, but sadness is not striking. The curiously consistent lack of lustre in lifestyle may be adroitly masked from the self and the observer. Nevertheless, one can capture the insidious failure of faith in life experience these persons suffer. The group of persons to whom I am referring are generally quite effective, and not infrequently gifted, individuals. They can be successful in this society which emphasizes skill, efficiency and canniness, and an eye to the marketplace. Spiritual miserliness, constrictedness, great self-absorption, vanity, and overwhelming pride, along with nagging uncertainty and fraudulent defiance are noteworthy character traits. The business world and the professions are well represented, and neither sex is exempted. Characterologically these individuals are best categorized as obsessional characters, in that in addition many of the character traits classically associated with that diagnosis are present.

I formulate my hypothesis as follows: Three specific forms of interpersonal relatedness — symbiosis, narcissism and necrophilia (which latter refers to activity against life, and not to sexual congress with the decreased) — constitute an underlying triad of processes composing what I call disordered affect in the obsessional character. *Disordered affect defines qualitatively a negation of life.* The severity or quantitative aspect of the negation modulates the overall degree of crippling. I further suggest the existence of a hierarchical organization along a temporal continuum in the evolution of these forms of relatedness. That is to say, the sequence begins with symbiosis followed by narcissism and then necrophilia.

Evidence for this assertion is empirical and constitutes the basis of the hypothesis that I am offering. How these affective states consistently interact or influence each other is not always clear. The composite suggests a syncytial process at times. Another metaphor that comes to mind is the musical fugue in which each theme has a separate identity and yet the sum of the individual themes comprise a unified whole which forms the substantive foundation of disordered affect. My hypothesis implies that if one could successfully tease apart the temporal organization of the themes, one would discover an ordinal arrangement to their evolution. Much that bears on the growth of the infant and child is unknown and inaccessible. We are thus seriously handicapped in this type of inquiry. We assume, however, that genetic factors, neurophysiologic factors, psychobiological factors and the texture of the relatedness of mother and offspring all contribute to the grand puzzle.

Undoubtedly, the first step or phase in the formation of this triad is the affective disturbance in the mother/offspring relationship; i.e., the developing symbiosis is already putting hopes for healthy individuation at risk. Because of the abnormal integration of mother and offspring, there evolves a narcissistic reparative device, the second phase, one that is truly faulty and is characterized by grandiose magical thoughts and feelings in the service of the offspring's protecting itself against an unacknowledgeable, insupportable terror of the mother. I say unacknowledgeable and deeply repressed by the offspring, but inferrible through the psychoanalytic inquiry. The symbiotic involvement at best provides only illusory advantages to the offspring with respect to preparedness to enter life. Consciously, Mother is usually an idolized figure, who alone really cares and understands and stands by. The repression of the offspring's terror is unexceptionable. In fact, if the inferrible terror is lacking, i.e., if the fear is easily acknowledged, then the severe symbiosis has not taken hold. The subsequent interpersonal travelogue is an ever-present narcissistic state, coupled with the third phase, the necrophilic phase, characterized by blurred — or even outright — fantasies of outrageous destructiveness. Sexual fantasies, when directed against the partner, are clearly sadomasochistic when fully conscious. In the case of the man, she, the woman, becomes a demeaned, gorgeous serf who serves willingly, to the point of exhaustion and death. To maintain a sense of well-being, the narcissistic state plays a cushioning yet misleading role, since minor setbacks, real and fancied, easily disorganize the dreams of glory. All relationships are constantly monitored in the search for an appreciative or adoring audience; failing that, seclusiveness is not infrequently the preferred style of existence. The necrophilic climax reinforces the ecstatic melodramatic dénouement. These persons, with their shaky support systems, suffer attacks of self-loathing leading to fantasies of punitive reprisals against the self. These are not depressive outbursts but stern, unforgiving assaults against the self; i.e., retribution for moral cowardice. Sexual involvement is fraught with humiliation and fears of impending impotence. At least the patient is always reassured in that he is still indentured to Mother and she to him, and the faith is kept.

In order to better clarify my thesis, I would like to introduce one of six case histories in illustration of what led me to my hypothesis. Following the case history I will focus in greater detail on topics of symbiosis, narcissism and necrophilia.

The patient is a physician of middle years who has revealed himself to be conscientious, compassionate and highly skilled in his profession. Emotional problems, however, have plagued him all his life. During childhood and into the adult years, one would have characterized him as fear-ridden; attending school, dealing with classmates and colleagues, and preoccupation with his health and his looks have all constituted unceasing challenges. Despite a good sense of humor and social charm, he confesses to no joy in life. It is said that shortly after his birth his mother left him for three months in order to recuperate from the burden of mothering this first and only child. He was allegedly cared for by a close relative during her absence. The mother of the patient was one of four daughters who grew up having little or no experience with the opposite sex, which reinforced her already well-developed inferiority feelings. Her attitude toward men has been uncompromisingly critical. She has always been socially uneasy, quick to feel offended, and unable to achieve a sense of worth; thus, it would appear she very early attached herself to her intimidated son, the patient, for her own salvation. Mother and son became inseparable; he turned to her constantly for reassurance, be it concerning his health or any aspect of human involvement. Just prior to marriage, the patient's father, a reclusive individual, entered and remained uninterruptedly in a lowly government post. The father, throughout his life, made no effort to improve the financial strain imposed on the family although it was amply clear that had he the urge or drive to earn a higher wage, it would have been possible. He was a remote person, basically unfriendly, and unwilling to be torn away from his newspaper or his books. The patient saw him as a frightening person, easily provoked to anger and to shouting.

It is important to depict what the patient described as the climate of family life. There was an eerie, unceasing, tacit awareness of who was paying attention to whom. His mother and father "were always at it." She nagged her husband about his obdurate unwillingness to seek gainful employment. He would sit in his chair angrily, trying to read. The patient could not stand his mother's shrewishness, but "she was right." He was furious at his mother for her incessant carping, but he was ashamed of his ineffectual father; yet he felt sorry for him, and was tied in knots about what to think and do about it. Each member watched the other. They could never enjoy a television program because it meant "you are more interested in the program than in me."

The atmosphere was one of choking possessiveness. The mother was absorbed in her son. The father crankily refused to express his needs and protested all efforts to pleasure him. The patient was living in a noisy, angry vacuum, frightened, guilty, and himself inert — yet never driven to leave his prison for the outside world.

Although family life was allegedly boring, this allegation simply denied a sense of affective turmoil which was, however, more manageable than the frightening expectations of life away from home. He lived with his family for many years following graduation from medical school. It was interesting that the subject of his moving from home did not come up for discussion. Neither parent approached the topic of his separating from his ties to them or theirs to him.

From early childhood, decisions were always difficult to make. The patient tired of toys he had, would want to have his friends' toys, would clamor to swap, and shortly thereafter would regret it. Although he completed his schooling and professional training quite satisfactorily, he never actively decided on which path to follow subsequent to graduation. He let himself be "guided" — he never felt strongly about any branch of medicine despite the fact that he "found himself" a member of two specialty boards. His competence (begrudgingly admitted) served to give him openings for hospital appointments; he made progress mainly because of his clinical acumen; he dared no interest in original inquiry. His conscientiousness and tenacity made up for his argumentative, negativistic style with colleagues. His secret fantasy is that he is the only one who truly knows anything, but this is counterbalanced constantly by his inordinate fear of making an error. In the sessions he frequently describes complex diagnostic situations in which from moment to moment he is hero and idiot in bewildering alternation. He is unattractively defensive, and at the same time clumsily ungracious when complimented. Trying to interest him in pursuing any problem in living in the therapy is met with loud negativistic charges that he can't understand what I mean, and that he is baffled by anything I say. He anticipates constant criticism, i.e., "I know, it's all my fault — I'm always wrong." Yet his intonation implies reproach at the great injustice I am directing toward him. This is quickly followed by, "I'm not getting anywhere — we've been wasting time." If I then say I can't follow the point he is making, he unleashes another impatient blast which is like a temper tantrum. From the transference standpoint, I explained: I am he, and he is his critical father toward me. This grappling style of engagement was fortunately terminated by the patient's providing, unwittingly, data which allowed speculation. The course of therapy — 4 hours a week — has been rocky but interesting in that more often than not there are dreams and illuminating anecdotes which break through his testing of my caring for him, which underlies his counterpunching style of conducting an exchange. In his prior therapeutic enterprise of many years' duration, where sexual impotence brought him into treatment, he describes a superficially similar style with an analyst who talked rarely, and who approached the patient's problems in the classical tradition. The patient was relieved that his prior analyst sat and listened quietly, without commenting, except for an occasional interpretation which the patient speedily turned to nothing. The patient felt deeply cared for by his prior analyst, which however was never acknowledged or discussed in the previous analysis.

The patient finally broke off his prior treatment, which had come substantively to a standstill years earlier. After several months, the patient became quite anxious and vaguely uneasy, and I believe deeply lonely, and sought a new analyst.

Progress in the present analysis has been slow, but there are evidences of more effort to relate to people and to adventure with women. Any material that hints at growth and individuation is cleverly concealed, particularly if he suspects that it augurs improvement. In particular, if he is involved durably with a woman, as he has been in the last six months, he criticizes her ruthlessly. In this phase of the treatment, I am Mother in the transference — I am possessive, jealous, and begrudge him his freedom from his indenture to me. His criticism of the girl is to reassure me that he won't desert me, and to reassure himself that he won't be deserted.

The patient's relationship with his father significantly molded the patient's set toward women. It was quite evident that marriage would hold little reward, even for an undemanding husband. His father, who for the last years of his life was invalided, refused his son's medical assistance; the patient kept trying to intervene and often did, but only with his father's minimal acknowledgment. Over the years the patient gave his father gifts of clothing and books which the father ungraciously accepted.

In the analysis, coffee is served at 7:30 A.M. meetings, and he has not felt comfortable accepting it; yet he does always "greedily" accept it, treating the experience, however, as making him beholden. It, he says in a childlike way, signifies at the same time my caring for him. When he has given me a cigar or when we have swapped cigars, it has never been a simple project. According to the patient; "Mine was O.K., but his was better." Then come apologies: he fears I will sneer at his gift, so he is apologetic before handing it to me and often behaves as if it would be important proof of my independence were I to refuse his gift (namely, show my not being needy).

We can summarize our discussion of the gift problem or the nature of giving and receiving as follows:

The giver become indebted to the receiver once the donor insists on giving the gift. How is that accomplished? Let us say that you offer me a cigar. What I do is to immediately make you feel that you are the needy one, not I: I don't need your gift, you *need* to give it! Therefore I am sacrificing myself to accommodate to your need to give me a gift. Since I am sacrificing myself to your need, you owe me something — you are now further in my debt. The more you give me, the more in my debt you become. This could account for your being in want all the time because you cannot need anything.

In this system, the therapist can't feel rewarded. The therapist "needs" to cure you — you don't need to be cured. Look at the leverage you have! I become more and more indebted to you because I need to cure you and I see how I am failing so I must continue to express more and more effort. You are doing me the favor letting me try to help you, and by your generosity, I owe you.

The patient bitterly complains that neither parent prepared him for life. Their inadequacy enrages him, and yet elicits his compassion toward them, as do his patients when they seem disconsolate, but also when they select him over other physicians. He continues to have stage fright at any conference he attends, even when there are no grounds for uneasiness. He is himself always on stage, usually secretly buoyed up when it goes well, but angrily fearing the simplest question posed him. He anticipates humiliation from moment to moment. He is extremely envious of the success of others. When attempting to achieve self-assurance he may present himself awkwardly, making contradictory statements when in conference with other physicians. He is especially upset if the other person is calm. Everyday living is a major struggle. When he feels outraged, he fears his occasional retaliatory outbursts will result in his dismissal, and he quickly humbles himself. He feels unrewarded and unappreciated by men. He sees them as crude, ineffective and helpless, despite the fact that he must know that this bias as a generalization is absurd. He always sees women as the intelligent ones, far more knowledgeable and calm than men. He feels this way about his mother and in the abstract has firmly adhered to this view, yet when he talks about specific women other than Mother, this attitude changes to one of disdain. He readily scorns women but anticipates that his sexual impotence has made him the object of deeper scorn in the eyes of all women. He is also convinced that women always look at the other man when he is in mixed company. He has clearly projected his unconscious sense of his mother's scorn for men and for him on other women. His overevaluation of his mother conceals a dread of her, again projected onto other women. Having interviewed his mother, I could quickly see that this woman had no sense of herself as a successful woman in the eyes of men. She "sees" homosexual trends in her husband and her son, although she has never confessed this to her son. I detect his unconscious response to this mother's unspoken assertion as an *unconscious placation* of the evil woman. He does not dare experience these feelings lest he betray them to his mother, who he fears could not tolerate a possible disturbance in the foundation of their secret form of relatedness. When she recently remarried, following the death of her first husband, she seemed to despise her new husband and said clearly that if the patient objected to the marriage, she would cast her husband out. In the last year the patient has met a girl who adores him, serves him in every way, sees him as basically the finest person she has ever met. Sexually she has brought him around to becoming a much better functioning male, yet as he reports his improved behavior, he is impatient and constantly critical of her, claims she cannot conduct a mature conversation and, although a good cook and housekeeper (she has washed and ironed all his shirts, scrubbed and waxed his floors), she is still not good enough for him. He says, "It sounds crazy, but no woman is good enough for me." He admits that were she able to discuss books, music, foreign affairs, etc., he would feel threatened and outclassed and would have to leave her. She is physically quite attractive, so he feels that she can be in his company, but he prays that she will keep her mouth shut. He constantly urges me to tell him to give her up. He says he is lonely, so he keeps on seeing her, but threatens to drop her. He "quietly" goes over for Sunday breakfast. "She makes pancakes just the way I like them." Overall, he cares deeply for no one, seeks constant adulation and when he gets it from this woman, he feeds on it, but feels guilty because he does not love her, and struggles with trying to decide whether he should break it off. Yet her simplicity, lack of possessiveness, suspicion, jealousy and rivalry draw him to her. She is the good mother. His miserliness is not taken on face value by her, and his criticisms of her do not defeat her. His need for self-aggrandizement is affirmed by this girl. He struggles to find grounds for being offended by her so he can leave her. He needs the woman to be ineffective, otherwise he feels like "a baby" — the inadequate male, the despised baby! If he yields, he suddenly sees himself under her scornful control. He does not grasp his deep terror of the woman's scorn.

His description of a recent sexual episode with his girlfriend puts the whole picture neatly together and reflects elegantly the ordinal arrangement of symbiosis, narcissism and necrophilia. She was having her menstrual period, so she practiced fellatio on him as he lay quietly on his bed. He is lying there in a state of ecstasy — he is thinking she is an expert — his comments are awkward because he has never admitted to ecstasy before in analysis. When she said she could continue all night, he explained to me disdainfully, "her passion is unnatural." "It never dawned on me she could be enjoying it." When I said, she enjoys you and sex, he was dumbfounded. What I said made no sense to him. He replied in effect that he was reveling in being the undisputed master; "She got nothing out of it!" he insisted noisily. "She was my slave; I can demand anything; she is willing to die for me!" "She is not worthy of me, therefore I will not acknowledge that she has any feelings!"

What is the patient actually saying? He is asserting that he is indispensable to the woman — she needs him for her survival. He can falsely deny his dependence on her and thus he achieves fictional leverage — he cannot be indebted! This is how he deals with his terror of Mother.

Symbiosis is defined in the Oxford English Dictionary as

follows: "(Biol.) Association of two different organisms (usually two plants or an animal and a plant) which live attached to each other, or one as a tenant of the other and contribute to each other's support." (This is to be distinguished from parasitism, in which one organism preys upon the other.) This definition includes mutual beneficial association without bodily attachment. Even though the definition does not specifically refer to animal/animal symbiosis, it would seem implicit.

The above definition includes a mutually healthy situation. Symbiosis in man, on the other hand, signifies an unhealthy association, in the sense that individuation is not only not facilitated, but is blocked. Further consequences of this form of relatedness undermine the individual's courage and determination to discover himself and to avail himself of the opportunities for interpersonal experience. Reality testing is often seriously ignored. The feeling of uncertainty that is part of the human condition is often extreme since little effort is expended in sorting out manageable from unmanageable tasks. Since involvement with others requires constant evaluations and decision-making, these individuals are unprepared and are thus either naively gullible or filled with distrust. When they test a relationship, their criteria are solipsistic; they get no reliable feedback and perforce return to Mother. Living is never an interesting adventure. In fact, the symbiotic relationship, in my clinical experience, can never be described as joyous. These individuals, i.e., the symbionts, are often warring with one another but at bottom their faith in their mutual connectedness is sufficiently powerful that they do not fear rejection or desertion one by the other. They can behave with each other in ways which they are convinced no outsider would tolerate, so that their "courage" is purely boundless with each other. Their perduring disdain for each other, as observed by the outsider, does no damage to the symbiotic relationship.

The symbiotic relationship is an idolatrous one. The persons involved attribute to each other powers and a unique sensitivity which presumably serve a mutual life-saving function. Each may be quite clear that neither can accomplish his or her respective missions, but they maintain a deep loyalty for one another which is more lasting than bronze.

Symbiotic individuals rarely collaborate usefully and certainly do so poorly with outsiders. They feel they are submitting when they accede to the slightest request, no matter how reasonable.

This "yielding" quickly arouses their rage, which may or may not be obvious to the outsider. Their sense of humiliation is always on the front burner, so that their fantasies are brutal, although suppressed. They are usually careful in response because in their minds there may be a showdown, a moment of truth; the showdown can lead to banishment: if I win, then I have banished my opponent into oblivion; in fact, I have killed off the world. Even though I am the master, I an now completely alone and once more terrified. The thought of Mother quickly comes to mind. Is she alive? Is she there? If I lose the exchange, I am a worthless despicable scum and cannot fact life any longer — I am the disgusting baby/infant who is disposed of, who deserves no place on this earth.

Collaborating with anyone is a vastly precarious enterprise for the symbiotic individual. Every encounter must end in disaster; there is no winning. The moment of truth must be avoided at all costs.

What I have said about symbiosis might suggest exclusively a mother–son relationship; however, mother–daughter symbiosis is equally possible. In other words, symbiosis is a crucial disturbance in relatedness; the sexual components are incidental in terms of dynamics and do not compose the foundation of the disordered integration with others.

Symbiosis and, of course, narcissism and necrophilia have been of central interest since the inception of psychoanalysis. Freud's monumental contributions led the way, and subsequent major contributors to psychoanalysis have addressed themselves to these aspects of human functioning. In my opinion, Erich Fromm has discussed symbiosis, as well as narcissism and necrophilia, more valuably than have many others who have made significant contributions to these topics. Fromm has concerned himself with the nature of these psychobiological states beginning with his authorship of *Escape from Freedom*. Throughout his 50 or more years as clinician and theoretician, he has continued to develop his views on man's nature and the human condition. Among his many impressive contributions, *Man for Himself, The Heart of Man* and *The Anatomy of Human Destructiveness* have dealt profoundly with symbiosis, narcissism and necrophilia. In the forward to *The Heart of Man*, Fromm (1964) states:

> ... the main topic here is his [man's] capacity to destroy [necrophilia], his narcissism and his incestuous fixation .... I try to show

that love of life, independence, and the overcoming of narcissism form a "syndrome of growth" as against the "syndrome of decay" formed by love of death, incestuous symbiosis and malignant narcissism.

In further discussion of incestuous ties and symbiosis, Fromm has summarized his views as follows:

> Freud's concept of the incestuous strivings to be found in any child is perfectly correct. Yet the significance of this concept transcends Freud's own assumptions. Incestuous wishes are not primarily a result of sexual desires, but constitute one of the most fundamental tendencies in man: the wish to remain tied to where he came from, the fear of being free, and the fear of being destroyed by the very figure toward whom he has made himself helpless, renouncing any independence.

Fromm's formulation is one with which I fully agree. There are, of course, unanswered questions in regard to some of the points made. Is the fear of Mother essentially rooted in the dependency upon Mother? This is both easy and difficult to resolve. It is easy to understand in that one senses one's helplessness, that one is completely at the mercy of the mother's whims; the host can easily parasitize or destroy its tenant. But more certainly, the fear or terror begins, I believe, mysteriously at a very early stage of growth and is repressed. Are we sure that we know what the symbiont is repressing? It would seem that some catastrophic danger, operating implicitly over a time span and of such magnitude that its conscious acknowledgment must be extinguished as incompatible with survival. The registering or prehending of experience and at the same time the blocking of its emergence into awareness is an awesome, poorly understood, process. Yet its phenomenal properties are met with in human enterprises when terror can be anticipated. In terms of a society, persons are prone to discredit the statements made by many Germans that they knew nothing about the concentration camps, and it is perfectly true that many lied in the hope that their innocence would spare them in some way. But I am convinced that the assertions of not knowing were often honest. The consequences of knowing something severely forbidden were so threatening that whatever information filtered through would have to be dissociated. Fromm has expressed a similar view in different terms. He has pointed out that the repression can be penetrated only when the forgotten language of the dream with its symbolism can spell out its terror-laden nightmares, inaccessible to awareness during wakefulness. I would go further by interpreting the conscious and unconscious denial of fear of the mother as a placation of Mother: never let Mother suspect you fear her! This placation is a reassurance to Mother, for to let her know of your dread of her would unleash her evil.

I am indicating that the terror has come into being before language has become even a rudimentary tool of communication. Assuming this to often be the case, the search for early memories could be futile. That is, in addition to repression, few if any recoverable engrams have developed.

To conclude my discussion of symbiosis, I want to present one more quotation from *The Heart of Man:*

> This pre-Oedipal attachment [of] boys and girls to their Mother, which is qualitatively different from the Oedipal attachment of boys to their Mother is in my experience by far the most important phenomenon, in comparison with which the genital incestuous desires of the little boy are quite secondary. I find that the boy's or girl's pre-Oedipal attachment to Mother is one of the central phenomena in the evolutionary process and one of the main causes of neurosis or psychosis.

The term, *narcissism,* is derived from the Greek myth about Narcissus. A myth is an allegory; in the same sense, a dream is an allegory. Allegories tell a story which can reveal important messages. These messages can be variously interpreted. Sometimes an interpretation can be sufficiently powerful that it can stand unchallenged and unmodified over many years until one day the myth and the dream are examined anew. Renewed interest reveals new messages; hopefully out of the extended inquiry, enrichment issues. Freud's concept of narcissism was considered by him to be one of his most substantive discoveries. The role of narcissism was regarded as of dynamic importance in respect to its distinguishing psychotic from neurotic organization. He saw its role in many other human connections such as in jealousy, castration fear, love, and sadomasochistic trends. Aside from the narcissism of the infant and the narcissism involved in the psychoses, which latter has not been phenomenologically a source of controversy in psychiatry, the question becomes more complex when one attempts to understand its placement and meaning in everyday human experience. Freud viewed narcissism as a phenomenon which is never truly eradicated but exists, or perhaps coexists, in a socially acceptable form with other aspects of normative human behavior.

Narcissism indicates an unhealthy type of integration with others and with self. To locate reliably at what period in ontogeny narcissistic patterns can emerge does not seem feasible so far. However, I do not believe that it would be incautious to infer its emergence in early infancy. Whether this will be eventually possible to establish clinically is beyond my ken. That narcissistic trends are recognizable in late childhood, adolescence and adulthood seems indisputable.

Narcissistic states can vary in severity and in the crippling effects they bring about in the human situation. Narcissistic persons are self-absorbed, supersensitive and touchy, and often unforgiving and vengeful. It is also true that they not infrequently demonstrate little genuine empathy and caring for others. It is a paradox that the narcissistic person shows no kindliness towards himself – no generosity and no encouragement. He protects himself gracelessly, and his self-appraisal rarely gives him joy any more than it does others. Erich Fromm sees narcissism as the antithesis of the capacity to love.

What we know about the nature of narcissism is still shrouded in mystery. It has, however, continued to be a subject of great interest to many investigators in the field of psychiatry. Outstanding among revisionists are Kohut and Kernberg, who have each made serious and constructive efforts to bring greater understanding to the subject, both in terms of theory and therapy.*

The last of the three interpersonal relatedness states that form the triad leading to the general condition of disordered affect is necrophilia. The literal translation of the word necrophilia means love of the dead. However, as used by Erich Fromm, the term denotes a tendency or tendencies "directed against life," which, when severe, can be regarded as "the essence of true evil." It represents with narcissism and symbiotic fixation to Mother, in severe form, the "syndrome of decay." Many of Fromm's writings over the years have been concerned with all three orientations. He has considered these orientations as indicative of destructiveness and inhumanity. It is important to bear in mind that Fromm, who contrasts this negative orientation toward life with the orientation of biophilia, asserts that they exist as a kind

*For an excellent critical review of their contributions, it is recommended that one read Mitchell's article, Twilight of the idols, *Contemp. Psychoanal.*, **15**, 170–189 (1979).

of blend. What has to be reckoned with is the quantification of these trends; it would be rare indeed to meet with either extreme in one's everyday practice. Hitler and Stalin have been cited as examples of pure necrophilia. In the case of Hitler, one sees a constant fascination with destruction. He not only wanted to destroy the enemies of the Third Reich, but eventually he turned his wrath and destructive rage against his own people, who failed him, and finally against himself.

In the psychoanalytic literature, necrophilia has never been described as a general orientation toward life, although as Fromm states, it is related to Freud's anal-sadistic character as well as to his death instinct. Freud postulated the repetition compulsion, which was allegedly representative of a phylogenetically archaic principle, reflecting the tendency of organic life to return to inorganic existence, i.e., back to where life arose. Thus, according to Freud, one sees the operation of a life instinct and a death instinct. Fromm has attempted to clarify and disentangle his own views from Freud's in his chapter, "Love of Death and Love of Life," in *The Heart of Man,* from which I will quote:

> I suggest a development of Freud's theory in the following direction: The contradiction between Eros and destruction, between the affinity to life and the affinity to death is, indeed the most fundamental contradiction which exists in man. This duality, however, is not one of two biologically inherent instincts, relatively constant and always battling with each other until the final victory of the death instinct, but it is one between the primary and most fundamental tendency of life − to persevere in life − and its contradiction, which comes into being when man fails in this goal. In this view the "death instinct" is a malignant phenomenon which grows and takes over to the extent to which Eros does not unfold. The death instinct represents psychopathology and not, as in Freud's view, a part of normal biology. The life instinct thus constitutes the primary potentiality in man; the death instinct a secondary potentiality. The primary potentiality develops if the appropriate conditions for life are present, just as a seed grows only if the proper conditions of moisture, temperature, etc., are given. If the proper conditions are not present, the necrophilous tendencies will emerge and dominate this person.

Although Fromm unquestionably acknowledges the validity of Freud's major contribution to characterology in his clinical description of the anal character, or as Fromm calls it, the hoarding character, they part ways on theoretical grounds. Fromm sees the anal character or hoarding character as one who is attracted to what is useless for life, "such as dirt, useless things, property merely as possession and not as the means for production and consumption." He recognizes that constitutional elements, the character of the parents and particularly the mother are important determinants. The need for continued research into the affinity for what is unalive is still an important task for students of psychoanalysis and psychiatry.

CONCLUSION

I shall briefly summarize:

I asserted that three types of relatedness with their affective correlates, namely symbiosis, narcissism and necrophilia, clearly seen in many obsessional characters, express an ongoing state of disordered affect. Further, the data suggest a hierarchical or ordinal arrangement in the evolution of disordered affect. The case material provides evidence which led to the hypothesis that these states of relatedness are central to the affective set of the obsessional character, which inclines toward a negation of life experience. It seemed to me the temporal organization is most clearly observable during the sexual act. Here we see the patient in a symbiotic relationship with his partner, having grandiose fantasies of power, fearlessness, and domination. With mounting ecstasy his partner, his loyal adoring slave, is willing to give herself to him to the point of exhaustion and death. These sexual acts, more fulfilling than ever before with any other woman, provide a vignette of his style of interpersonal relatedness. During the sexual act he has managed to transcend his terror of Mother. His partner is the one woman of whom he is not totally afraid. He does not have to slay her – she is willing to die for him.

Can these observations and the working hypothesis have any therapeutic value? I tend to believe so, since the overall inquiry is focused on exploring human trends revealing negation of life. If one can capture these themes broadly and also in detail, and not get lost in the symptoms, one gets a truer overview of what the patient struggles with. This area of negation of life is difficult for both the patient and the therapist. It is an area still in need of serious study.

References

Fromm, E. (1941), *Escape from Freedom,* Farrar & Rinehart, New York.

Fromm, E. (1947), *Man for Himself: An Inquiry into the Psychology of Ethics,* Rinehart & Co., New York.

Fromm, E. (1964), *The Heart of Man,* Harper & Row, New York.

Fromm, E. (1973), *The Anatomy of Human Destructiveness,* Holt, Rinehart and Winston, New York.

Oxford English Dictionary, Oxford Press, Oxford.

CREDITS

The chapters in this book have appeared in the following issues
of *The Journal of The American Academy of Psychoanalysis:*

Chapter 1 — Volume 9, Number 3, July 1981, pp. 399–414
Chapter 2 — Volume 8, Number 4, October 1980, pp. 473–495
Chapter 3 — Volume 9, Number 3, July 1981, pp. 415–434
Chapter 4 — Volume 8, Number 4, October 1980, pp. 497–520
Chapter 5 — Volume 8, Number 4, October 1980, pp. 521–538
Chapter 6 — Volume 8, Number 4, October 1980, pp. 539–554
Chapter 7 — Volume 6, Number 3, July 1978, pp. 325–352
Chapter 8 — Volume 8, Number 4, October 1980, pp. 591–614
Chapter 9 — Volume 4, Number 3, July 1976, pp. 347–372
Chapter 10 — Volume 4, Number 3, July 1976, pp. 327–345
Chapter 11 — Volume 8, Number 4, October 1980, pp. 615–631
Chapter 12 — Volume 4, Number 1, January 1976, pp. 7–12
Chapter 13 — Volume 5, Number 2, April 1977, pp. 215–232
Chapter 14 — Volume 6, Number 3, July 1978, pp. 281–300
Chapter 15 — Volume 9, Number 1, January 1981, pp. 33–49

Index

Psychic discharge processes, affects and, 15
Psychoanalysis, affect in, 12-17, 52, 81-83
  defenses against, 15, 16, 81
  depression, 211-217
    case report on, 217-228
  ego psychology and, 15
  libidinal zones, 82-83
  motivation, 30-32
    Descartes and, 46-48
  neo-Freudians, 167-171
  pain and, 16
  physiologic reporting process, 82
  positive and negative affects, 21
  precursors of affect, 82
  problems inherent in, 81
  psychic discharge process and, 15
  psychodynamic awareness process, 82
  screen affect, 15
  secondary affects, 14
  signal and communication function of affects and, 14, 16
  structural theory and, 15
  therapeutic process and, 16
  see also Freud, S.; Therapy
Psychodynamic awareness process, 82
Psychosomatic ailments, 67-68
  alexithymia, 68
  therapy for, 180-181
Psychosomatic phenomena, affects as, 29
Psychosomatic studies, emotion and, 76
Psychotherapy, see Therapy
"Pure" states, in core model, 61, 62

Quasicognitive aspects of emotion, in core model, 63-68

Rado, S., 170-174
Rage, in core model, 61. See also Anger
Reason, emotions tempered with, 42
Regression, in therapy, 232, 235, 237
REM smile, in infancy, 97, 99
Representations, Descartes and, 35
Resistance, in therapy, 179-180
Riddance, 60

Sadness:
  in depressed school-age children, 143-144

Descartes and, 43-45
  see also Depression
Satiety, 60
Schachtel, E., 168-169
Schemactive core, 64
  in core model, 66, 67
Schemata, of infant, 103
Schizophrenia:
  diffuse arousal in, 57-58
  severe depression compared with, 227
Screen affect, 15
Secondary affects, 14
Secondary loneliness, 279
Secondary pain, 55-56, 60
Secondary pleasure, 55-56
Security, anxiety through loss of, 120, 122-123
Self:
  anger as basis for sense of, 249-254
  loneliness and, 274-275, 282
  otherself, 64, 65
Self-sufficiency, Thoreau's Walden and, 282-284
Self-system, 123-129
Self-worth, loss of in depression, 196-198
Sensory apperception, in core model, 53-56
Separation:
  anxiety aroused by, 116, 117, 119-122, 125-126, 279
  attachment reducing fear of, 266-268
  attempts to resist, 288-289
  loneliness and, 275
  see also Loneliness
Separation anxiety, 116, 117, 119-122, 125-126, 279
Severe depression, see Depression
Shame anxiety, 121
Signal anxiety, 115
Signal function, 21
  of affects, 14
Signal-scanning affects, 21
Significant third, therapist as for depressed patients, 224
Simple affects, 21
Sorrow, 60
  Descartes and, 40-41, 42, 46, 47, 48
  see also Depression
Split-brain studies, 77